old DEAD white men's PHILOSOPHY

Old *DEAD* white men's PHILOSOPHY

Laura lyn INGLIS

and

Peter k. STEINFELD

Humanity Books

an imprint of Prometheus Books
59 John Glenn Drive, Amherst, New York 14228-2197

Published 2000 by Humanity Books, an imprint of Prometheus Books

Inquiries should be addressed to
Humanity Books
59 John Glenn Drive
Amherst, New York 14228–2197
VOICE: 716–691–0133, ext. 207
FAX: 716–564–2711

04 03 02 01 00   5 4 3 2 1

Library of Congress Cataloging-in-Publication Data

Inglis, Laura Lyn, 1952–
    Old dead White men's philosophy / by Laura Lyn Inglis and Peter K. Steinfeld.
        p. cm.
    Includes bibliographical references (p.) and index.
    ISBN 1–57392–823–2
    1. Feminist theory. 2. Philosophy. 3. Religion. I. Steinfeld, Peter K. (Peter Klaus), 1952– II. Title.

B29 .I54 2000
108'.2—dc21   00–025097
                                                              CIP

Printed in the United States of America on acid-free paper

CONTENTS

PREFACE

THIS BOOK IS DEDICATED to all the women (and some men as well) who are in conversation with the classical texts of Western civilization. The setting for this enterprise is the need to study the mainstream of the Western heritage of ideas from a new vantage point which is provided by the margins. As women speak and offer new directions and perspectives, there is a need to reflect upon the interaction between the old tradition and the new voices. The old tradition has been dominated by white, European men who are now (mostly) dead. The context of the learning of these old dead white men is now de-centered and contextualized. The opening of the Western tradition to the voices of those who have been systematically excluded has cleared spaces for new interpretations, new meanings, and new dialogues.

Our point of departure is the teaching of the classics of the Western tradition in classrooms in which women are full participants in the process of making sense of a tradition that has denied these women access. In the courses we teach, we are able occasionally to add a text authored by a woman, usually written in the past fifteen years, or we are allowed to offer a course with a focus on women. Some of us manage even to split our position between philosophy or history or political science or religion, and women's studies, so that our "women's" courses have a permanent listing in the catalog and a place in our preparation. The rest of the time we teach courses in which the major focus is on men, their past, their ideas, their contributions, their reality. And we do it well, giving full credit where credit is due. We were trained in a corpus dominated by men, often trained by men, and we teach what Man has to say for himself. We are careful that no one can say of us that we lack objectivity, nor do we let that "feminist stuff" get in the way of our being real scholars.

This book is dedicated to all the women (and some men as well) who study the classical texts of Western civilization, all the while wondering about the relevance of it all to women. Occasionally, such students encounter a text authored by a woman, though she speaks largely about the original ideas contributed by men, or at least uses those ideas as the measure of truth. Sometimes such students manage an elective course that focuses on women. Some of these students even manage to handle a minor or second major in women's studies, so that courses on women form a part of their outlook on the whole. The rest of the time they wonder why the views of women seem to have had such a limited impact before, even as they feel the impact of their views now. But most of the time is spent on Men: their past, their ideas, their contributions, their reality. And such students do a good job of showing that they can master the material, if only they are allowed once in a while to offer a paper on the place and contribution of women to all of this.

Nonetheless, we continue to be trained by men, in a corpus dominated by men, though we occasionally have a woman (who was trained by a man) as a teacher. We can truly testify that we have learned what Man has to say for himself. We have considered giving it all up to focus on women's studies. However, we pride ourselves on being practical and objective and not getting lost in the peripheral issues, no matter how relevant to our personal views.

This book is dedicated to ourselves, our feminist colleagues, and to women (and some men) students who are beginning to demand that we discuss women outside the protection of the limited women's studies courses available. We teach philosophy and religion. We love the old masters. We insist that our students read Plato and Kant and Heidegger and all the rest as primary texts, as their introduction to philosophy. We want the ideas that challenged us to challenge them, and we are always amazed and delighted at our students' capacity to respond with power and originality to the ideas that shaped history. These are the books and the ideas that can change lives and open minds. We will not give them up for predigested compilations, "desexed" and sanitized through the perspective of modern authors, male or female. Nor will we rob our students of the breadth of potential that is the living repository of history. So we are dedicated proponents of old dead white men and their living texts.

This book is dedicated to the task of becoming self-aware of the contradictions involved in a task we love. The silencing of women is not something done once upon a time, a long time ago. Even we are engaged in the ongoing project of the silencing of women. Many of our students rarely even notice that there are seldom any women who merit attention in our classes. But they learn from that fact also. We carefully monitor our own language and theirs, and we explore the philosophical implications of the various forms of the generic. Then we read the old dead white men who could care less about including women in their language. Is it enough to model a woman who thinks, if she thinks, and can think, only in paths worn by men's tread? We discuss such questions regularly in our feminist classes or among our feminist friends, but seldom in any other context. It takes time and effort to teach the classics, and this would make it impossible to proceed. Must such questions be discussed only in the context of a marginal course, such as the last chapter in a book on "humanity" in which we get at last to the question of women's role? Will a little frosting of Hannah Arendt change the taste of the classical cake? Or do we need to throw out the cake and return to the kitchen, carrying with us our own undigested training in men's thought?

Man continues to be the measure of all things and, most especially, of the legitimacy of feminist texts in philosophy. Women continue to get jobs in which their feminist perspective is expected not to interfere with their major responsibilities to the full scope of their discipline. Their papers are reviewed and rejected on the basis of too much of a feminist bias. Students continue to be encouraged and evaluated on their ability and to become cognizant in one or more great thinkers of the past—who happen to be almost always men. Indeed, the power to maintain the criteria for inclusion in the philosophical heritage rests on the power of that heritage to determine the terms of the present. The old dead white men are our past. We live in it. We live it. We live out of it into our future, where we meet it again. Because the past cannot "go," it is time to do some living history. Oppressive history is a history of answers given by the oppressor to our questioning. Yet the history of our questioning is missing. Dominance is the right to claim the answers as absolute, beyond questions and questioning. History begins to be liberated from the power of erasure the moment anyone asks, "What is the concrete, historical question to which *this* is the answer?" The makers of history have long struggled with the oppressive results. Paulo Freire states: "Human existence cannot be silent, nor can it be nourished by false words, but only by true words, with which men [the question here is whether women also] transform the world. To exist, humanly, is to *name* the world, to change it. Once named, the world in its turn reappears to the namers as a problem and requires of them a new *naming*."[1] History becomes human only when it becomes a problem to be addressed by humans. The problem for women is why history is not theirs, why even Paulo Freire makes history a project for men and not for women. If women are to be engaged in the naming of their world, they must begin by naming history, and they do so by addressing the texts that form the context of this world.

The question, which we pose to our oppression as an ongoing, violent, repressive reality, is currently stimulating remarkable changes in a variety of disciplines. It has already changed the nature of anthropology, especially archaeology, and turned the study of history, at least in its most dynamic form, into the study of social history. These transformations have, in turn, given rise to new possibilities of affirming the presence of women as active participants in both surviving and resisting patriarchy.[2]

Most exciting and relevant to this project is the re-searching which has led naturally and often unconsciously to the developing of methodologies for reevaluating texts, traditions, and ideas. "E-valuating" is a process of judging value. "Reevaluating" implies reexamining the values once again. What these re-searching, reevaluating, feminist methodologies do is to examine the values expressed in the light of the question that informed their process of valuing and thereby attempt to change the system itself. More specifically, patriarchal values are being reevaluated as they are embedded in sacred texts. Texts are sacred, because they answer the deep questions of a culture: questions of origin, questions of meaning, and questions of legitimation (power and authority). All these questions and their answers rest on fundamental values that are sometimes hidden from view in the texts. The intended result of such reevaluating is a reversal in key values that support oppression, a trans-valuing.

This kind of methodology is essentially a hermeneutical act, an act of textual interpretation. Hermeneutics has a long history of bringing to view values and meanings in sacred texts, that is, values and meanings that go beneath the surface to open the text to ever deeper levels of understanding. The relevance of hermeneutics to the structure of oppression is that texts give access to the formulated values that underlie the social construction of meaning. Every act of interpretation draws forth values: both those values it proclaims and those values it rejects. Hermeneutics, as a way of bringing values to consciousness, has the capacity of undermining dominant values by challenging their underlying assumptions. Nowhere is this more obvious currently than in the original home of hermeneutics in the interpretation of biblical texts. Here, women, committed to the liberating meanings embedded in sacred biblical texts, have found ways to directly engage the symbol systems of oppressive religious communities.

Suppose for instance that one were to teach a course on the Hebrew Bible while reading Merlin Stone's *When God Was a Woman*.[3] The accident of reading Merlin Stone simultaneously with the biblical text would change the way the course was taught and might even result in a "paradigm shift."[4] A conventional reading of the Exodus story involved placing the story in the context of the values of creation, promise, liberation. God gave his[5] people a Promised Land and liberated them from bondage. If in our course we discussed the status of women, it would focus on the story of Adam and Eve. Even here, the condemnation of women in the story of the Fall would remain buried in the issues of obedience and freedom to God's will. The response of God to various challenges by his human partners sometimes make God an enigma but would not threaten the central values implicit in historic monotheism. While reading Stone, however, the traditional reading would take on a new context.

Merlin Stone's book introduces a shift in fundamental assumptions regarding the structure of divinity and value in the biblical text. One might once have seen God as the beneficent, if disappointed, judge of human frailty. But this interpretation was always contorted in the face of the acts he required and condemned. It was always problematic why God should so tempt and so condemn his newly created beings on the basis of such a trivial act of disobedience. With Stone, however, the story requires much less redaction and qualification. The contorted readings that could never avoid the question of theodicy cease to be puzzling. The placing of the serpent in a story of human innocence now indicates the collision of two texts: an older story that praised wisdom, particularly female wisdom, identified with a serpent/Goddess, and this new story of a jealous God drawing a line in the sand. Stone's interpretation discloses that the Genesis account of creation carries within it a condemnation of women and an exclusion of female divinity. The overt text reveals a covert text "between the lines" of the surface of the story. If the serpent is a stand-in for another sort of value, the value of wisdom in a culture seen as a threat to the ancient writers, there is no puzzle.[6]

In Stone's writing, the original inhabitants of Canaan, the Promised Land, come alive, as having an equally valid culture which was destroyed by violence. To justify that act of violence, the conquerors produced a narrative. The narrative serves directly to justify an act of genocide and indirectly discloses why the Canaanite culture posed such a threat that violence was necessary. The key to the whole was the status of women in the two cultures. Women as powerful posed a threat to a misogynist Father god who never married. Now the entire biblical narrative begins to make sense, as a coherent ideology which was founded in the need to maintain his sovereignty and his right to eliminate the competition.

That simple answer, which one might draw out of Merlin Stone's fascinating discussion, would not be, of course, the final conclusion of the reevaluation of the biblical narrative. Instead, it represents one starting point for the new approaches to biblical interpretation. Feminists have long had to deal with the misogyny of the biblical texts, and they have come up with a variety of answers. The approach of the nineteenth-century *Woman's Bible*, for example, demonstrates the way in which women chose the least repressive pieces and dropped or rewrote the rest. This was the only alternative to leaving the tradition altogether and starting over elsewhere.

Stone's book might offer another path, a hermeneutical path, by which the text as it had previously been read is set in juxtaposition to another reading of the same text. Hers was an effort aimed at a popular audience, as she herself was not a biblical scholar. Independent of her efforts, feminist scholars have developed similar approaches that provide amazingly enlightening and constructive ways through which women within the traditions that inherit these texts can appropriate them creatively.[7] What they find within the text is evidence of a struggle between woman-affirming religious traditions and the dominant biblical orientation of repression. Stone poses this struggle between the Hebrews and their Canaanite neighbors, the first violent and patriarchal, and the other peaceful and woman-centered.[8] As feminist scholars have begun to examine the structure of valuation of powerful female figures, they have reclaimed the voices suppressed by the dominant voice of patriarchy within the text. The voices condemned within the text are voices that belong to the text, as clearly as do the voices of the victors. The process of interpretation frees the texts to speak about other possibilities, possibilities that affirm what the overt texts rejected, possibilities that now are available to women to claim as their sacred inheritance.

When Merlin Stone wrote *When God Was a Woman,* she made connections that went beyond noticing that women are not authors, nor major actors, in the biblical narratives. She saw exclusion as representing a positive acknowledgment of something so powerful that for the text even to mention Her name was too dangerous. For many of us, her book marked the turning point that went far beyond the immediate quality of its scholarship. Her approach represented a positive step in the understanding of the traditional texts. She offered a way of seeing in exclusion a report on events that could not be directly acknowledged but which nonetheless remain represented within the text. Implicit in her work is a methodology that can and has been extended by feminist scholars. Hers was one stone thrown into a pond, one ripple among women who have discovered a way to re-search old paths to discover what is hidden behind, beyond, and beneath the stated relevance of the text.

Much of the current appropriation of these hermeneutical alternatives has clustered around *Sophia*, the name of Wisdom to which a multitude of psalmic texts are addressed.[9] Her relevance is hidden in the translations that remove her as an independent name for the deity. *Sophia* is neither a "new" god, nor a god exterior to the biblical tradition.[10] *Sophia* is God, Herself, present and available as a biblical reality. *Sophia* is a minority voice. Even so, *Sophia* represents a direct challenge to the dominant voice and an implicit re-valuation of the images of God, the King, and the Father. The challenge is mounted, not against the texts, but within the texts. To affirm a biblical Goddess has never been claimed to be the "intention" of an author or authors or an editor or subsequent redactors. It is quite certainly in direct opposition to all the forefathers of faith in the Hebrew Bible and its sequel. Yet this is not an objection, but a realignment with that in the biblical tradition which had been silenced by the fathers of the faith. It is a beginning for what is new and a new beginning, a rebeginning to what was original, a return to what is old. It is our inheritance from our mothers, who died leaving their words in the fathers' mouths. That the fathers rejected them, said them with disdain, changed the pronouns, denied their power, destroyed their proponents, makes them no less a source of primordial power. The fathers' own record contains them, the nemesis of the Godfather hidden in his own words. *Sophia* springs to life in the reversal of the fathers' intentions and the reevaluating of the values that inform the text.

The revival of *Sophia* at the heart of the biblical tradition has made it possible for women involved in the professional study of religion to move out of the margins and into nearly every aspect of religious thought. There is still oppression in the structuring of institutions and the continuing project of silencing women in the religious discussion as it reaches out into religious practice. Yet increasingly, the fathers of the church are sitting on a powder keg. Women have *something to say*, and the saying is now a fact of life in scholarship. As a result, there is life and excitement in the corridors of the academy.

This book is dedicated to carrying that revolution over into the still exclusive halls of philosophical thought. Here, too, there is quite open disparagement of women's power and virtue. Here, too, there is a discipline dependent on interpretation of a collection of sacred texts. Here, too, there is *Sophia*. What men study when they study thought is named *Sophia*, and the practice of the wondering about things is called "philo-sophy": love of *Sophia*. So far philosophers have essentially remained sternly independent of and unaffected by the challenges posed by feminists, preferring to reproduce the analytical study of a genderless philosophy. Women chip away at the corners of the tower, however, looking for the weakness at the foundations.

This is where the current investigation begins. Just as *Sophia* as a name for the biblical deity is the outward symbol of women affirming the voice that was suppressed (but never entirely destroyed) in the biblical narratives, here *Sophia* will name the voice of woman's wisdom which has yet to be heard in the philosophical texts of the Western tradition. The purpose of this book is to attempt to locate that voice in a few selected texts, some of the sacred texts of Western philosophical thought. If we can find such a voice within the texts themselves, then we have the grounds for introducing women's reality into the very heart of the fathers' corpus.

Such a voice, if it exists and if the texts can be illuminated by listening to the voice, would not belong in a course called "women's studies." It would make possible the reexamination of the dominant interpretations, and would belong at the heart of each discipline. No one, at least in a nondogmatic context such as the liberal arts, dares ignore the possibility that what we thought the texts said was not all that they might be saying. The reexamination of the texts opens a way into the act of philosophizing itself, and above all, gives a foothold for resisting the marginalization of feminist philosophy. The purpose of this text is to make it worthwhile for anyone practicing philosophy to address the critique raised by feminists.

New points of departure in philosophy always begin by reinterpreting what came before. In this sense, philosophy is essentially a hermeneutical enterprise. It is also the only way philosophy ever gets anywhere. Philosophy never gets beyond its history; rather, philosophy carries history on its back. This is really no different from any other discipline, but for philosophy it is a self-conscious task. To find a new point of departure in philosophy always means being original in the sense of seeking the origins. As such, feminist philosophy must become self-conscious in the appropriation of patriarchal texts. To do so requires a way, a path, a hermeneutical method. We propose that this hermeneutical method be informed by and infused with subversion, a subversion that can transform the whole of the past. Subversion might be a kind of guerrilla warfare for feminists within a repressive tradition of thought. Subversion plays upon and with sub-verses, to open alternative meanings beneath the surface of the text.

This book is dedicated to the humble enterprise of rethinking philosophy from the ground up. We will seek the ground to dig up around and among and underneath the graves of the old dead white men. This book is dedicated to all those philosophers among whose bones we will be excavating. This book is dedicated to all the teachers and students who already practice subversive hermeneutics without using that term and to all the thinkers eager to make love to *Sophia*.

Though this book is birthed out of a desire to develop a feminist methodology of appropriation via subversion of the classical texts of the Western philosophical tradition, it also originates more personally as a lover's quarrel. We have been together nearly twenty years, arguing unmercifully with each other about everything from the nature of commitment and birth politics to the meaning of Heidegger's ontology and Kierkegaard's dialectics. Our friends have often wondered whether our marriage would last. And now our kids (all three of them) wonder about us, too. Philosophical marriages are dialectical marriages.

We want to share a bit of the process that goes into our writing together. Truly joint authorship is an oddity. Typically, Laura throws out a wild idea, usually late at night when Peter is tired and ready for sleep. Her ideas come from classes, readings, dreams, and visions. He is the respondent and critic. We argue and we dance around the idea (if he can stay awake). Sometimes we yell and scream and get mighty angry at each other. When this happens, we know we are probably getting at something really important. But it is a painful endeavor. So sometimes we just let the argument go—maybe for a day, or a week, or a month, or a year, or longer. But the fruitful arguments always come around again, and the battle is fought all over again. The trick is to find the center of the argument, that single point around which the whole debate revolves. When we arrive at this center, it is magical. It is as if the center has found us rather than us finding the center.

There have been many detours along our way. There were years worth of diapers to change. There were philosophy and religion classes to teach. There were kids to whom bedtime stories must be read. There were departmental school meetings. Lots of distractions and lots of interruptions. But the arguments did not disappear. Magically they returned, waiting for their turn to be faced.

This is the magic of our writing together. The arguments return, as if by their own momentum. In some sense, neither one of us is the author of this manuscript. What is written here is created out of the argument that is between us. This writing is by neither one of us, nor really by both of us. This writing comes from that magical space in between us. And so we venture forth this project, which belongs to neither of us. This is our "autonomous text."

The labor is completed, the child has emerged. We thank the book's siblings, Coryn, Nathaniel, and Gwendolyn for showing no more than the appropriate ambivalence about sharing their parents' time with another demanding presence. We also thank the subversive and thoroughly critical voices of the Faculty Writing Group, especially but not exclusively, Susan Seitz, Nadine Brewer, Hollace Drake, and Ed Cohen. We thank our Academic Assistants, Shawn Nauman, who was there at the project's inception, Garrick McFadden, and most especially, Tom Klett, whose willingness to learn new skills taught his teachers. Thanks to Buena Vista University for financial support, and our new friends at Humanities Press, who never gave up on us. Thanks also to Verity, our familiar spirit who understood how to play even with truth.

NOTES

1. In *Pedagogy of the Oppressed* (New York: Continuum, 1970), 76.
2. "Patriarchy" is now a term that has been used so often that the edges have begun to blur. The word breaks down simply into *archy*: "rule by" and *patri*: "fathers," so it means "rule by the fathers." Once this had a sort of innocence attached to it, for who should better rule than the father, who was made in the image of God-the-Father? Now it has come to mean all those various and manifold systems that have dominated the world since the beginning of time—man's time, that is, what we call 'history.' There is not just one patriarchy for all times and all seasons, yet all patriarchies have this in common, that they resisted and resist any sharing of power with women and children. Often patriarchal systems will fight wars with each other. In all these wars, as in all the peace that momentarily follows, it is the women who lose.
3. Merlin Stone, *When God Was a Woman* (New York: Harcourt, Brace, Jovanovich, 1976). Merlin Stone is not necessarily the only pathway by which one might come to retell the biblical narrative. But for many of us, the timing of her realization was also the time of our own coming to consciousness of the patriarchal nature of our own tradition as embodied in biblical texts.
4. Thomas Kuhn in *The Structure of Scientific Revolutions* (Chicago: University of Chicago Press, 1970) uses this term to refer to dramatic shifts in the framework of viewing a problem or a theoretical understanding in science. The term "para-

digm," however, works equally well for understanding the framework of assumptions that shape any systematic knowledge. A shift in any discipline is a
major event, one that will be resisted by most of those trained in the discipline.
Even the fact of Merlin Stone's being trained in discipline other than biblical
interpretation fits the pattern of such shifts. Being trained in another discipline
makes it possible for her to see the texts in a way excluded by the very structure
of training in biblical hermeneutics. Also, the continuing revolution among biblical
scholars mimics the pattern of social change that Kuhn describes. There are, of
course, many points of entrance into such a shift. The anomalies raised into
consciousness by the feminists have become a major source of tension and change—
and excitement—within the discipline.

5. Perhaps God is neuter, and perhaps he's not. Because this work is in conversation
with the text as it is, we will let God maintain his properly masculine dignity.
Since he is, after all, God, we will let him keep his capital "G." It is his deeds,
as God, that interest us here, not his apologies.

6. So many wonderful rewritings of the story of Adam and Eve have been done
that it would be a major effort just to catalog them all. Our own version, compiled
from many others, runs something like this: God's people had invaded and now
lived in the midst of people who revered the Goddess. These people were willing
to teach the newcomers how to farm, but to do so they had to teach them about
fertility, and that was divine, and divinely feminine, knowledge. So, Yahweh's
neatly patriarchal views were being distorted among his followers by all this
new knowledge about babies not being seeds put in women by the fathers and
so forth. The cult of Yahweh felt it necessary to condemn the new knowledge in
terms that would make it clear that you couldn't trust anything told you by a
woman (especially a woman who was priestess). The story of Adam and Eve
resulted. God makes the man who, quite properly, is the real originator and
source of the human species. He gives birth to the woman. Thus her act of
birthing is put in its proper place as a derivative power. The snake, so deeply
associated with the Goddess, becomes a clever deceiver. The Goddess' tree of
knowledge, especially knowledge about sex, is forbidden. The woman, of course,
breaks the rule. Eve's name, by the way, happens to echo the divine "mother of
all living." The two are thrown out of the garden and made to work for a living,
proof that all those knowledgeable farmers around them are the real sinners.
And woman is to be ruled over.

7. For a nice summary of many of the major approaches, see Phyllis Trible, "Five
Loaves and Two Fishes: Feminist Hermeneutics and Biblical Theology," *Theological
Studies* 50 (1989), 279–95.

8. Though Stone's book has provided for many of us a way out of the patriarchal
mind lock, her book also raises some difficult problems between feminists coming
from a Jewish background and those of a Christian background. Beneath the
surface of many feminist attacks on the Hebrew patriarchs is an implicit anti-
Semitism. Even though the same methods apply equally well to New Testament
materials, Christian feminists tend to focus on the Old Testament/Hebrew Bible
while ignoring or minimizing the same patterns in the New Testament, or at
least the Gospels, or at the very least in Jesus himself. Jewish feminists have
challenged this anti-Semitism by focusing on the conflict within the Hebrew/
Jewish history between elements that imply earlier nonpatriarchal traditions that
have been suppressed or destroyed by the dominant interpretations and theological
conclusions.

9. The recent "Re-Imaging Conference," held under the auspices of the Presbyterian Church—U.S., shows the power that such imagery can bring to women within the Christian tradition—and the continuing willingness of the patriarchs to repress such reawakenings at all costs.

10. The name *Sophia* actually belongs most originally to the Greeks, being an ancient name long associated with Wisdom as a deity and an object of thought. *Sophia* was the Greek translation of the Hebrew term for Wisdom. Greek-speaking Jews translated the Hebrew term *hochmah* (also a name and also feminine) in the Septuagint. *Hochmah*, translated as *Sophia*, had its divinity disguised in the neuter term "Wisdom." This allowed interpreters to absorb the term as an attribute of God, its feminine inflection entirely erased. The hymns to Wisdom occur throughout much of the Wisdom literature of the Hebrew scriptures.

INTRODUCTION:
LOVE SONG FOR SOPHIA

PHILOSOPHY BELONGS TO OLD dead white men. On the simplest level of analysis, this statement says no more (and no less) than the truism that women have been excluded from the corpus of classical philosophy almost without exception. Women did not "think," or so one must assume, prior to the twentieth century. From Socrates to the present moment, the tradition of Western thought is a tradition of men, and more often than not a tradition of men who felt perfectly comfortable excluding women consciously and actively. Now that the old dead white men are dead, perhaps there is room for women in philosophical circles. Even so, the ghosts of the old dead white men continue to haunt academia because it is their ideas that define both the content and the meaning of all philosophical discussion. No current speech by women, no multitude of women-who-are-also-philosophers can ease the tension created between the present speaking and the echoing absence of female speech in the tradition.[1]

So far, this is a merely formal claim of sexual oppression. One takes note of the lack, but no more. No immediate meaning can be drawn from the absence of women in and of itself. Indeed, the silence of women is likely to go unnoticed without some way of approaching the meaning of the silence philosophically.[2] There are social, historical, and political reasons for the dearth of women in the philosophical heritage, even if no one any longer argues "biological" reasons for their exclusion. It is much more complicated still to show the relationship between the systems of abstract thought and the structures of sexism in Western culture.

Indeed, there is an implicit claim that the nature of philosophy makes the fact of male exclusivity irrelevant to the content of their thought. Claims about the status of women in philosophy's history are seldom seen as having any philosophical implications. Though it is clearly possible to study the misogynist tendencies of the men who "do" philosophy, such discussions are bracketed off from the "real" substance of philosophy. After all, these men reflected their times and its prejudices, as well as their own personal

1

histories and relationships to women. Feminists are encouraged to look at those isolated instances in which the great philosophers speak directly about women. Of course, any such information does not affect the value of their abstract, their truly philosophical, conclusions.

The difficulty is to show how these personal and historical elements affect the immortal truths of the systems philosophers create. The claim is easy to make but difficult to substantiate. These men, by definition as philosophers, have transcended the mortality of the conventions and psychological limitations of their times and mores.[3] They are philosophers. They *think*. They are the immortals, preserved for all eternity by the productivity of their conceptions. More than science or business or politics, Thought is not limited by time or place or, perhaps, gender. Thought, like God, is transcendent. If so, it is of merely accidental interest to know that the philosophers who shape Thought are, almost without exception, men. Thought, if not the thinkers, is the true generic.

The current participation of women in philosophy assumes the pragmatic reality of the gender neutrality of philosophy. Every woman who attempts to philosophize today does so by first being trained in the thought of these old dead white men. Her assumptions belong to the corpus handed down from the old dead white men. The gender-neutral character of thought remains operationally true and indeed is reinforced by the current participation of women in philosophy. Women have made it abundantly clear that they are capable of studying and duplicating the structures and conclusions of their male colleagues, but in so doing they have also reinforced the claims to transcendence made by those men.

A more delicate question is whether or not women are capable of thinking independently of those old dead white men. If the claim to gender neutrality should not hold, then women must find some alternative way to begin. Certainly it is possible not to know philosophy, or even to refuse to read thought generated by men. However, philosophy is not so easily evaded. Every thought of every feminist, from the most shallow to the most profound, can be shown to stand in some sort of a dependent relationship to one or more of the old dead white men. Feminists are Hegelians, or realists, or Kantians, or deconstructionists, or marxists, or phenomenologists, even as they attack the sexism of past conclusions. Thought draws on the assumptions and structures of those who came before. This can be a conscious process or an unconscious process, but the conclusions of thought and thinkers' pasts permeate the present and its thought.

How, then, is one to go about beginning the task of challenging the mastery of the masters? If the first step is the recognition that women's voices are missing from the past; the second step is the recognition that women's voices are currently stifled by the ongoing, historical, social, and political (but of course, no longer "biological") limitations that result from that domination of thought by men. The problem is not dead and gone. The measure of a woman's thought remains the 'generic' man and also the man that is her husband, or a doctoral committee, or a review committee, or a description of the number of courses on old dead white men that she must teach. It doesn't matter that women sometimes "do" philosophy, for they have been trained by men in a territory controlled by men. The style of women's thought must remain as dry and desiccated and as analytical as a man dead for a thousand years. It is, in other words, not just men, but *old dead white men*, the standard of thought and the subject of all "real" thought, that continues to control the destiny of philosophy.

The transcendence of philosophy allows a claim of gender neutrality that preserves the good old boy's network even over death. The claim of gender neutrality in philosophy covers over the unremitting exclusion of women. Women are excluded from the network by virtue of having been excluded from the system of immortality. Thus, because women as philosophers remain isolated instances among the creators of original thought, it becomes clear that philosophical thought belongs to men. For those women who pass all the tests for proper male thought and are admitted into the territory, there is no way to connect with anyone but by means of the old dead white men. For women as women there is no way in and no way out.

The preserve of thought exists as a male territory by virtue of the preservation of thinkers. The conspiracy to exclude women from thought is a conspiracy of memory. The loss of the memory of women's thought prevents women from creating a heritage, a tradition of ways of thinking from which to create new ideas. As long as those few women who manage to carve a foothold in philosophy must do so by studying under and in the shadow of the old dead white men, there can be no woman's thought as such. The cost of entrance into man's preserve is to forget one is a woman and grant the assumption that men's thought is thought. For women who choose or who are forced to remain outside philosophy, there is no memory. Their room in academic halls is the women's room.

Beyond the fact that women are missing among the makers of philosophy, there remains a methodological step. The lack itself becomes a positive datum. The feminist critique begins with the recognition that women's voices are missing from all the important expressions of civilized thought. However, women's thought is not simply missing from the Western tradition. Rather its status as "missing" shapes and informs the whole nature of man's thinking, creating, and describing of the world. This is the philosophical move, the move that creates the possibility of claiming the "missing" within the texts as a starting point for thought.

Every thought, every methodology that can be named today, either begins by addressing the methodological implications of women's exclusion or must add weight to the drag of the old dead white men upon philosophy. This is not true because the relevance of women's absence has been understood but for precisely the opposite reason. The nature of the exclusion has not been understood. Therefore, methodologically and from the foundation, all "neutral" and "generic" projects are suspect. The past, by its rejection of women's voice, takes on the character of simple oppression. Men have owned philosophy. Thought has been claimed, colonized, and occupied. Thought is the territory held by man, the rational animal. Is not this still the case? If women rarely speak, or when they speak do so only within the confines of male institutions, male methodologies, and male assumptions, the old dead white men's inheritance remains intact. Philosophy is not free to resume its normal enterprise, free either to women or to men, until women can speak, for themselves and in such a way as to open up that speaking into the past.

Those who speak for the present always speak to and out of the past. How then are we even to begin, since in some sense we must begin before our own beginnings? Re-beginning is not as impossible as it may seem, for philosophy always starts over again, always goes back to the beginning of thought to understand itself. Since Hegel, that "beginning" has been given a historical twist. To be philosophical is to start over at the beginning of thought. That is why philosophy never "progresses." To progress requires a kind of forgetting that brackets off the relationship to the past. Philosophers are historians of a past that lives. Therefore, the silence of women in the past holds us to it, making all projects of speaking questionable, even now and perhaps even tomorrow as well, or else the silence of women is broken open in the past and, therefore, now as well. The speaking of women becomes heard by the discovery of a voice that predates and echoes throughout the corpus of the old dead white men, a speaking that is first hinted at by silence.

The primordial possibility of women's speaking is hinted by the gendered nature of philo-*sophy* itself. The nature of thought is given the name *Sophia*. Women are not just lacking in the tradition; the tradition is named "Woman." The exclusion of women is an exclusion from *Sophia*. The negative, the lack of women, reveals the positive, that somehow what they are excluded from has a feminine nature. Woman is silenced *in* philosophy, and, therefore, men have presumed to speak for Her who *is* philosophy. The interpretation of the history of philosophy is the interpretation of a feminine presence, which is under a spell of silence.

The silence at the heart of philo-*Sophia*, and the multitude of men speaking, both require hermeneutics, the art of interpretation. Hermeneutics, as a self-conscious, methodologically conscious discipline, developed along two paths, as biblical and literary interpretation.[4] Perhaps it is not surprising that it is in biblical hermeneutics women have most emphatically broken the silence. It is among feminists struggling to appropriate a sacred past which has vilified, erased, and subjugated them that *Sophia* has become a living source of transformation. This change has broken loose from the confines of academia, and now women who are not biblical scholars and who are therefore not trained in their words can speak and begin something again.

A sacred past is one that cannot be discarded nor forgotten. A sacred past is a living past, a collection of texts that has the power to shape living dialogues today. Interpretations of a sacred past demand precisely the kind of transformative hermeneutic that is also required in philosophy. Here it is not sufficient to note that women were silenced, nor is it simply sufficient to substitute new words that we wish more adequately reflected our reality. In theological reflection from out of the biblical tradition, any new beginning must address a sacred text which cannot be changed nor abandoned. It can only be interpreted in a fashion that frees the listener by freeing the text.

The biblical texts have been a crucial testing ground for the development of a specifically feminist hermeneutic. Investigation of the book of Genesis by women employing such a feminist methodology uncovered the curious exclusion of any mention of the matrifocal traditions that formed the context within which the Hebrew traditions emerged.[5] Even the word Goddess lacks a Hebrew equivalent.[6] Yet the story of Yahweh's creation makes use of terms that tie that story to other creation stories built on the destruction of the Great Goddess.[7] Yahweh moves across the face of *tehom* (the "deep"). The relationship between *tehom* and Tiamat, the already established female divinity of the ancient Middle East, invites feminist reconsideration.

Feminist hermeneutics approaches the story in Genesis, therefore, suspicious of intentional exclusion of feminine divinity. Such suspicion becomes intensified in light of the cultural and religious interface between the patriarchal Hebrews and their matristic neighbors. In light of this exclusion, the myth of Adam and Eve becomes transparent. Eve's subordination and guilt provide the justification by which the story legitimates the rejection of female authority encountered by the Hebrews in the ancient peoples around them. The story justifies the maintenance of violent repression of Hebrew women who might sympathize with their Canaanite neighbors and the legitimation of violent destruction of the matristic cultures around them. The story that once signified God's promise and God's love, the giving of the Promised Land to his people, now becomes the story of a God who gives away someone else's land—in exchange for the genocide of its people and their heritage. And somehow, it is the fact that they worshipped Goddesses, that their women were not quite as thoroughly enslaved as the Hebrews, that must be suppressed in the text. The story of that story goes on, continuing to teach a promise—and an exclusion. The importance of the story throughout the tradition hints at the ever-present need to prevent women from connecting with the ideas and heritage that lurks in the background.

The purpose of this book is to establish a methodology appropriate not only for biblical texts but for all texts of the old dead white men. The subversive task is to understand the way in which all texts, all the old dead white men's texts, can be opened to reveal another text beneath them. We need to find the snake in the philosophical garden,[8] to speak to the midwife from whom Socrates learned, to hear in the texts the ideological justifications for the violent silencing of women of power. The exclusion of women's voices from the corpus of classical thought shapes patriarchal thought as a missing person defines a crime. Feminist hermeneutics takes the exclusion of women as the starting point for understanding the past record of history as patriarchal history, as 'his' story and as containing a hidden denial. The denial of women's original thought shapes the tradition, and thereby provides a methodological premise for reopening the tradition to examination. The result is another text, a text that is the reverse image of the surface text, a text that somehow belongs, not to the man who made it, but to the women whose tongues he cut out.

The exclusion of women's voices from history marks, in feminist hermeneutics, the point from which the tradition itself becomes transparent. Just as a detective determines the identity of the missing person by the imprint of a footstep in the mud, the imprint of silence in history traces the process of exclusion. The more central and sacred the text, the more likely the text will carry concrete information in the pattern of its exclusion, for the control and suppression of women was always both a central and a sacred tenet for all the forms of patriarchy. Feminist hermeneutics represents a subversive rethinking of the texts, a kind of detective work that seeks out what is hidden within the tradition. The guilty conscience of patriarchal exclusion presents an opportunity to access what it was written to reject, an opportunity to reanimate the suppressed memory of women's speaking in power. The current excitement concerning the Goddess emerges precisely from women rethinking men's foundational texts and thereby opening up new ways of interpreting women's own immediate experience. And this is only the beginning of what can be discovered.

Such a feminist reopening of the biblical texts provides a model for the rethinking of the entire Western heritage. Feminist hermeneutics is subversive in its relationship to the basic texts, because it is prepared to address the classical tradition in light of the shadows it casts even into the present. Such a hermeneutics cheerfully welcomes the opportunity to explore the biblical texts on their own literal terms, rejecting attempts to use symbolic language to soften the vilification of women and the glorification of men. Instead, the materials of the whole biblical history are placed in relation to our discovery that women were never absent or silent but that they were suppressed, because they represented cultures that posed a theological threat to the biblical authors. And strangely enough, it is the texts themselves that best document this threat. Where the past has been erased, one must turn to the victors for information about those they destroyed.

Feminists turn to the texts to find women's past and the terms of their exclusion. Feminist hermeneutics focuses the light of its examination on constant reexamination and rethinking of history. It requires finding and putting together pieces of historical facts already accepted by patriarchal scholarship so as to disclose a new pattern. It also involves recognizing the potential of texts to carry messages about those opposed by the overt intentionality of the text. The conversation within the text is dialogical in its inherent structure. Patriarchal texts are, by intention, monological in their assertion of exclusive truth. The exclusivity of "truth" as proclaimed by the text excludes that other possibility which is, by the definition of the text, nothing, voiceless. However, there is that in the nature of the text that always calls out the *con-text*, as both "with" the text and "contrary" to the text. Pure monologue is impossible. That is, every monologue is a bifurcated dialogue. The monologue of the texts of patriarchy have as their context the manifold voices of women. The whispers of the forbidden voices are everywhere in the frozen conversations of male thought. Feminist hermeneutics begins with the recognition of sexism, the recognition that the voices of women are missing. It becomes concrete in the discovery that the shape of one particular set of missing voices remains imprinted in the shape of the denial and can, therefore, unlock the doors of denial. Behind those doors there are hidden a multitude of voices, of stories, waiting to be heard. Feminist hermeneutics is a dialectical enterprise of reconstituting dialogue. Such a dialectic is more interested in reconstructions than in letting even the deconstructed text stand. Feminist hermeneutics seeks to reawaken the multiplicity of meanings, of stories, of myths, and of metaphors which were distorted by the monologic intentionality of the patriarchal world.

The task of seeking to hear the background in the thought of the old dead white men opens the texts, rendering them into the form of dialogue once more. A feminist hermeneutic reconstructs the voice of the lost dialogue, the dialogue that exists as a "might have been," as a possibility within the text. This dialogue is the positive implication of the missing voices of women within the text. The lost dialogue conflicts with the overt meaning of the text, which is the text in which the dialogue is excluded, though it always stands in relationship to it. Feminist hermeneutics relates a new message by means of bringing forward the background of the existent text. In this sense subversive hermeneutics is not revisionist. The standard meanings of the text require preservation even as the text is opened into other readings. One still knows that God promised a land, but now one also hears the genocide which is the underside of that promise. The text remains intact; its intentionality remains vehemently in opposition to the proposed alternative. But now *two* texts are visible, standing in dialectical relationship to each other: the message affirmed by the text and the message negated by the text. The subversive text stands as the con-text in the background of the intended text. As an alternative text, the silenced text in some measure explains the text and, in some measure, criticizes the text. Above all, what the text does not say, but implies by its silence, provides an avenue to another world. Just as the Goddess is missing but implied in the book of Genesis, the text that stands behind the intentional text reestablishes dialogue—with *Sophia*.

Biblical interpretation remains the primary example of the power inherent in a feminist interpretation. The tools of feminist interpretation have been shaped by the need to address the issues raised by women's exclusion from full participation in the religious foundations of our culture. The potential implicit in subversive interpretation reaches into all aspects of man's thought. It is often harder to see the background in contemporary thinkers, where the interpreter herself participates in the foreground of men's triumphant "neutrality." The victors can afford to be 'neutral,' because they never have to admit that women were excluded. To participate in scholarship, feminists are required to accept the neutrality of their teachers for lack of an alternative foundation. The methodology of subversive hermeneutics offers the possibility of applying the insights of women's revolutionary discoveries in biblical hermeneutics to the male thinkers who still primarily shape the mainstream of academic discussion.

What would it mean to claim that the old dead white men wrote their philosophy in some measure to maintain the mastery over women, a control that was always in doubt? This thesis assumes that the history of oppression is a dynamic story of forces at odds with the ongoing project of Western society to establish dominion over all the earth. It presumes that a major factor in that dynamism is the continual reoccurrence of the memory/dream of a radical alternative to the given history controlled by the patriarchs. This alternative has never ceased to be identified with woman as such and thus has necessitated total erasure of women from power and from thought. The possibility of women making connections with women introduces forces that men in control must always resist, by thought as well as by arms. Philosophy is therefore at the center of the mechanisms of control. Philosophy is an incredible repository of ideas and a means of connecting ideas and thinkers across time. The old dead white men represent, support, maintain, and extend the power of patriarchy in its historical struggle with a diversity of alternatives—somehow identified with women—just as the old dead fathers of the church were preserved, because they served to exclude minority voices in Christianity. Women have always been allowed in both institutions, but the power to connect across time, to preserve the memory of speaking, remains with the fathers of thought.

In tracing the involvement of the philosophers with the forces of exclusion and destruction of female-identified alternatives, we will look at the structural metaphors that preserve the patriarchal control. In so doing, we attempt more than simply to deconstruct the sexism of our forefathers. Nor do we merely implicate philosophy in the other institutions of sexism. Instead, the purpose is to draw from the fathers of thought some hint of what might have been. We seek in the texts moments of vulnerability, in which openness threatens. Such moments allow access to another past, available by virtue of the essential dialectical nature of metaphor and valuation within the text. We seek the Canaanites who were killed and the Hebrews whose god had a consort. We seek that which the overt message of the text would deny, the recollection of alternative histories. We might call these histories "prehistory," as a way of designating their status as prior, as original, and as the background for history.

Prehistory is the history of peoples who came before the patriarchs, before the onslaught of violence, before the way things have always been.[9] Prehistory is not just a possibility that existed once, if at all, in the distant past. Rather the potential reorganization of society that prehistory represents has acted as a dream and source of revolution throughout the history of patriarchy. Prehistory as historical reality is something for archaeologists to argue over. Prehistory is, however, also a metaphor for the heritage of otherness with which women might connect. The mothers have always been restive and only continual warfare (private, public, and philosophical) has suppressed their rebellion. The erasure of the memory of their rebellion necessitates that each generation reinvent the goal and the memory, and this energy-draining process is perhaps the most potent of the weapons used to control women. Therefore, learning to discover the traces of the erasure in the documents of the oppressor can provide methods to guide the re-calling of the dream of change, of liberation.

Change is a hermeneutical task. Self-conscious change is a rethinking of a past in such a way that its directionality is changed. This is how we will attempt to approach our philosophical task, looking for the odd elements, the traces of old struggles, looking through the lenses of the philosophers' support of patriarchy for the terms of that commitment. From there we can seek the negative impression of the positive possibility of "prehistory." Knowledge of periods and institutions that preserved women's power has begun to come from re-searchers in a variety of disciplines concerned with the "facts" of the past. These provide external verification. The texts, however, remain the internal criteria of meaning, for we seek meanings that are not foreign to the texts. In many cases, our resources will be to obscure references in the texts, points at which the valuations that underlie the corpus are not quite fully digested by the texts' primary reference. These odd points can be our guide for reorganizing the evidence, anthropological and otherwise, and for discovering within "the facts" the existence of nonoppressive alternatives to patriarchy.

The task of interpretation, however, is not thereby made simple. There is not a single answer that can be pronounced whenever an old dead white man is announced. The work of interpretation is to engage a text. What we have attempted to formulate is a method by which feminists may engage the classical texts on their own terms. Upon whose terms? Upon the terms of the text itself which promises, even as it withholds, a dialogue. It is, of course, presumptuous to claim that the dialogue was with women when the old dead white men in their various life times never bothered to speak with women. This is nonetheless the claim: that the texts carry within them, independent of their creators' intention, a meaningful message for women's appropriation.

It is worth noting that this hermeneutic of subversion is a violation of the unspoken covenant between interpreter and author. The deal involves a commitment either to disagree openly with the text from some other standpoint or to be willing to carry forth with the project as stated. Any other use of a text is prohibited and labeled a fallacy, of quoting out of context. As an interpreter, one has a profound responsibility to be honest in letting the text have its say.

> Of all the empty academic exercises, the most futile are perhaps the attempts to interpret a text against the grain of its own premises: The Philosophy of Schopenhauer: An Optimistic Interpretation; *Das Kapital*: A Free-Market Interpretation; St. Thomas as Process Philosopher. That sort of thing is nowadays often called Deconstruction. A text can fruitfully be criticized from an utterly alien point of view, but to *interpret* it in such a topsy-turvy way is either naive or perverse.[10]

A subversive hermeneutic is a perversion of all the promises the old dead white men have made to each other over the centuries. It is, however, an honest perversion, for it maintains a close relationship to the overt meanings of the text while drawing forth a subtext of excluded meanings. It is neither an agreement nor a disagreement with the text, because each of these would require a place to stand within the heritage of men's thought. This it lacks. A subversive hermeneutic treats the text as a sacred text and as a dialogue rather than private property claimed by copyright of an old dead white man and his heirs.

Only recently have we begun to realize that texts may be independent of authors and their intentions. Ricoeur's *Interpretation Theory* is only one of several texts that have explored the way in which the voice of the author is, and is not, embedded in the text.[11] The text speaks for itself. The 'I' who narrates is a voice in the text. Nor does the author have privileged access to the text. Only the power of interpretation, its ability to open up, to clarify the text itself, has privilege. In this way, all texts gain the ambiguity that biblical texts have by nature of the hiddenness of their authorship. More than that, the texts lose the dated quality of being the product of a being who is, after all, dead. The text is a bridge to a past that comes alive within it. But what is alive can be changed, is as responsive to the present as to its original context. The aliveness of the past comes of its transformation into metaphor through the text. The meaning of the text reverberates between past and present in constantly changing patterns of interpretation. It is only the text that is independent of its author, which is important to anyone other than the author's psychologists and counselors. The text belongs to no one. Therefore, it is in play, as a ball is in play, with its interpreters.

If the right to speak with the text is determined by the power of an interpretation in making sense of it, then it may be that the text may not mean what one might assume the author meant. It is this possibility that opens the way for a feminist methodology, a methodology that takes seriously women's exclusion from the tradition. Suppose that there is that in the text which suppresses women's voices? What then? The text, by its silence, speaks of what it withholds from meaning. What is it that the text supposes about women's voice that makes such exclusion necessary? What must be excluded must also pose some risk to the text. Or, to put it another way, where there is exclusion, either there was nothing to be heard, or there is power. The confidence with which women now begin is the confidence that we have something to say and have always had something to say. This is a hard-won confidence, grounded in current experience and the breakthroughs of scholars who have been able to find traces of women's footprints even where women's voices have been erased. We, therefore, dare to claim that where there is silence, there is something of power to be silenced.

This confidence is not proof that the text has as its primary intention the project of silencing women. The supposition of the presence of women with something to say, who were nonetheless not included, supplies the hypothetical potential, the right to rethink old interpretations, to see if the hypothesis of another hidden text can actually be made to work. The proof is in the pudding, in the meaningful interpretation of texts. And, therefore, the bulk of this book will be the development of a methodology of feminist interpretation in the midst of and by way of doing interpretation. This book is one attempt to look for those moments in the texts of the old dead white men in which alternative projects might emerge. The goal is the development of a methodology broad enough and profound enough to be applied (and which is already being applied) by some feminists seeking a point to begin. That goal will be reached, not in the abstract but in concrete dialogue with points in the corpus of philosophy.

The choice of works to be interpreted in this book is somewhat arbitrary, governed by familiarity and success at gaining insights by using this methodology. Interpretation is the art of hearing and speaking with a text, an art that assumes that special kind of relationship which listens. It is not a science, to be applied arbitrarily or mechanically. Nonetheless, the imprint of women's exclusion suggests that all across patriarchal history there are texts with hidden messages. We have attempted to choose a range of works by old dead white men across the history of philosophy: Plato, Anselm, Kierkegaard, Nietzsche, Heidegger. In addition, these authors work particularly well, because valuations borrowing from metaphors familiar to the author in each case serve as a pivotal point in the argument. Also, these authors managed to achieve within their own works a kind of reflective distance and self-awareness which lets the text be multivocal, clearly offering up a variety of possible meanings.

Beginning with Plato, the book will exhibit its claim: that Plato's thought at several significant junctures shows signs of silencing the women's voices of his time. The goal is not to address the totality of the dialogues, as if Plato were on trial before us. Rather, we will take a small piece of thought, a metaphor perhaps, that somehow fits oddly into the whole or that gives insight into the whole of a dialogue or perhaps opens a way into several dialogues. In the case of Plato, this odd piece is the metaphor of the cave.[12] The metaphor of the cave in the *Republic* is a piece that hints at the directionality of the works as a whole, but in itself also depends on a set of valuations of light and dark, sun and earth, cave and surface. The interpretation will look at the metaphor of the cave as a silencing of a kind of meaning available in the concrete caves of Plato's time. It is here the rejected message of the Eleusinian women leaves an imprint on Plato's text. This unspoken dialogue about the nature of truth is our point of access to the cave they experienced. Certainly the master of dialogue cannot object to a few questions. Perhaps in the process we might learn something of an alternative truth, associated with caves, which stands in dialogical relationship to the parable's assertion of one ultimate truth.

With Anselm, the crucial discussion will focus on the hierarchical valuation of being that underlies his famous proof for the existence of God in the *Proslogium*. Here, we will look at the possibility that value is not something which can be ranked. Ranking itself reflected the hierarchical structure of the medieval church in its resistance to the multiplicity of religious meanings that persisted even into Anselm's time. If there is an ambiguity at the heart of the conception of "greater," of that than which nothing greater can be conceived, then it might be possible to conceptualize something even greater than the God Father. The ranking of value turns back upon the fathers and opens the question of any particular naming of divinity. Against monologic values, we will rethink the role of imagination in the wonder that makes Anselm's proof glow.

Kierkegaard has already opened his texts to reappropriation by setting them in the context of pseudonymity. The pseudonyms remove Kierkegaard's texts from any direct relationship to his own personal investments. The dialectical method that he employs allows the text to stand in conversation with itself and its reader, as a context for self-examination. Our argument will focus on the implications of the discussion of the genius, as he develops it in the curious little book *On Authority and Revelation: The Book on Adler.* Here there is a point for women to think through the implications of their own revolutionary turn, for his notion of the genius as *extraordinarious* provides an insight into the nature of any serious social change. But the question of revolutionary feminist thought has implications even for the nature of God. Here there is a collision between the transcendence of an immutable God and the claims of justice. This collision echoes the ordeal of Abraham that Kierkegaard investigates in *Fear and Trembling.* Abraham's confrontation with God hints at the dilemma facing revolutionary women, who would also like to speak with God.

Nietzsche echoes continually in the creating of this manuscript, if only because he also has engaged in the trans-valuing of meanings and metaphors he has received from the tradition. The structure of valuing and re-valuing, which informs his notion of "the will to power," open his texts to alternative meanings. In this case it is to Nietzsche himself that the reversal of values will be applied, as we examine *Beyond Good and Evil* and *Thus Spoke Zarathustra* in light of Nietzsche's own longing to ensure the maximization of masculine control in the face of the continuing threat from weakness and womanly values. Nietzsche, in his very commitment to a language of violence, speaks quite clearly of the reality of patriarchy. In so doing he betrays the trust of the fathers, who are most effectively in control when their power is most hidden. Nietzsche says what should have remained known only to the creators of euphemism. He thereby gives an opening for the saying of what he most fears, an opening to the reversal of the values and power sources of patriarchy.

The final text we will examine is Heidegger's *Poetry, Language, Thought.* Here we will follow the default of the gods back to the abyss that opened in the faulting of the earth. Heidegger's commitment to holding a place in philosophy for language, not as an object but as a Saying, opens into a horizon grounded in that original darkness. We will wander into the darkness, because as women all our speaking has long been confined to the darkness and the silent, and therefore we know something of what has been concealed. Here also, as with all the thinkers we have discussed, our project remains deeply in dialogue, deeply wedded to the thought and approach developed by Heidegger. Even so, our conclusions will seek another horizon than that available to patriarchy, with all that it dare not say about its origins.

Just as the most radical meanings in biblical interpretation have occurred in the works of women most committed to staying within a faithful conversation with the biblical truths, the purpose of this work is to be friendly to the texts themselves. The goal is not the disposal of the past but the possibility of reinhabiting it. These are *our* texts. We live with the past and we live within it. The past is not dead. Only the old dead white men are dead. Their texts live on as the context of contemporary meaning. With those dead men are buried our mothers. This will be our way of paying tribute to all the old dead crones who have resisted before and made life among the patriarchs a tenuous social reality, even for the philosophers.

Texts speak. They speak to all their interpreters, their lovers. We are their lovers, just as much as those who loved them for their power to perpetuate women's silence. What this methodology hopes to accomplish is the opening of the texts, the reveling in the multiple possibilities of meaning which exist within them. As an oral tradition preserves by its multiplicity of retelling, we will offer a new way of telling these old stories and thereby release the texts into their primary multivocity. Our hermeneutic will be "anarchic" in its approach to the text, in that it denies any single "true" meaning to the text, in favor of allowing texts to contain a multiplicity of competing meanings.[13] In this case the meaning sought is subversive. The meaning is quite intentionally not the accepted or the obvious meaning. However, the method proposed should intensify awareness and thought of the majority voice within the text, even while it offers up a minority voice. Only the monologue of meaning, which is the voice of patriarchy, will be lost.

Philo-*sophia*. The love of *Sophia*. *Sophia*, your sisters call you, look for you, among the graves of the old dead white men. If there is life and voice for women now, then it was always there. We will hear through the past to that other past, the one that always seemed to die a-borning. We will hear backward and beneath and beyond to that voice that was always and will always be the nemesis of conclusions and endings. All can be reopened. Then we will begin anew the beginning again.

NOTES

1. The silence of women in philosophy is so blatant as to need no documentation. More interesting is to examine the justifications of that silence men have given throughout the history of philosophy—including its most recent history. Of particular interest is Andrea Nye's discussion of this silence and its relevance to the deconstructionists. See Andrea Nye, "The Voice of the Serpent: French Feminism and Philosophy of Language," in *Women, Knowledge and Reality*, ed. Ann Garry and Marilyn Pearsall (Boston: Unwin Hyman, Inc., 1989), 233–49.

2. Michelle Walker identifies Luce Irigaray, Genevieve Lloyd, and Michele Le Doeuff with the project of attempting to understand the silence of women in philosophy, in a philosophical fashion. Irigaray, Lloyd, and Le Doeuff investigate the systematic silencing of both woman and women from the discourse of Western philosophy. They understand silence as involving an absence of women's voices from the dialogues that constitute the philosophical enterprise as a tradition. Michelle Walker, "Silence and Reason: Woman's Voice in Philosophy," *Australasian Journal of Philosophy* 71, no. 4 (December 1993), 400.

3. No one would, of course, claim any longer that their thought is factually independent of time and place. This is a naive claim. Yet operationally this transcendence is still true. It is still possible to be a Platonist, a Kantian, a Whiteheadian; indeed, it is impossible to be a philosopher and not be somehow attached to one or another of the old men. This is the practical immortality which is the lure of remembrance that Hannah Arendt so aptly describes. To reduce a philosopher to his history is to stand outside of philosophy and do something that is not philosophical.

4. Hans-Georg Gadamer, *Truth and Method* (New York: Seabury Press, 1975), 153–54.

5. The term "matrifocal" is one of many possible terms used to describe cultures that are matrilineal in terms of descent (inheritance through the mother) and that see the metaphors of birth and woman as primary sources for imagery of the divine. The use of the term is in contrast to "patriarchy," while rejecting the obvious alternative, "matriarchy," because these cultures were not "ruled by mothers."

6. See especially Stone's chapter "They Offered Incense to the Queen of Heaven" in *When God Was a Woman*, 163–79.

7. The Genesis story echoes parallel stories, such as Marduk's destruction of Tiamat in the Akkadian creation myth, the *Enuma Elish*. In this account, the splitting of the heavens is quite literally an act of dismembering the unity of the Goddess. In the Genesis version, the relationship to the feminine divinity who is ripped apart to form the two firmaments is hidden. Yet the name of the deep, *tehom*, and the nature of the violence hint at the preexistent feminine divinity. See Mary Daly's discussion of Goddess murder in *Gyn/Ecology* (Boston: Beacon, 1990), 107, 110.

8. Andrea Nye, "The Voice of the Serpent: French Feminism and Philosophy of Language," in *Women, Knowledge, and Reality*, ed. Ann Garry and Marilyn Pearsall (Boston: Unwin Hyman, Inc., 1989), 233–49. Nye uses the metaphor of the snake in the garden, and the wisdom it represents, as a powerful way of reexamining various philosophical conclusions arrived at by men.

9. "Prehistory" is another of those terms that has come to carry the immense weight of longing and controversy. Its traditional use was intended to contrast the time

of history, which began with the Egyptians or the Mesopotamians, with all the time before. The one was history, with dates, written texts, "civilization," and most especially, a direct continuity with our own present. The other, the prehistory, was primitive, obscure, important only for its necessity to produce history when it was finished. This set of assumptions began to break loose when it was discovered that those "prehistoric" times saw huge, sophisticated civilizations, buried beneath the rubble of "historic" societies. Feminists began to claim a certain relationship between the structure of those gynocentric societies and their erasure from the tomes of history. (Marija Gimbutas is an excellent source of technical discussion of the archaeological sources of such claims.) These civilizations are now seen as having existed across the globe. They were consistently destroyed by the patriarchal hordes that perfected only one art: warfare. The dating of the end of prehistory is subject to change without notice. Perhaps we may use as rule of thumb the date given to Yahweh's "creation" of a new universe, one week in 4004 B.C.E. God's creation was dependent on a full-fledged set of materials that he "separated" but did not create.

10. Stephen Crites, "*The Sickness unto Death*: A Social Interpretation," in *Foundations of Kierkegaard's Vision of Community: Religion, Ethics, and Politics in Kierkegaard*, ed. George B. Connell and C. Stephen Evans (Atlantic Highlands, N.J.: Humanities Press, 1992), 144.

11. Since Ricoeur, many thinkers have explored the idea of the self-referential nature of the text; that is, the way in which the text exists in reference to itself independent of the intentions of the author. Paul Ricoeur, *Interpretation Theory* (Fort Worth: The Texas Christian University Press, 1976), 12–19. There is, of course, here also a possible avenue for feminist interpretation. The relationship of 'text' to 'textile,' as explored by Mary Daly in *Gyn/Ecology* (Boston: Beacon Press, 1990), 4–5, shows how the dichotomy between the two served to reinforce male control. This approach also suggests the possibility of replacing the text in the tradition of spinsters who spin as a community, texts that "belong" to the wearer and the tradition from which they were spun. The question of authorship, which has proved so problematic in biblical studies, then discloses itself as the peculiar product of the self-aggrandizing tendencies of Western thought, in which the value of the thought was directly proportional to the name of the old dead white man to whom it could be attached. Once released from the author as immortal, the text is freed to speak to and out of a context that is in some sense identical with an individual human being and in some sense independent.

12. Luce Irigaray makes use of the same metaphor in her discussion of Plato's cave in *Speculum of the Other Woman*, trans. Gillian C. Gill (Ithaca: Cornell University Press, 1985). For Irigaray, however, woman herself operates as a metaphor within the philosophical corpus, as reflected in Plato's cave. "Woman" in this sense is an ontological other, rather than a historical reality which confronted Plato with concrete challenges. We seek the particular voices of particular women, silenced first by the violence of their fathers and brothers, and then again in the legitimation of their erasure posited in the philosophical texts.

13. Gail Stenstad, "Anarchic Thinking: Breaking the Hold of Monotheistic Ideology on Feminist Philosophy," in *Women, Knowledge, and Reality*, ed. Ann Garry and Marilyn Pearsall (Boston: Unwin Hyman, 1989), 331–39.

O n e

PLATO'S CAVE: SUBTERRANEAN EXPLORATIONS

THE HISTORY OF PHILOSOPHY begins in a conversation. Socrates walks about the city of Athens talking with those he encounters . . . and thereby begins something new. This is the foundation upon which Western civilized thought is based: an eccentric man who had peculiar conversations. Socrates seeks truth in many conversations that are generated only "from living day to day with the matter itself."[1]

> The term translated 'conversation' here is *sunousia*, which includes among its various meanings forms of social interaction that are not primarily verbal, such as dinner parties and cohabitation. But as Plato uses it, the term often refers expressly to verbal intercourse, of the sort that occurs in dialectical conversations specifically.[2]

The list of his conversations hints at the wider context of thought that already existed. The names of the dialogues are the names of partners in conversation: Crito, Euthyphro, Phaedo, Parmenides, Meno, and so forth. These men also thought and also talked. They also are philosophers, partners in this new enterprise.

The names have expanded now. The conversation has gone on and on, reaching across the centuries all in conversation with that man who walked the streets of the Agora in Athens and wondered about things. Philosophy is not simply sometimes a dialogue. It is conceived in speaking between people, born of the professional midwife, the man who delivers thought into the living presence that will grow up to be philosophy. Socrates has delivered up to history a child whose identity is grounded in speaking.

Socrates has delivered a child and named her *Sophia*: his love. But whose child is this? The conversations preexist Socrates. Thoughts are conceived before Socrates. The men with whom Socrates speaks were already thinkers in their own right. The audience of the young men of (what is to become) the Academy are to be impregnated by the conversation between Socrates and the thinkers with whom he converses. Socrates' method is maieutic, in

17

which he makes explicit the thoughts that have already been conceived. Even maieutics itself, Socrates self-proclaimed methodology, is an idea borrowed from his mother.[3] Socrates claims he is only a midwife for what already has been conceived.

Yet the Socrates handed down to philosophy, the Socrates who said all those clever things, does not exist except as a poetic invention of Plato. Plato conceives of Socrates as the one who then brings Plato to give birth to philosophy. Plato is Socrates' poet. Socrates is both Plato's father and Plato's son, for he comes both before and after.

> S. is P., Socrates is Plato, his father and his son, therefore the father of his father, his own grandfather and his own grandson.[4]

The relationship between the two is tangled, but what tangles it further is that it is neither Socrates nor Plato that is conceived but the beginning of philo-*Sophia*. Within this tangled relationship, a child is conceived, the child *Sophia*. Here is the reversal of the whole project of birth, and this reversal serves as the myth of origin for philosophy. The philosopher who comes after creates the philosopher who came before who is a midwife for that which must therefore also predate him. The whole project begins before it begins. The conversation is something that is inherited and picked up from those who came before.

Perhaps then the true beginning is in the conversation, the partners with whom Socrates converses. Their speaking makes possible his speaking, makes possible the poet Plato. Philosophy emerges out of their thought, to which Socrates' own ideas are but the riposte, the response. The list of the dialogues tells us something about philosophy's origins. It tells us who was speaking. Before Plato was Socrates. Before Socrates was the pre-Socratics. Before the pre-Socratics was Homer.

> For literature Homer is the beginning, though every scholar is aware that he is nowise primitive; for theology, or—if we prefer so to call it—mythology, Homer presents, not a starting-point, but a culmination, a complete achievement, an almost mechanical accomplishment, with scarcely a hint of *origines,* an accomplishment moreover, which is essentially literary rather than religious, sceptical and moribund already in its very perfection. . . . Beneath this splendid surface lies a stratum of religious conceptions, ideas of evil, of purification, of atonement . . . at once more primitive and more permanent.[5]

The beginning begins with Socrates and maybe a few old dead white men from before. The beginning traces a starting point, and it tells us who was not speaking. The dialogue between thinkers defines philosophy as an inside circle and therefore raises the question of criteria, of what (and who) is outside. The dialogue consists, of course, solely of men. This is the beginning of philosophy as it is its end: all men. Once again the question arises backward. From the course of philosophy, in which only men participate, we are not surprised that only men constitute its beginning. Of course. The conception of philosophy is homoerotic, emerging out of the love men have for each other, for their speaking and thinking and being.

> So when someone rises by these stages, through loving boys correctly, and begins to see this beauty, he has almost grasped his goal.[6]

This is the conception which has no need of women, to which women are not invited, and Socrates is the midwife. The question of woman does not even arrive as a philosophical question. It is a moot point, a mute point. Women are not in the conversation, are not invited to the delivery, and thereby the birth of the child, *"Philo-Sophia,"* gains the proper respectability. Like *Athena*, without a mother, philosophy springs fully clothed in armor from the head of man. Thus the beginning.

So begin all the myths of men. God births man from the dust and delivers woman by cesarean section from the man. The man posits his own beginnings, complete and whole, without approximation, growth, or the participation of woman.

> Only God who refuses all determination and has nothing behind him, nothing that goes back earlier than he does, is. Extrapolation of the copula of all existence, of all that is, effectively. Has been, one day, conceived. . . . Eclipse of the mother, of the place (of) becoming, whose non-representation or even disavowal upholds the absolute being attributed to the father. He no longer has any foundation, he is beyond all beginnings.[7]

Socrates' mother was a midwife. The metaphor calls up an earlier possibility, that Socrates learned his skill from a woman. The images of midwifery tie the dialogue to the missing women. The images point back before the beginning.

The history of philosophy takes Socrates as the beginning, but the beginning is a man-made determination, like claiming the death of Christ as the beginning of the calendar. We mark time from *anno domini* (A.D.), but then find that in order to make sense of those times which are A.D. we must also speak of what is before Christ (B.C.). The beginning points back. The beginning is a political and ideological claim rather than a true representation of time. Likewise, to speak of Socrates as the beginning of philosophy still necessitates the acknowledgment of the pre-Socratics. Socrates' claim to be a midwife points to the practice of midwifery as belonging to women. Socrates' philosophy points to the pre-Socratics as the thought before thought.

Socrates' dialogues emerge whole and complete out of the darkness of what was before, which remains as fragments and hints. The fragmentary remains of Thales and Heraclitus exist to tantalize us but offer no path back behind the beginning. They remain men but still tied to yet earlier realities of thought, hints of hints back into darkness. When they speak, their speaking is tied to and responsive to religious traditions that once venerated the divine as woman. Thus Parmenides begins his exercise in logic by quoting the revelation of the Goddess.

> The steeds that draw my chariot were conducting me to the farthermost reach of my desire, bringing me at length on to the resounding road of the Goddess, along which he who knows is borne through all cities. Along this road I was carried—yes, the wise horses drew me in my chariot while maidens led the way . . . When these gates were flung back on their hinges, . . . [t]he Goddess greeted me kindly, and taking my hand in hers she spoke these words: . . . "Never shall it be proven that not-being is. From that path of inquiry restrain your mind. Do not let custom, born of everyday experience, tempt your eyes to be aimless, your ear and tongue to be echoes. Let reason be your judge when you consider this much disputed question. The heart when left to itself misses the road."[8]

The *Logos* of the pre-Socratics is still bound and beholden to its birth mother, *Mythos*. Myth does not exist outside of logic but the two are entwined, and their roots point back to a time in which thought gained its power by association with the divine feminine. The logic of those who come before Socrates is a dreaming, poetic wondering about the universe. And even then, the fragments of pre-Socratic thought (so-called because they are philosophers only because Plato regarded them so, and thus preserved them) that remain are too careful, too complete, too clearly responsive to yet other ideas to be the real beginning. Before the pre-Socratics, there may well have been a wealth of thought and speculation and wondering. The fact that it is missing, and Socrates is complete, tells us more about a process of destruction than it does about the beginning.

This is a historical claim about philosophy based not on archaeological evidence but rather textual evidence. This is the methodology upon which this project is based: to seek out the metaphors that hint at alternative histories of philosophy. The historical claim that our philosophical heritage is truncated rests on the same "nothing" that allows philosophy to claim that its history begins with Socrates. It is, in fact, the same claim. The "nothing" from which philosophy emerges whole and complete in the dialogues of Socrates is the "nothing" of a tradition that began by repudiating what came before. It is a thought that emerges whole and complete, out of a tradition of war and violence and annihilation, that erased peoples and their memories.

> Yet for thousands of years before the classical myths took form and then were written down by Hesiod and Homer in the seventh century B.C., a rich oral tradition of mythmaking had existed. Strains of the earlier tradition are evident in the later myths, which reflect the cultural amalgamation of three waves of barbarian invaders, the Ionians, the Achaeans, and

finally the Dorians, who moved into Greece from 2500 to 1000 B.C. These invaders brought with them a patriarchal social order and their thunderbolt God, Zeus. What they found when they entered Greece was a firmly rooted religion of Goddess worship.[9]

Philosophy participated in that destruction, depending on violence to ensure the triumph of its self-generating truth. In exchange for the conqueror's patronage, philosophy provided the conquerors with legitimation for their new order. The philosophers continued to derive meaning from the myths which they nonetheless rejected. All that remains of what went before is what is preserved by the philosophers as notes in a museum of lost ideas, as defeated enemies' heads might be arranged decoratively upon a city's walls. What was before was destroyed; therefore, the Platonic dialogues are the beginning. The only place to begin, even to begin again, is with the texts that remain: the texts of the tradition.

Perhaps someday archaeologists may discover the philosophical equivalent of the Dead Sea Scrolls or the codices of *Nag Hammadi*, but until then what we have is what the fathers of philosophy, the old dead white men, chose to preserve. Historians can tell us much about the destruction that marked the times from which patriarchal civilization sprang.

> The study of mythical images provides one of the best proofs that the Old European world was not the proto-Indo-European world and that there was no direct and unobstructed line of development to the modern Europeans. The earliest European civilization was savagely destroyed by the patriarchal element and it never recovered, but its legacy lingered in the substratum which nourished further European cultural developments.[10]

Feminist historians have redirected and intensified that search by linking the fragments of the great wars that precede and inform history with the destruction of societies that honored women. The dialogues of Socrates rest upon the triumph of those men and those wars.

The dialogues of Socrates also replay the defeat and exclusion of women from civilized discourse. The dialogues speak of women, but never with women. Only in the *Symposium* does a woman participate. In this "symposium" of men, which is not tied to any man's name, Socrates credits his information to a woman, a priestess named Diotima (*Symposium* 201d-215a).[11] But the woman who participates in that dialogue is absent. Socrates speaks for her. She, like Socrates' mother the midwife, comes before the beginning. She appears in the history of philosophy only after a man has claimed her words.

There are those who would say philosophy is excused from taking seriously the absence of women as a philosophical problem, because their absence reflects only the social situation of ancient Greece. For these people,

Diotima exists only as a creation of Socrates, to be ignored except in foot-notes on the historical background of the time. The silencing of women continues in men's notes of the irrelevance of their absence. The women of that time remain mute, in the background, before the beginning.

If women are going to speak, the speaking must begin in the beginning, that is to say, now. Luce Irigaray represents such a return to the origins that lie behind and within the artificial beginning point established by Plato. She is both our contemporary and a voice with the past. She returns us to the point of exclusion and opens up the conversation. Her essay entitled "Plato's *Hystera*"[12] is the beginning of a constructive feminist reclaiming of the beginnings of philosophy.

Irigaray notes the desire of men to claim for themselves the right to begin, a claim that originates in a forgetting of the place from which human existence originates. Irigaray posits the "before" as a reference to the universal precondition of existence in the experience of birth. The man, the philosopher, strives to forget that there is anything before his coming into self-awareness.

> *He who has never dwelled within the mother will always already have seen the light of day.* The oblivion of incarceration in the shadow and the water of the mother's cave, room, womb, that immemorial home, the blind-ness shrouding the memory, blocking reminiscence, that inoperable leucoma covering the eye (of the soul)—all this the Father vows to do away with by dazzling you with an endless day. It is too early, however, to put such an *alētheia* into operation. *Forgetting you have forgotten* requires a long and methodical initiation. Some time must elapse, some distance must be covered, some turns managed, mimes enacted. There must be a continu-ing and overlapping of operations which repeat and seek to transpose traces that are effective particularly perhaps because they resist appearing. Scenographies which precede and prepare the possible re-inscription of ideal forms. Within the soul.[13]

Irigaray ties the exclusion of women to the desire of man to forget the ontological priority of woman. She traces the metaphors through the process of denial, showing the underside of the careful erasure of memory. She lo-cates her analysis of the forgetting in the allegory of the cave, with its echoes of womb and its centrality to Plato's thought in the *Republic*.

The *Republic* is a strange dialogue, barely remaining within the pretense of conversation. Perhaps this is because the missing speaker is so closely present. Following Irigaray, we shall look at this dialogue in hopes of dis-covering a voice for the missing speaker. We will be following hints, as does Irigaray, though perhaps in a different way, a way more linked to an archaeology of texts than to the ontogeny of the soul.

We begin with the banter, the typical banter of men who have no need to concern themselves with a woman's sensibilities. The dialogue establishes itself as without women, as men talking to men. Yet talk of women (a women's religious festival, women's sexuality, women's desirability to men) helps set the stage for the serious discussion to come. Socrates, and the implied male audience, is "charmed" by the words of Cephalus:

> Indeed I was present at one time when someone asked the poet Sophocles: "How are you in regard to sex, Sophocles? Can you still make love to a woman?" "Hush man, the poet replied, I am very glad to have escaped from this, like a slave who has escaped from a mad and cruel master." I thought then that he was right, and I still think so, for a great peace and freedom from these things come with old age: after the tension of one's desires relaxes and ceases, then Sophocles' words certainly apply, it is an escape from many mad masters. (*Republic* 329c-d)[14]

The overcoming of the "mad masters" is something that men must achieve, which is why old age is something to be desired and something that makes possible philosophy. Once women are out of the way, men can begin thinking. The conception has disappeared, and the birth belongs to the male midwife, Socrates.

The *Republic* takes place in the midst of a festival, the festival of Bendis. The men come to watch. They watch the women, though being beyond such things, prefer to talk with the young men.[15] Socrates and his friends are mere spectators; they are present but do not participate. They are removed from what is going on and thus begins their reflection.

The topic of these reflections is justice, which is raised as if by chance. Such a conversation, a *sunousia*, is made possible because old men, old rich men, are independent of conditions, just as these men are unconnected with the festival that they attend. Having begun by disrelationship, the dialogue is freed to pursue Truth. Men rise above their surroundings, and contemplate rising above their mortal conditions. For this Socrates is well suited to be midwife, for he has consistently shown how one might, as a man, transcend the conditions of birth (and thus death) to find what cannot be born of woman. Socrates is the preeminent male midwife who births away from women, out of women, free of his wife and all wives: the man who brings men to birth as the ideal of man.

Let us step back into the negated context, the festival of Bendis[16] on the nineteenth of the Greek month, *Thargelion*.[17] Socrates reports in the opening lines:

> I went down to the Piraeus yesterday with Glaucon, the son of Ariston. I intended to say a prayer to the goddess, and I also wanted to see how they would manage the festival, since this was its first celebration. I thought our own procession was a fine one and that which the Thracians had sent

was no less outstanding. After we had said our prayer and witnessed the procession we started back toward the city. (*Republic* 327a-b)

The worship of Bendis is something new to the city, as indicated in the quote. The festival was introduced to the Athenians from Thrace, more or less as a diplomatic move to ensure Thracian cooperation in the Peloponnesian war.[18] It is thus of historical interest, no more. The festival is a mere occasion; speculation is the thing.

The *Republic* is only superficially like the ironic interchanges of other dialogues. Justice as a subject of debate gives way to speculation on the ideal society. The substance of the reflections is a proposal of an alternative to the society of Plato's own day, as symbolized in this new, popular festival. What good is it for men to speculate about the Good as such when society offers the easy out of divine propitiation?

> They offer in proof a mass of writings by Musaeus and Orpheus, offspring, as they say, of Selene and the Muses. In accordance with these they perform their ritual and persuade not only individuals but whole cities that, both for the living and for the dead, there are absolutions and purifications for sin by means of sacrifices and pleasurable, playful rituals. These they call initiations which free from punishment yonder, where a dreadful fate awaits the uninitiated. (*Republic* 364e-365a)

The Muses and the Moon (Selene), whose descendants still influence society, corrupt the very conception of justice. The conversation has not merely left the festival; it turns away from what the festival represents. To discuss justice, one must posit a society grounded in rationality. Plato poses against what is, another "what is," a possibility. The irony is not absent but is present in its relationship to the concrete festival to be negated.

The religious festivals of Athens, represented by the context of the dialogue's beginning, celebrate the popular religious life of the Greek people, especially women.[19] The festivals point bodily back before the beginning by which philosophy posits itself. In order to begin, philosophy must negate all origins and begin again . . . with a reconception of the gods. The poets must be limited, brought within the limits set by philosophy.[20] The limit is the censorship in the name of the good, the removal of all images that point to that which is not rational, not perfect, not under control:

> Such then are the kinds of stories which should be heard about the gods, and the kinds that should not be heard from childhood on, by those who are to honour both their gods and their parents, and who will attach no little importance to friendship with one another. . . . We must then, it seems, supervise such tales and those who undertake to tell them, and beg them not to rail at things in the underworld in the unrestrained manner they do, but rather to praise them, as their stories are neither true nor beneficial to

future warriors.... We shall expunge all that sort of thing. (*Republic* 386a, b-c)

The voice that is not to be heard is identified with the popular religion as represented by the festival at hand. It is not that Bendis is untrue, or that any of the myths are untrue, but they are injurious to the production of warriors/thinkers.

It is important to keep in mind that the context of this dialogue is the other voice to be refuted. The whole dialogue, the *Republic*, is a dialogue and an argument against. Adeimantus tells Socrates:

When all such sayings about the attitudes of men and gods toward virtue and vice are so often repeated, what effect, my dear Socrates, do we think they have upon the minds of our youth? One who is naturally talented and able, like a bee flitting from flower to flower gathering honey, to flit over these sayings and to gather from them an impression of what kind of man he should be and of how best to travel along the road of life, would surely repeat to himself the saying of Pindar: should I by justice or by crooked deceit scale this high wall and thus live my life fenced off from other men? (*Republic* 365a-b)

This popular wisdom that might corrupt youth is the stuff of the festival of Bendis. The gods must be put in their place, far away from human affairs. The mothers, who make cowards of us all, must be silenced. Socrates tells Adeimantus:

Then, my dear sir, I said, let no poet tell us that "like unto strangers from every land the gods in various shapes frequent our towns" nor tell us lies about Proteus and Thetis; neither in their tragedies nor other poems bring on Hera in altered form, as a priestess begging for "the life-giving sons of the river, Argive Inachus," and many other such lies they must not tell. Nor must our mothers, believing them, terrify their children by telling bad stories, saying that some gods wander at night in the shape of strangers from many lands. These stories slander the gods, and at the same time make children more cowardly.—They must not be told. (*Republic* 381d-e)

The philosophers must replace the gods of the festivals with the realm of the Ideal.

The apparent targets of the dialogue are the poets, and, specifically, Homer and Hesiod. The poets preserve the unreason of the gods. Once again the dialogue is between men, but someone is missing. Homer is not available for discussion, but he is taken as the spokesman for the dramatic representations of the acts of the gods and goddesses. It is too bad that Homer cannot reply, but after all, who can argue with a poet? Perhaps this is why Homer is not given a chance to reply. Poets must be controlled, because they cannot be refuted. Yet Homer himself is also not the ultimate target.

The festivals, such as the one "speaking" with Socrates in the present dialogue (even though it is not allowed a word), in some sense exist independently of Homer and predate his poetry.

The act by which poets bring the gods into the human realm, *mimesis*, connects the different levels of being together. It calls back into being the time prior to philosophy, when *Mythos*, not *Logos*, ruled. Plato limits the meaning of the term *mimesis* to the making of images, the mimicry, which is by definition not the true.[21] Mimicry is not so much untruth as it is a way of participating experientially in truth. The threat posed by the religious implications of myth is that the imitation also changes the nature of those who participate. By the recalling, the ritual reenactment calls back up other kinds of interactions, other kinds of knowing and being. The space of ritual in Socrates' time was ostensibly controlled by the *polis*, yet within popular religious ceremony, the status distinctions of the state were blurred. Ritual acts, such as the festival, create a space in which the divisions between truth and untruth, mortals and immortals, slaves and free, even men and women, are broken down.

Socrates explains to Adeimantus the danger of mimetic imitation in drama and the training that Guardians ought to provide the children of Athens:

> We shall then not allow those for whom we profess to care and who must grow up into good men to imitate, being men, a young or older woman who is railing at a man, or quarreling with the gods, or bragging while thinking herself happy, or one in misfortune and sorrows and lamentations, even less one in illness or in love or in labour.—Absolutely. Nor must they imitate slaves, female or male, performing slavish tasks.—Not that either. (*Republic* 395d-e)

The poets and the festivals exist to some degree independent of state control. Such independence could prove disastrous for the commonwealth, for order is replaced with disorder.

The *polis*, as a rational, male-controlled invention, is dependent for its existence upon the rigid distinctions between free men and slaves. Plato's ideal state reflects and reinforces the distinction between those who are free to explore higher matters and those who live in bondage to support such enterprises.

> What all Greek philosophers, no matter how opposed to *polis* life, took for granted is that freedom is exclusively located in the political realm, that necessity is primarily a prepolitical phenomenon, characteristic of the private household organization, and that force and violence are justified in this sphere because they are the only means to master necessity—for instance, by ruling over slaves—and to become free.[22]

From where we stand now, within the edifice built upon the philosophical contemplation of Plato's thought, this appears to be the only possible way in which philosophy can exist. The *Republic* exists as the structural under-pinning of philosophical speculation. Thought belongs to those men who can live off the labor of others. This social vision is the foundation Plato built. This is the dialogue in which that vision is delivered by the male midwifery of Socrates.

The dialogue, for most of its overt structure, is a monologue. Socrates speaks and his friends agree. Its internal structure, however, draws its energy from what it negates, what it stands against. But this dialogue has taken on a dangerous enemy, an enemy that it wishes simultaneously to argue against and to silence. This is an argument, but it is also a war against softness, femininity, a war against all that would undermine the structure that makes philosophy a male enterprise. Plato's Socratic dialogues are carefully crafted, but here he has stretched that medium to its limit. This is a dialogue with one who cannot be allowed to speak, a refutation of an argument too dangerous even to be allowed to be heard. Even though Socrates converses with his friends, the real dialogue in the *Republic* takes place in a far more subtle fashion.

The *Republic* is in dialogue with a festival. The lack of details about the festival suggests that this festival stands in for festivals in general, and, indeed, the comments about the "messiness" of Greek religion suggests a general reference. Yet somehow this festival provides an appropriate context for a hidden critique of popular religious tradition, the religion of the people. And there is something about the festival that points to what is not named in the dialogue, that one (or ones) who are not allowed to speak on their own behalf.

The festival of Bendis, the *Bendideia*, is an appropriate place to discuss the interaction of state and religion, because it was, probably from its beginning, a state-sponsored event.[23] Plato would certainly have known its introduction from Thrace, and could quite possibly have witnessed the discussions that led to its establishment. The *Bendideia* was a civic creation and would have involved discussions that may well be reflected in the initial discussions in the *Republic*. The *Bendideia* reflects the tradition of rational discourse on the use of religion for political security within the polis.[24]

The *Bendideia* also was an appropriate context for the discussion, because, even when affirmed by rational discourse, it participated in a tradition that countered rationality. The celebration of the festival linked Bendis with the Thracian worship of Dionysus.[25] Though chosen to cement the relationship of Thrace and Athens, the festival that Socrates attended was full of the irrationality associated with the orgiastic side of Greek religion. The festival of Bendis represented what must be countered if ever the project of patriarchal philosophy was to triumph.

The festival of Bendis is our access to the missing voice. Bendis was a

Goddess, the wife of Dionysus, from Thrace.[26] *Bendideia* was linked to the mystery religions by association with Dionysus and possibly by practice.[27] Yet its association with a Goddess, and a foreign Goddess at that, might well identify the festival with the earlier periods in which the mystery religions were still grounded in women's rites of initiation.[28] The festival creates a unique space in ancient Greece in which women shared space with men in a (nonpolitical) public space. The dialogue makes no mention of the purpose of the festival, nor the nature of the participation, nor of the participants. Information about the *Bendideia* must come from elsewhere.[29]

In contrast to the open participation of men and women in the festival, the dialogue removes itself from the festival and concentrates the conversation on the social interaction of men in isolation from women and practical concerns. Indeed, the removal of the discussion from the festival represents a fundamental move within the text away from all real spaces and realms of discourse and into a specially constructed ideal world. The discussion of justice, which appears to be of concrete concern to a group of enfranchised male citizens of the political world of Athens, serves as mere point of departure to an abstract discussion of the male ideal.

> A suspension within the dramatic frame gradually takes place when a new method of inquiry is chosen and it is resolutely agreed 'to walk it' to its very end (369b). The interlocutors have shifted their attention from the ongoing festivities as well as from the rest of their business, and embarked on the discursive journey that will last several hours at the very least. Whatever they had in mind before, and certainly their desire to see 'those things worth seeing' at the night festival, is put aside. . . . Displaced from the event for which they have gathered, suspending the hectic night with its promised excitements, they are immersing themselves in a flow of discourse that knows no nights and days, having a very different promise in mind.[30]

The dialogue removes itself from the festival and also internally from any real concern with the actual world as it is lived. There is a yet deeper level of removal, a historical removal of women from all conversations. The seclusion and isolation of Greek women in the home represents their removal from the realm of public discourse.[31] Within the structure of the religious festivals, their sequestering in women's quarters is temporarily suspended.

The relationship between the dialogue and the festival reflects the relationship between philosophical speculation and women. Women are relegated to the lower levels, the levels of labor and mortality, the levels of the irrational that is not fully amenable to male control. From this reality the discourse of the *Republic* withdraws itself to discuss that which cannot be corrupted by those who have removed themselves from the corrupting influence of women and their mysteries.

Women are absent from the discussion, both in the sense that they do not speak and in the sense that nothing is said of their exclusion. Yet their absence shapes the discourse, especially in the implicit disgust for all things associated with them—and all aspects of lived reality increasingly fall into this category. The relationship of the dialogue to women is negative in the sense that it denies them entry into the discussion. Beneath the tension is the suppressed memory of the defeat of those cultures that honored women's participation. The attempt to make this argument from a mere lack is, of course, difficult. The festival hints at a potential point of departure and of context, given that it is a festival honoring a Goddess and that women's participation is indubitable.

The festival hints at the hidden discussion of the relationship of women and women's wisdom to the enterprise of philosophy. There is no discussion of the festival, yet the placing of the dialogue in relation to the festival opens the question. The discussion soon leaves the festival behind as a setting and as a possible topic for discourse. The dialogue does return to it in due course, however, in a yet more hidden fashion. The mystery of Bendis disappears, but a deeper mystery serves as the setting for the section of the text that has been most influential upon generations of students to follow. The allegory of the cave is the story of a mystery and an echo of a mystery now hidden from our view.

Socrates' audience was familiar with the way in which caves had played a part in the search of the populace for enlightenment, but Socrates' approach would have come as something of a shock. Caves had in ancient times been associated with the Goddess, and for his Greek audience, probably carried a degree of sanctity.

> Rituals in her honor took place in womb-like caves, often with vulva-like entrances and long, slippery corridors; both the cave entrances and grave sites were often painted with blood-like red ochre, a clay used as pigment.[32]

Now, so many centuries later, we have no memory of a time when the nature religions linked caves to the mystery of birth and likened them to the womb. Yet Socrates' use of the cave reflects that earlier sanctity. The women of Socrates' day still retained some trace of their ancient power, if only on festival days. And one of the most powerful of all their mysteries was at Eleusis. By the time of Socrates, men had been allowed into the mysteries. But even so, the mysteries of Eleusis retained their relationship to women through the myth of Demeter and Kore/Persephone.[33]

The relationship to the allegory is more tentative, for nowhere does Socrates acknowledge that his cave is an inversion and a parody of the mysteries. Yet for his listeners, the parallels must have been striking. By not acknowledging the relationship, Socrates could mock the sacred elements without danger of a direct confrontation with devotees of Demeter. This means that our discussion also is a dialogue in possibility. The claim we would like to make is a claim upon thought and from within the confines of philosophical speculation rather than historical fact. Just as Plato invented a Socrates who both was and was not the historical Socrates, this discussion will focus upon a dialogue between the truths proposed by the Eleusinian mysteries and the *Republic*, a dialogue that both is and is not historical.

Our enterprise is not without precedent. We follow in the footsteps of Luce Irigaray, who has explored and developed a conversation with those men of Athens.

> The myth of the cave, for example, or as an example, is a good place to start. Read it this time as a metaphor of the inner space, of the den, the womb or *hystera*, sometimes of the earth—though we shall see that the text inscribes the metaphor as, strictly speaking, impossible. Here is an attempt at making metaphor, at trying out detours, which not only is a silent prescription for Western metaphysics but also, more explicitly, proclaims (itself as) everything publicly designated as metaphysics, its fulfillment, and its interpretation.[34]

The "detour" she has in mind is in line with the structure of the dialogue itself, which is full of detours. Even the conversation, which is the dialogue, is itself a detour taken by the men who are attending the festival. Irigaray's detour returns to the conversation what is missing, the missing voice that informs the project. Irigaray fills out the myth, returns to it the meanings that shape its metaphors, the images that make the myth work for the men that hear the myth and the men who come after. Irigaray's project reaches, therefore, beyond Plato's myth to the underside of the myth that shapes Western metaphysics, which is also a metaphor and which also appeals to men because it supports the patriarchal project of meaning.

Irigaray's discussion is grounded in the modern philosophical conversation. It participates in the interpretation of texts that "de-constructs" those texts by relating them to internal and external structures that exist independently of the text's overt claims to meaning. Socrates search for "Truth" decouples truth from the authority that spoke it. At the same time, the texts beginning with Plato's dialogues form a new kind of authority. The authority of the classical texts has been such that the only routes of interpretation allowed were either based on agreement or disagreement with the text. Both possibilities assume the transparency of meaning in the text. But texts are not transparent. They gain their meaning from the interplay of metaphors and symbols, which exist independently of the overt intentionality of the text or its author.

Irigaray exemplifies this kind of hermeneutic. She neither agrees nor disagrees with the overt claims of the *Republic*. Rather she turns the claims into an internal conversation of metaphor. She makes the allegory of the cave speak with itself, as a series of competing claims that are generated from within the metaphors themselves. From Irigaray's point of entry into the dialogue and the method she uses to deconstruct its meaning, a pathway is opened into the metaphoric structure of Western metaphysics. From this conversation, women are not excluded. Indeed, the images of the feminine clarify the inner workings of Western metaphysics in "its fulfillment, and its interpretation."

Irigaray's exploration into the metaphoric underpinnings of the text removes the truth claims from the univocity of authority. Words speak on many levels, and these levels arrange themselves in relationships of overt and covert meaning. Socrates' argument attempts to counter the multiple meanings of words by pointing to an absolute, if inexpressible, meaning. This argument suppresses the relationships between words, metaphors, and meanings and substitutes an authority of argument that is itself removed from argument. It is this extratextual claim to authority that has prevented the audience from participating in the exploration of meaning from within the text. Only those already committed to the maintenance of the authority of the text over life and over textual structures of meaning are allowed into the discussion. And from this discussion women are forever barred, or rather, as Irigaray paraphrases the *Republic*, woman shall participate only insofar as she can "fulfill the same functions as man, as guardians of the State. But, apart from the fact that she will perform her duties *less well*, as a result of her inferior nature, she will also participate only insofar as she is the *same* as a man."[35] Man is the standard and the authority on reality. But this is a limited reality, a reality without depth or dream.

When Luce Irigaray analyzes the language of the allegory of the cave, she releases the language into a kind of dreamlike self-exposé. Rooted in the traditions of psychoanalysis with its assertions that consciousness reflects meanings which it did not intend, such analysis goes beyond analysis of 'slips' to reflection upon the subterranean meanings of the fully conscious creations of human intellect. Such deconstruction uses the independence of the text from the structures of the conscious intentionality, to create alternative interpretations. Irigaray's discussion of the allegory floats in the same intellectual space as does the subconscious. The relationships between the text she reconstructs and the text traditionally handed to students of philosophy are shocking and revealing. This is not an argument that proves anything about the text at hand. Rather one comes across realizations and re-cognitions; one is twisted from the course set by the text and its interpreters to see through the text's intentions to the text's submerged meanings. Just as the captive in the cave is dragged into the light, there is a sense that one does not want to see what Irigaray wants to show, but one recognizes it when one sees it.

Irigaray is inherently critical of the overt voice of Plato's text. Irigaray is to Plato's text what Xanthippe (Socrates' wife) is to Socrates. They are both excluded and present within the text. Irigaray is the strident voice that stops speculation in its tracks, even as Xanthippe must be dismissed by Socrates as a distraction. Irigaray brings up what Socrates has forgotten, suppressed, locked up with his wife in the women's quarters. She is within the text, but in a dialectical way. By overcoming her exclusion, she participates in the ideality that shapes the form of her own discourse, which is always with Plato and not about Plato.

Her analysis is a dialogue with a submerged voice within the text. She introduces the suppressed ideality of woman in the form appropriate to a dialogue that has escaped real space for the unreal space of ideality. Irigaray in this sense is very close to Plato. Irigaray participates in the same floating space of myth and possibility that forms the methodological structure of the Platonic dialogue. Yet the myths and possibilities that Irigaray draws out into the light of day are opposed to the explicit intentionality of the text. She, like Plato, creates myths that are responsive to the ideality of meaning. She adds the missing voice who dreams along with Socrates, drawing out the image into new realms of ideality, yet leaving the ideality itself intact.

Irigaray imagines the cave as a womb and carefully follows Socrates through the metaphor of the cave, but now that metaphor is disclosed as also being a metaphor for the womb. Her text is in dialogue with the existing text in a way that almost demands reading the two together. Socrates tells his story: the cave, the captives staring fixedly at the shadows on the wall, the release into daylight, the slow adjustment to the light which is also the Good. Irigaray walks with him through the same story, but her seeing lets us into the story from another point, showing us how the captive is being forced, not allowed, out of the cave, which now echoes our maternal inheritance.

It is this inheritance that we have lost by virtue of a long project of thought constructed by men who have rejected their own origins in exchange for a story that places their own gender in a position of transcendent value. The consequences of this transmuted story shape the interiority of every metaphor and every metaphysics. Metaphysics recapitulates ontogeny. Every metaphysical question reverberates with memories of that from which we originate, namely, the mother. The questions of metaphysics are all answered by more or less disguised memories of the relationship to the mother.

And, but, what of the "*first matter*"? What is this unknowable entity that has an existence in itself? Something that eludes the question "what is?" (*tode ti*). Might this not be the body of the mother, and the process of becoming flesh within the mother? Of becoming *phýsis* always already constituted as the *hypokeimenon* that defines the substance of man? Might it not be this bodiliness shared with the mother, which as yet has no movement of its own, has yet to divide up time or space, has in point of fact no way of measuring the container or the surrounding world or the content or the relations among all these? It cannot be shaped in any distinct mold. Fusion, confusion, transfusion of matter, of body-matter, in which even the elementary would escape any static characterization. In which same and other would have yet to find their meaning.[36]

Plato stands at the beginning of the forgetting and denial of origins, a point of some importance for the history of philosophy. Irigaray returns with him and participates with him in the beginning of that project, skillfully unwinding the knots as he ties them in the cords of meaning. She moves within the metaphors that are within the dialogue. The price of her admittance, however, is to share in Plato's denial of real time and real space. Her approach is grounded in an abstract, universal understanding of the womb and of woman that can serve as a measure equally for every philosopher and every metaphysics. Irigaray unlocks the authority, the closure on the argument, opening it for feminist deconstruction. What is still lacking is location, a possibility of grounding the project in the concrete struggle of women to reply to the theft of meaning by men.

In all times and all places the suppression of women took energy and thought. In all times and in all places, women resisted. In all times and all places men talked and thought about women, and their thought and their talk served the purpose of maintaining the social situation and common assumptions of their time about the place of women in the background. Now as much as then, men would like to have claimed to have risen above, to have transcended the frame of the real, to have reached the place in which pure thought and the Idea reigns without contamination by daily life as embodied in women. The rising above is the direct philosophical contribution to the oppressors' justification of the putting down of the "other," the other that is none other than woman.

The ideal world is a transcendent world, a world "on top" of the other world. Its images are all images of hierarchy and superiority, of heavens and suns. The place of woman is below, in body and mortality and messy labor. This relationship is sometimes recognized, but always it is as if woman is regarded as less because of her association with that which *is* less. If woman is associated with body, then woman will be regarded as less. The history of the denigration of the body, of bodily functions, and of the experience of being embodied parallels the history of denigration of woman. The linkage between woman and body goes back so far in our cultural history that its roots are invisible. The invisibility makes it possible to mistake the historical roots of this interconnection of symbols (woman/body) as ontological rather than as historical. The difficulty in doing such a history is that this event happened prior to history as his-story. What we see in Plato is the remnant of this ancient linkage.

And it all begins with Plato and his cave. Here the nature of truth is once and for all removed from the realm to which women have been assigned. Plato can only justify his claim by making an ontological argument about the necessary priority of the new transcendence. How are we to argue that justice does not have to address the oppression of women? We remove the question of justice from the earthly realm, from questions of more and less, from the issues of give and take. But how can we claim that such a discussion is still about justice, given that it no longer addresses what is at hand? There is no argument that could positively establish justice as disembodied, as removed from the concrete exploitation of concrete human beings. Hence Plato's need for irony, for a style of argument that always moves away from the fuzzy logic of actual existence. Always the question is asked of the one thing that is virtue, but the question points away from the actual practice of virtue, away from the questions of those who suffer and of those who profit. When the time finally comes for claim to be made of what is it we are after in searching after the Good, Plato replies with an allegory that denies the embodiment which it nonetheless represents. This turn to transcendence is a historical act. What makes Plato the father of philosophy is that he is the first one to bury the historical act of man's priority as ontological Truth.

The allegory of the cave represents the foundation stone upon which patriarchal thought will rise. Plato's argument offers a recognizable alternative to another myth and another story, which have become invisible. The allegory of the cave is a strange and contorted story. The images of men chained as prisoners since childhood, forced to watch shadow plays, of strange, invisible magicians whose sole purpose is to make shadows, is bizarre. Yet this allegory is to serve to claim philosophy as a "rational" enterprise. The oddity of this claim points to another possibility. The allegory of the cave resembles another strange tale of origins, in which a woman who eats an apple is supposed to explain all of man's inhumanity to man. In both cases, the irrationality of the rationale suggests that something else is going on.

The allegory of the cave is not good philosophy. It works on some other level than the rational. It works ironically, by feeding off the strength of what it counters. What is the alternative telling of the allegory that it counters? Who is the argument with? The partner in conversation is missing but is present in the possibility of reversing the present myth to tell another story, its shadow, the subverse to which it appeals even as it is told to deny.

This is a story, clearly, of going into caves. The alternative story claims that truth is found in shadows, that the sun somehow cannot answer the essential questions of human meaning. The alternative is a story of firelight and shadow play, a story of truth as mystery. Plato's allegory of the cave is an inversion of meaning whereby the cave/womb becomes prison and freedom becomes authoritarian reason. Let us try going one step farther and claim that the womb that is the cave is not Womb as Idea but the concrete womb of the Mother Goddess already concretely symbolized and enacted yearly by the women at Eleusis. This is the story that was embodied in the Eleusinian Mysteries, a story dangerous enough that it must be refuted and erased. Plato's text becomes our way into the mysteries destroyed by the fathers so long ago. Thus begins philosophy, but before that, what?

The Eleusinian Mysteries point back toward an earlier time and earlier traditions. The myth that is recorded in the Homeric *Hymn to Demeter* is but an echo of an earlier mother/daughter story.

> Whatever the impulse behind portraying Persephone as a rape victim, evidence indicates that this twist to the story was added after the societal shift from matrifocal to patriarchal, and that it was not part of the original mythology. In fact, it is likely that the story of the rape of the Goddess is a historical reference to the invasion of the northern Zeus-worshippers.[37]

Yet even in the patriarchal version of the myth, the power of the mother is still evident. Zeus gives his daughter Kore to his brother Hades, a good solid patriarchal match. He hides the nature of his "gift" from Demeter, mother of Kore, knowing she will not approve. Hades is given permission to abduct Kore to be his wife in the underworld. Tempting Kore with a flower, he rises out of the earth, grabs the girl, throws her into his chariot, and disappears into the underworld. Demeter hears her daughter's cry but arrives too late to intervene or even trace her disappearance.

This story is but the introduction of the real action, which is Demeter's acting out of her grief and resistance to the gods. The ostensible purpose of the myth is to explain the seasons. Demeter's grief creates winter, in spite of all the pressure the gods can bring. Nor can they reverse her power. They, like the mortals, are subject to the most essential power of change. Only when Kore is returned to her mother does spring arrive. The seasons change, reflecting the changing relationship of an essential mother to an essential daughter.

There were several festivals that reflected the seasonal aspects of the myth of Demeter.[38] However, the Eleusinian Mysteries identify with the deeper traditions of Demeter and Kore leading into the heart of the mystery of mortality. Kore/Persephone understands death, has penetrated the depths of mortality, and can teach her mother and her *mystae* (the initiates of the Eleusinian Mysteries), the knowledge that is inherent in the experience of dying. By choosing to go into the underworld, one can learn what it can teach and be released from the fear of it. The truth they teach is the truth within mortality that overcomes fear and frees from grief. The initiates of Eleusis retrace the steps of Demeter, learning as she learns, concluding as she does at the temple of Eleusis. There she and they await the revelation brought by Persephone.

The temple of Eleusis becomes the tomb of death and the womb of rebirth. In the darkness of the cave, one will learn the mystery of the unity of death and birth, by seeing and knowing. The mystery that is mortality will be revealed. What was actually shown is lost. Though many ancient authorities speculated about its substance, no one ever recorded the full rite. But all Athenians knew of the Mysteries and the basic shape of its truth, by reputation and by familiarity with the Homeric hymn. They knew that the truth taught was taught in darkness, that it centered in the Mother, and that it transformed its participants.

Plato's allegory of the cave begins with a story, therefore, that was already familiar to the listeners that evening in Piraeus. The allusion to the cave could be recognized as suggestive of the various caves in Greek popular religion and to the underworld of Demeter in particular. It would be dangerous to confront the Mysteries of Eleusis directly, for they had powerful supporters. If the allegory refers to the Mysteries, it does so in the context of a mystery not yet fully accepted by the populace, the festival of Bendis, linked to the mysteries at several points, but also a mere Thracian import. His technique, as always, is ironic, indirect, and recognizable only by those prepared to agree.

> Next, I said, compare the effect of education and the lack of it upon our human nature to a situation like this: imagine men to be living in an underground cave-like dwelling place, which has a way up to the light along its whole width, but the entrance is a long way up. (*Republic* 514a)

The allegory begins by describing the men who dwell in a cavernous underground chamber, not quite a cave, yet invoking that image. By Athenian times, these caves associated with the Goddess had been absorbed into cavernous templelike complexes, such as those at Eleusis.[39]

The temple at Eleusis, about fourteen miles west of Athens, consisted of a temple complex including two small caves which were identified with the portals of Hades.[40] The focus of the temple complex was the initiation hall, the *telesterion*. The *telesterion* was a huge rectangular building, supported with many columns. It was designed to re-create the experience of the underworld. Plato goes on to describe the conditions of those within this cavernous chamber, which might resemble the *telesterion*.

> The men have been there from childhood, with their neck and legs in fetters, so that they remain in the same place and can only see ahead of them, as their bonds prevent them turning their heads. (*Republic* 514a-b)

The allegory ties the initiates to a whole system of captivity, which en-
slaves them as children. According to the allegory, the Athenian religious
traditions prevent the people from appreciating new truths, such as the one
Plato wishes to introduce. Irigaray identifies the place of captivity with the
womb. They are trapped in the womb, the *hystera*/hysteria.

> So let us make reading the myth of the cave our point of departure. Socrates
> tells us that men—*hoi anthrōpoi*, sex unspecified—live *underground*, in
> a *dwelling formed* like a *cave*. Ground, dwelling, cave, and even, in a
> different way, form—all these terms can be read more or less as equivalents
> of the *hystera*. Similar associations could in fact be made for *living, dwelling*
> for a certain time or even for all time, in the *same place*, in the *same
> habitat*. As the story goes, then, men—with no specifications of sex—are
> living in one, same, place. A place shaped like a cave or a womb.[41]

The resistance of popular culture, of the Greek common people, to the
new order established by the *polis*, to all things imposed by the free men, is
in the allegory translated as a kind of captivity to ignorance. Irigaray links
captivity to the feminine image of the womb. The people are enslaved to
their past, to their mothers, to their childhood, and to their Mother, the Goddess.
Their chains are the chains of superstition, centering in religion, in traditions of worship and celebration that temporarily at least allow them to escape the rigid distinctions of male and female, slave and free, rich and poor,
imposed on them by the *polis*.[42] The resistance of the common people was
not true action but mere captivity to the past. Resistance to the Truth of
absolute distinctions that support the *polis* is here called slavery. From this
"captivity" they must be forcibly released.

The Mysteries at Eleusis, like many of the religious traditions rooted in
an ancient, now nearly forgotten time of equality and commonality, was
open to all without distinction. Only murderers and those who spoke no
Greek were excluded from participation.[43] All are the same when in darkness, and none escape the mystery of death. Certainly the people who had
worked so hard to arrive at Eleusis would not have seen their search as
enslavement. The Great Mystery was preceded by a year of preparation, the
lesser mysteries that culminated in that dark cave. Plato's use of words like
"chains" and "captivity" are probably not objective descriptions of the chamber
but rather represent his resistance to the ties that bind human beings to the
earth. Mortality had become, for Plato and the new order, something that
must be escaped, and the *mystae's* acceptance, their search for understanding of its mystery, ran directly counter to the new ideas that sought to transcend the bounds of death by denying and overcoming the ties to birth.
Kore/Persephone and Demeter in their dance with death, spiraling around in
the seasonal passage from summer to winter to spring, always leaving, always

returning, was a truth best discovered by firelight, whose flickering alternation between light and darkness suggests the nature of the mystery at the heart of human affairs. It is against this mystery that Plato conceives the allegory.

> Light is provided by a fire burning some way behind and above them. Between the fire and the prisoners, some way behind them and on a higher ground, there is a path across the cave and along this a low wall has been built, like the screen at a puppet show in front of the performers who show their puppets above it. —I see it (*Republic* 514b)

The actual nature of the mysteries is buried with its initiates. What we do know, we know from the archaeological evidence. One of the puzzles implicit in the layout of the temple is how anything could be shown to the assembled crowd. Though a "showing" is at the heart of the mystery, the temple is set up in such a way that it appears to have no point which is visible to all. At the center of the *telesterion* is another enclosure, the *anaktoron*.

> The *telesterion* was a rectilinear building built around a much smaller rectangular chamber, the *anaktoron* or 'lord's dwelling.' In the later *telesterion*, at least, the roof above this *anaktoron* was constructed as a "lantern," admitting the only light from outside and affording ventilation for torches and fires. . . . On one of its sides, the *anaktoron* had a door, beside which was the high-backed and roofed throne of the hierophant, affording him protection from the great fire within the *anaktoron*. The interior perimeter of the *telesterion* consisted of several steps leading up to the wall. Here the initiates presumably would sit or stand, with others perhaps also on the main floor of the hall. The line of view obviously was obstructed from many angles. With the forest of columns that supported the roof, and the high back on the hierophant's throne, and the sacred chamber itself all blocking the view, many candidates within the hall would have found it impossible to see what the hierophant did at the moment of the 'vision.'[44]

Perhaps it was a shadow play, images dancing across the walls and columns from the central enclosure: the *anaktoron*. The *anaktoron* contained a central fire, a source of light and shadows. Perhaps dancers performed around the fire, casting shadows to be interpreted by the initiates. Or perhaps the *anaktoron*, the "Lantern," was surrounded by a curtain, separating the affairs of the people from the performers who realized the divine drama by embodying it. The initiates did not look at the center, but their gaze was fixed upon the outer walls, letting the mystery stay mystery even in revelation—the reveiling that lets something be seen from the inside rather than the out. Whatever there was, the viewers did not face the performance, could not see it directly, for there was no point which could be viewed from the whole hall. Perhaps that which was to be seen was viewed by moving about the hall, following a track through the drama, by being participants as much as spectators.

We know there was a "hearing" and a "seeing" with the power to interpret the nature of life in a way that overcame the fearfulness of death. The "seeing" was never lit by the sun, which obscures by its glare, but was half-seen, half-assumed, in the light of fire, a truth of wondering dream. The nature of truth was something seen indirectly, grasped by intuition and heart rather than intellect.

Plato's description of the activities in the cave continues.

> See then also men carrying along that wall, so that they overtop it, all kinds of artifacts, statues of men, reproductions of other animals in stone or wood fashioned in all sorts of ways, and, as is likely, some of the carriers are talking while others are silent. . . . Do you think, in the first place, that such men could see anything of themselves and each other except the shadows which the fire casts upon the wall of the cave in front of them? (*Republic* 514b-515a)

The holy objects were carried into the temple at the start of the ceremony.[45] The viewing of the objects was clearly the center of the ceremony, though what the objects were and how they were shown is not known. Perhaps Plato also did not know, or perhaps they were too holy to be mocked, but he does hint at what he thinks they represented: figures dancing out the images of life. The meanings of those figures was left to those who view them, again the echoes of participation in the event.

> What if their prison had an echo which reached them from in front of them? Whenever one of the carriers passing behind the wall spoke, would they not think that it was the shadow passing in front of them which was talking? Do you agree?—By Zeus I do. (*Republic* 515b)

Echoes and shadows, the mysteries point at reality hidden by and in firelight. It is possible to imagine a chamber, a cave, perhaps Plato's cave, perhaps another, filled with shadows dancing against the wall, where echoes whisper among the pillars. The truths that are shared speak as if from within the participants, the darkness aiding the illusion and the disclosure. The leaders of the ceremony take on roles, are hidden behind the roles they enact. The distinction between metaphor and meaning, symbol and reality, is blurred. The myth ceases to be the story of distant beings and becomes each man's and woman's own story, the story of mortality. The center of the ceremony is magic, the art of changing consciousness and thus of changing being. The people recognize the truth, because it is the truth that they have lived, have known, since childhood, which has been made explicit and transformative.

From the outside, from the standpoint of the patriarchs (who participated only stripped of their power and reduced to the status of children), the mysteries were the last remnants of unreason from an ancient time. Plato was one of those patriarchs; from our modern vantage point, he appears to be one of

the old ones. From the standpoint of his contemporaries, he was a spokesman for a new myth. From the standpoint of the new myth of reason, the
cave was a place of dark, superstitious tomfoolery. It was dangerous because it was outside of the control of the new Logos. Magic had been dis-
credited by might. A few centuries later, the temples all would be torn down,
and a new patriarchal religion would rise on their ruins. But first Plato must
provide the transition. First the myth that underlay the return to the Mother
must be overthrown.

> Consider then what deliverance from their bonds and the curing of their
> ignorance would be if something like this naturally happened to them.
> Whenever one of them was freed, had to stand up suddenly, turn his head,
> walk, and look up toward the light, doing all that would give him pain,
> the flash of the fire would make it impossible for him to see the objects
> of which he had earlier seen the shadows. (*Republic* 515c)

The change, from *Mythos* to *Logos*, must be made. What if they should
resist? Then they must be forced. This is a strange prescription for a man
who stands for the power of reason to propose. Yet this is a battle, not an
argument, and the "captives" will resist. The process will be painful, and
irreversible. The allegory will set men free . . . by force, will drag them
from their chains, will render them unable to return. This is a freedom without choice. A freedom that no one would, of their free will, wish to make.
They will be overwhelmed by the Truth, by the light, unable to see into the
shadows, unable to evaluate what they might have seen, forced into a new
reality which provides no point of reference by which to ask questions that
might challenge the value of what they will be shown.

> What do you think he would say if he was told that what he saw then
> was foolishness, that he was now somewhat closer to reality and turned
> to things that existed more fully, that he saw more correctly? If one then
> pointed to each of the objects passing by, asked him what each was, and
> forced him to answer, do you not think he would be at a loss and believe
> that the things which he saw earlier were truer than the things now pointed
> out to him? (*Republic* 515d)

Strange that the Truth does not enlighten nor make obvious the deception
of the cave! Instead somehow the Truth misses the mark, does not relate to
the questions that the cave answered. The newly released captive is shown
the curtain, the basket of objects, the setup by which the magicians did their
tricks. But far from recognizing and being enlightened, the ex-captive rejects what the daylight shows. These objects are not nearly so real, are only
indirectly related to the shadows. Having looked into the symbolic heart of
things, the captive is shown the bare nature of things and does not recognize them. The water, the crystal, the mirror, the grain, the chalice are more

than they appear when seen through the shadows of symbol. They can open up mystery, and are more than the water, the crystal, the mirror, the grain, the cup as objects merely objectified, to be stared at by unholy eyes. The context is magic and provides self-discovery viewed through the ordinary. It is from that context of revelation that the captive has been forcibly freed. The one who has been forced to be free does not recognize the Truth, but still holds out for what was shown from within, within the cave and within the art. The outer truth is not even now as real as the inner, not even when the "mystery" has been uncovered as mere shadow-play.

> If one then compelled him to look at the fire itself, his eyes would hurt, he would turn round and flee toward those things which he could see, and think that they were in fact clearer than those now shown to him. —Quite so. (*Republic* 515e)

There is a cure for the obdurance of ignorance. Stare into the firelight, be forced into night blindness until nothing less forceful can be seen. Even the *hierophant* sits with his back to the great fire, so that it will not blind him from what the firelight shows. Now the darkness is to be violated in its relation to the light. The freed one is forced to turn from what was revealed through its veil of shadows to stare at the fire. When this ex-captive has been sufficiently blinded, the shadows will leave, be drowned in "Truth." Perhaps the prisoner will try to escape, to return to ... captivity. This is a curious play upon the image of captivity. Freedom is forced, the prison is that to which the captive longs to escape toward, away from captivity now forced upon one ... by freedom. The words turn around and around, the meanings reversed until one no longer knows what is meant. This is necessary, if the inner truth is to be replaced with a truth manipulated by men in sunlight.

What is it that the prisoner, even now, even blinded and no longer able to see the shadows, still desires enough to prefer blindness to the new sight? Irigaray places the reversal in the very exploitation of images by which Plato redesigns the cave into a place of captivity.

> The shadow-reflections of their marvelous tricks, which trace and outline both themselves and the *silent virginity* of the back of the cave, begin to speak, we are told, eclipsing the staggered artificial system of their pro-ductions-reproductions. Shadows of statues, of fetish-objects, these and none other would henceforth be named truth—*to aléthes*—by the men in chains. Projections of symbols for men's bodies, raised high enough so that they show over the top of the little wall so as to dominate and sub-limate it—though the wall has been raised in the cave artificially—would, theoretically, be the only possible representation of the truth for the pris-oners because they provide, in addition, the echo of the words pronounced by the same men. The echo is possible because of the reflecting property,

the so-called *virginity and muteness of that back of the matrix/womb* which a man, an *obstetrician*, turned round, backward and upside down in order to make it into the stage, the chamber, the stronghold of representation.[46]

The cave is the matrix, *hystera*, the mother-place, whose truth is engraved on the deepest level of the psyche of the child. This is a hard truth to up-root. Every man, as much as woman, stands in relation to its meaning, re-members it, can recognize it in the shadows. It is hard to tear out that truth, that recognition. To do so one must first change the womb, make it a place without mothers. Men take over, turn the womb around, make it a prison, not a place of return. They turn its inwardness into the illusion, its walls into places of men's projections. The myth that underlies and draws the initiate into mystery is a story of motherhood. In Plato's version of the myth, the allegory, the mother has been destroyed, erased, the womb turned over by the obstetrician, turned inside out, and now the prisoner, the child will be forced into the light.

> And if one were to drag him thence by force up the rough and steep path, and did not let him go before he was dragged into the sunlight, would he not be in physical pain and angry as he was dragged along? When he came into the light, with the sunlight filling his eyes, he would not be able to see a single one of the things which are now said to be true. —Not at once, certainly. (*Republic* 515e-516a)

The Eleusinian Mysteries of Plato's time were already run by men, by the *hierophant*, the family of priests who ran the initiation. Yet the nature of the Mysteries connects them to the ancient women's mysteries, to the real-ity not yet controlled totally by men. These dark truths, shadowy realities, mysterious meanings are an alternative, an opening into inwardness. But now the captive has been released from inwardness, severed from the mother and from what is also the captive's own heart. Torn from the cave by steep and rugged ascent, the captive is commanded to see. And in the sunlight, the free captive is unable to see a single thing. Here is Truth. Here is the beginning of authoritarian reason.

> I think he would need time to get adjusted before he could see things in the world above; at first he would see shadows most easily, then reflec-tions of men and other things in water, then the things themselves. After this he would see objects in the sky and the sky itself more easily at night, the light of the stars and the moon more easily than the sun and the light of the sun during the day. —Of course. (*Republic* 516a-b)

The upper world, the superior world, the transcendent world is now at-tained. It will take a while to grasp this world of things in themselves. These are things without depth, without darkness, without meanings, except the single meaning of themselves raised to the status of the Idea. Here a tree is a Tree, no more, no less, but thereby idealized. This tree has no spirit, whispers nothing on the wind. It is. It is an ideal form, but its form is totally abstracted from its nexus of symbolic interconnectedness, its context. The captive must learn a whole new way of seeing. For Plato, each instance of a thing is a dim reflection of its absolute abstracted form in the Idea. The uniqueness of instant, of accident, of context, and of relation, is now to be overcome in the Idea itself. The reality which lived and breathed with inwardness is now frozen into eternal self-sameness. Whereas the seeing in the dark revealed the potential of each thing seen both to be itself and to be another, the Idea rises above the accident, rejecting all interconnectedness. In the dark, every instance re-presents the whole and makes it manifest in its hiddenness.

In the sunlight, the task before our tearful captive is to become accustomed to the one thing that will replace all the multiplicity. The captive must face the coming of the night, now no longer seen through the prism of the cave. Captive to a new master, the one who is free will view the moon and the stars. In looking at them, no longer will there be a relation between the self and what it views. Now the captive must learn to look at these objectively, at a distance, as if they had no meaning to him. All this is preparation for the coming day.

> Then, at last, he would be able to see the sun, not images of it in water or in some alien place, but the sun itself in its own place, and be able to contemplate it.—That must be so. After this he would reflect that it is the sun which provides the seasons and the years, which governs everything in the visible world, and is also in some way the cause of those other things which he used to see. —Clearly that would be the next stage. (*Republic* 516b-c)

Now at last the captive is totally blind. Looking at the sun means that everything else becomes pale and washed out. Nothing can be seen but the one thing. The world is now totally dark in comparison. Yet it must all be worth it. Certainly nothing is as bright, as glorious as the sun! Nothing can touch it. It remains unchanged while everything around it changes. Therefore it must be in control. What does not change is essential; what does change is accidental. The goal is to move into control, via the sun. The goal is to escape the wheel of change, to leave behind Demeter and her daughter who move with the seasons. Zeus's mistake in the first place was to be dependent on the earth. Because he was, he could not simply give his daughter away to death, to Hades. He had to bargain with the mother for the sacrifice. The result was a messy deal. The old myth must be replaced by a new myth in which the One power, the top, can rule even over the seasons, without being influenced by that which it changes. This is the ultimate power over, to control without being in relationship to that which is controlled.

Here the uncaused cause can be seen—but of course the price is blindness.

The truth of the cave is a way, a wisdom, not an absolute knowledge. The power of the cave is power which is always power with and within, never power over. Having seen the Sun, who will settle for shadows? But then again, having seen the Sun, the shadows are no longer visible. There is no room in the cave for that kind of conqueror's ambition.

> Reflect on this too, I said. If this man went down into the cave again and sat down in the same seat, would his eyes not be filled with darkness, coming suddenly out of the sunlight? They certainly would. And if he had to contend again with those who had remained prisoners in recognizing those shadows while his sight was affected and his eyes had not settled down—and the time for this adjustment would not be short—would he not be ridiculed? Would it not be said that he had returned from his upward journey with his eyesight spoiled, and that it was not worthwhile even to attempt to travel upward? As for the man who tried to free them and lead them upward, if they could somehow lay their hands on him and kill him, they would do so. —They certainly would. (*Republic* 516e-517a)

The new way of knowing negates absolutely the old meanings. Stare into the Sun and the whole world is a shadow realm. Stare into the Good and lesser distinctions become meaningless. One can see the one thing, but only the one thing. If there is but One Great Truth, other people's realities, other people's truths become real only insofar as they are reduced to the One. This is the imperialism of unity. Every time there is a call to unify the world, someone has seen the Sun and been blinded. Every time some guru or some teacher announces that all beliefs are really One, remember the Sun. If there is but One Truth, then all other truths are reduced to shadows. Distinctions are lost, blurred into the eternal sameness of objects under too bright a light.

> For Being's domination requires that whatever has been defined—*within the domain of sameness*—as "more" (true, right, clear, reasonable, intelligible, paternal, masculine . . .) should progressively win out over *its* "other," its "different"—its differing—and, when it comes right down to it, over its negative, its "less" (fantastic, harmful, obscure, "mad," sensible, maternal, feminine . . .). Finally the fiction reigns of a simple, indivisible, ideal origin. The fission occurring at the beginning, at the time of the primitive conjunction(s) is eliminated in the *unity of concept*.[47]

The longing to find the one thing that explains everything can be achieved; this is the promise inherent in the allegory. But once the One thing that explains everything has been found, the everything has disappeared. The captive must settle for the Sun, being blind to all else. That is the nature of Truth with a capital "T."

But, being blinded, the captive is now ready to be a missionary. Not content with having found the Truth, the captive must free other captives. Suppose the captive attempts to reason with the prisoners in the cave. Will they listen? What can he say, this ex-captive who is now a son of the Sun? Be free, like me? But he has chosen, now, to be a hired servant, a landless man, in a hierarchy in which the top is already filled. Power over is attractive only if one is the one that is over. He needs new converts, to be over someone. The new converts laugh at the offer; they reject the kind missionary, perhaps even boil him for supper (or so he fears, unless perhaps he fears the laughter more).

> Anyone with intelligence, I said, would remember that the eyes may be confused in two ways and from two causes, coming from light into darkness as well as from darkness into light. Realizing that the same applies to the soul, whenever he sees a soul disturbed and unable to see something, he will not laugh mindlessly but will consider whether it has come from a brighter life and is dimmed because unadjusted, or has come from greater ignorance into greater light and is filled with a brighter dazzlement. The former he would declare happy in its life and experience, the latter he would pity, and if he should wish to laugh at it, his laughter would be less ridiculous than if he laughed at a soul that has come from the light above. —What you say is very reasonable. (*Republic* 518a-b)

Don't laugh at the patriarch's ideals. They may not make sense, but that is because they have rejected "sense" for higher things. The ideal proposed by Plato is one removed from ordinary things, rendering them so worthless that ethics can barely even be applied to them. No longer does ethics speak well of the world, now it rises up to the sun, contemplating that which cannot be corrupted.

> Come then, share with me this thought also: do not be surprised that those who have reached this point are unwilling to occupy themselves with human affairs, and that their souls are always pressing upward to spend their time there, for this is natural if things are as our parable indicates. —That is very likely. (*Republic* 517c-d)

On this foundation of the removal of the Good from the world, the world is left to the rule of brute power. Indeed, the good men blame the bruteness of the world upon the shadows of the cave. After all, what is not light is darkness.

The tyranny of the One is that it must always at the same time destroy all others and spawn the other in a new guise, as evil. If the good is One, then what is not good must be evil. The sun in its heaven is untouched by the shadows, pure and undefiled, but it casts a long shadow. In the cave the shadows and the light intermingle, hinting, suggesting, implying a relationship that binds the many together in the manifold. Death and birth, and birth and death, the wheel turns; the soul learns with Demeter to wait upon the return and rejoice in it even in grief.

In Plato's new order, the goal is an immortality that casts out mortality; the model is untouched by relativity. The earth drags upon the soul, holds it back from the heavens. Socrates welcomes death, because it gets rid once and for all of the weeping women, who are nothing to him. He rejects grief and escapes life's ambiguity. To the end, he rejects the relevance of other people to his own being. Having risen above them all, he gives to everyone, except his followers, contempt.

Upon this foundation rises the edifice of philosophy. Removed from the task of teaching human beings to search their own hearts, it examines a Good that is always beyond the cave of existence. The Good is preserved from contamination by issues such as why women never find a voice in the discussion. Philosophy, the product of a social situation, never needs to examine the relation of its thought to the social situation. In the *Republic*, the implications of the relation between the noninvolvement of philosophy in politics and the way in which it shapes and makes possible a repressive politics are made clear. The allegory of the cave idealizes a Good removed from human society—in the context of a discussion of a militaristic ideal society led by a philosopher/king. From the common laborers through the warrior/guardians to the philosopher/kings, the ideal is authoritarian, hierarchical, and founded upon force. The ideal, the sun, the Good, is a form which is, at the same time, removed and on top of existence. That is, it justifies and embodies a hierarchical system, a ranking of goods, and ultimately of people with all legitimacy concentrated at the top. But its absolute nature as the unapproachable Good removes it from accountability to what is below. Since evil is what is not Good, the Good is not responsible.

Who is responsible? Clearly, because this is what the sun shows, it is the woman. The woman is the cave, the repository of birth and death, the source of all that is bodily and messy in the world. The sun, the Good, the God, promises victory over death, or at least over woman.

> The eternity of the Father's Good. Since he has been promised a share in it, provided it is made over in his image. All this, of course, requires that he turn his back on any beginning that is still empirical, still too material and matrical, and that he receive being only from the one who wills himself as origin without beginning.[48]

The goal of reason is immortality. Immortality is the opposite of mortality, as reason is the opposite of body. Reason lifts us beyond what can be corrupted, by removing us, by blinding us to nuance and shadow-play. It seeks the definitive as if that were the same as the eternal. To know is to be eternal, that is Plato's promise. To know and deny the eyes is to know the sun which does not change. Humans can mimic the sun only by denying their origins, which is what reason does in the heritage of philosophy. Reason is man not born of woman. Such a man can be immortalized by other men. By creating the idea he creates himself in the image of creator, just as Plato creates Socrates and immortalizes them both. Here there is no room for woman, who always smells of the cave.

The cave that woman represents is the ontogenetic cave of human beginning, but it is also the cave entered into by the *mystae*. Plato rejects woman as beginning, and women as representatives of an alternative way of knowing. The Eleusinian Mysteries are a lost way of knowing that stand in dialogue with Plato. The cave that Plato rejects is a cave we might wish to enter. By entering the cave, we seek hints and shadows of old ways of knowing. We reconstruct the alternative negatively, on the basis of what Plato excludes. This is the sub-verse, the speaking behind the speaking we inherit from our fathers. It is subversive, quite consciously. It echoes back against Plato's project and seeks to undermine the directionality that the tradition took from the beginning which Plato represents.

Such an enterprise is in contra-distinction to Plato's apparent intention but hopefully not foreign to Plato even so. Grounded in Plato's images, it is also grounded in the multivocity of Plato's irony. Perhaps Plato himself mocked the political ideals of his times.

> The story of the guardian 'ideal' city is a peculiar textual act. Is it a radical political platform or a surrealist parody on the politics of reforms? Where exactly should the reader place this absurd narration, in which all propositions are perfectly logical? Is it a playful game or a serious argument, a kind of speech which constitutes a political act or a philosophical reflection on its very possibility? In order to understand the political significance of the guardian city one must understand where its referent lies, whether it is placed in the political realm or in the sphere of fantastic fictions, and whether its utterances refer to reality or to its fictive representation. But this is precisely what one cannot do with the story of that city, for it is a story, *mythos*, in the symbolic sense of the concept of myth discussed above. The myth of the ideal city blurs the very distinctions which it articulates, violates the classificatory system which underlies it, and ingeniously problematizes its own status as a textual as well as a political act.[49]

Throughout the corpus of Plato's work, there is an ironic edge that culminates in a negative conclusion about the Good in whatever dialogue he participates. The participant proposes a position about some good; Socrates dismantles it, carefully and with the full agreement of his partner in dialogue. The discussant is forced back into a thoughtful questioning that does not result in answers. Turned away from what is given, the discussant must find within the means to respond. Socrates is the midwife, delivering the listener back to the truth of recognition.

Perhaps, as seems evident from the surface of the *Republic*, Plato here answers all questions. His answer, if so, is a disappointing one, full of metaphors of autocratic philosopher kings and absolute Good. Perhaps Plato wants to be king! Or perhaps Plato is making fun of people who wish to proclaim themselves king on the basis of their philosophy! Yet whatever Plato's own intentions are, the intentionality of the text stands in a dialogic relationship to an alternative. The captive that sees the sun may escape also his new masters, may come to understand the sun shines only on the surface of things, and may pause to argue with those who drag him along toward the one conclusion. Against the hierarchy pointing upward toward supreme rulers and absolute Truth is the movement downward, into the depths of hidden revelation. Against the unitary movement of reason is the multivocity of metaphor, and this second truth is as present in Plato as the first. Against the sun of reason is the sun as metaphor, as the repository of multiple meanings waiting to be played with and left to suggest yet new horizons of possible truth.

Socrates as a midwife resembles, in practice, the male midwives who turned the gentle art of waiting on birth into the deliveries of the obstetricians. Perhaps Plato really intends to drag out the initiates from the cave and destroy that ignorance and superstition once and for all. Even so, the cave remains, and the dialogue turns on its own inner potentiality. There is that which still waits to be birthed. Kore longs to return, bringing another spring. Her mother's tears are enough to hold back the sun, giving the grateful earth the chance to become fertile under her rains once again.

The Socratic method is a pedagogy appropriate for the women who danced at Eleusis, for Demeter was a goddess of childbirth. Midwifery is the feminine art of actively allowing another to give birth. Maieutics is the gentle art of the midwife who holds open a space for the birth of knowledge within concrete sensuous reality. The fundamental task of maieutics is to bring a thinker into self-awareness, into the truth already known within. Maieutics weaves together unique experiences of birth with the transhuman patterns and rhythms of mortality.

The skill of the midwife is based on watchful presence, which beholds the wonder and mystery of the birth process with a minimum of intervention. The crucial element in the metaphor is the confidence of the midwife in the process of birth. Her power lies not in the act of creation itself but rather in her mediating role and her recognition that truth does not conform to some prescribed formula. Socrates was able to appeal to a living tradition of midwifery that everyone recognized. Yet he did more than merely appropriate an image. He stole maieutics from its proper location in birth and from the world of women. Maieutics has come to be totally abstracted from its context with women in the throes of labor. Today, the term maieutics has become virtually obsolete.

Maieutics gives access to the hidden roots of feminism. It recalls a past in which women's space encompassed a world, a world of shadows and firelight and the inwardness of vision. By the time of the Eleusinian Mysteries, men had entered into the mysteries. The mythological space of the cave has shrunk with the encroachment into and confiscation of women's sacred spaces. Yet the ties to the ancient myths of Kore/Persephone and Demeter keep open a link to the gentle art.

The cave suggests even so a way back to the ground of knowing as the interplay of all the senses. The shadows hold a truth beyond the intellect, which can only be known by bringing into play the full bodily participation of the one who seeks to be initiated into mystery. Sensuality gives birth to action. Action is magical, transforming the world and the actor by passionate involvement in thought. The passion of conception is intimately linked with the birth process, with the labor of life, and with the constant renewal of the seasons. To think is to conceive. To conceive is not to conceive a new conception; thought's aim is not to ground itself in its own self-deceptive story of origins. To conceive is to participate in the inward turning of truth, which gives birth to action. Thought aims at action, praxis, birth. Sensuality is the mediating term; it is the maieutic mediation between thought and action in a way that rejects the deadly isolation of the immortal Idea.

The recovery of woman's experience is the recovery of the metaphors and myths of sensuality. Birth is a space shared with every animal and with every star. The passing into and the passing out of being, the essence of mortality, is the structure of the universe itself. Demeter and Kore/Persephone show the way through the cave, through darkness and firelight and shadowplay, to where we belong as mortals. We belong as always passing through, as always returning.

> One buries children, one gains new children, one dies oneself; and this men take heavily, carrying earth to earth. But it is necessary to harvest life like a fruit-bearing ear of grain, and that one be, the other not.[50]

Plato gives us access to what was buried with the cave, though only negatively. The sun represents one truth, one good, one answer. We turn from the One to the dark comfort of the many, embracing it with our bodies and our symbols.

The sun in the allegory of the cave represents alienation from the very pattern of the universe. To become what Plato envisions is to strive against the rhythms of birth and death, to achieve an immortality that breaks the bounds of the natural order. But this immortality violates the integrity of human existence and can only be achieved at the cost of oppression. Oppression serves the purpose of freeing someone from the natural order by enslaving another. Insofar as women necessarily participate in the elemental structure of mortality, their oppression is required as the price of men's escaping the natural order.

Maieutics weaves together a new and an old way of thinking. What existed long ago, surviving only as hint in men's texts, offers a model for a way into an alternative future. Woven together in this other republic, in this community of thought and being, are the cosmic and the human, integrating the rhythms of the natural order with the experience of the unique moment. The tapestry grows from the weaving together of sameness and uniqueness. The task of the midwife attending the birth of thought and metaphor is to be the gentle hands that guard the tension of the weave: watching, waiting, holding, making space. The skill of the midwife is an intuitive skill that balances knowledge against the unpredictability that may signify the emergence of new patterns in the weave. She is sensitive to both change and constancy in the birth process, waiting with age-old patience for the emergence of the new.

The cave is dark, filled with shadows from a fire, that burns in the center. The seekers face away from the fire that their eyes may not be blinded by the light. Sounds echo and whisper among the columns, changed and distorted, until each listener, straining to hear and see, finds it necessary to interpret what is seen and heard in the light of her own birth and the inevitability of her own death. The stories that are told (and there are many) are all true and are all waiting to be filled with truth. Dreams and experiences interpenetrate and inform each other. What is said is always said as a hint, is always half-spoken, designed to lead the listener to fill in what is missing with what is needed. When the night is over, the *mystae,* who have encountered the mystery, leave the cave by the vagina-like entrance. The way may be hard, but the seeker is not forced. Reaching the open air, the initiated notices the sun is about to rise, and responds with wonder. And *Sophia* is born again, with the spring.

NOTES

1. Plato's *Seventh Letter*, 341c-d.
2. Kenneth M. Sayre, *Plato's Literary Garden: How To Read a Platonic Dialogue* (Notre Dame, Ind.: University of Notre Dame Press, 1995), xiv.
3. Sayre, *Plato's Literary Garden*, 220.
4. Jacques Derrida, *The Post Card: From Socrates to Freud and Beyond*, trans. Alan Bass (Chicago: University of Chicago Press, 1987), 47.
5. Jane Ellen Harrison, *Prolegomena to the Study of Greek Religion* (Cambridge: Cambridge University Press, 1922), vii.
6. *Symposium* 211b.
7. Luce Irigaray, *Speculum of the Other Woman*, trans. Gillian C. Gill (Ithaca: Cornell University Press, 1994), 306–7.

8. *Parmenides* Fragment, 1, 2, in Philip Wheelwright, ed., *The Presocratics* (New York: Odyssey Press, 1966), 95–96.

9. Charlene Spretnak, *Lost Goddesses of Early Greece: A Collection of Pre-Hellenic Myths* (Boston: Beacon Press, 1992), 17.

10. Marija Gimbutas, *The Goddesses and Gods of Old Europe* (Berkeley; University of California Press, 1982), 238.

11. Diotima is important also because the language of the argument credited to her duplicates the language of the mysteries, of the ancient mythological images associated with women. See Chrys Caragounis, *The Ephesian Mysterion* (Uppsala, Sweden: CWK Gleerup, 1977), 20.

12. Irigaray, *Speculum of the Other Woman*, 243–364.

13. Ibid., 295–96.

14. All translations of the *Republic* come from G. M. A. Grube, trans., *Plato's Republic* (Indianapolis: Hackett Publishing, 1974).

15. *Republic* 328a.

16. We know that the festival was the festival of Bendis from the *Republic* 354a.

17. Louise Zaidman, and Pauline Pantel, *Religion in the Ancient Greek City*, trans. Paul Cartledge (Cambridge: Cambridge University Press, 1992), 103.

18. Robert Garland, *Introducing New Gods: The Politics of Athenian Religion* (Ithaca: Cornell University Press, 1992), 112.

19. Kraemer argues by quoting from Strabo's *Geography* 7.3.4:

    It was a commonplace in Greco-Roman antiquity that religion was women's business, and it was not a compliment. Strabo of Pontus in Asia Minor said it most clearly: "Women [are] the chief founders of religion (*deisidaimonia*) . . . women . . . provoke men to the more attentive worship of the gods, to festivals and to supplications, and it is a rare thing for a man who lives by himself to be found addicted to these things."

    See Ross Kraemer, *Her Share of the Blessings: Women's Religions among Pagans, Jews, and Christians in the Greco-Roman World* (New York: Oxford University Press, 1992), 3.

20. Socrates states: "You and I, Adeimantus, are not poets now, but we are founding a city, and it is proper that founders should know the general lines which the poets must follow in telling their stories. These lines they will not be allowed to cross. We are not to compose their poems for them" (*Republic* 379a).

21. Jean-Pierre Vernant, *Mortals and Immortals: Collected Essays* (Princeton, N.J.: Princeton University Press, 1991), 164–65.

22. Hannah Arendt articulates clearly the distinction between the public sphere of the *polis* (the arena of speech and action) and the private sphere of the household (the arena of labor). See *The Human Condition* (Chicago: University of Chicago Press, 1958), 31.

23. Garland, in *Introducing New Gods*, analyzes the state funding of cults in the context of the Peloponnesian War. See 110–11.

24. Ibid., 112–14.

25. David Rice and John Stambaugh analyze the writings of Strabo (late first century B.C. geographer), who describes the music and the dance associated with the *Bendideia* and the cult of Dionysus. See their *Sources for the Study of Greek Religion* (Atlanta, GA.: Scholars Press, 1979), 197–98.

26. F. Guirand, "Greek Mythology," in the *New Larousse Encyclopedia of Mythology* (London: Prometheus Press, 1973), 160.

27. Rice and Stambaugh, *Sources for the Study of Greek Religion*, 197–98.

28. Kraemer in *Her Share of the Blessings* explores how the Eleusinian Mysteries and the worship of Demeter have naturally been associated with women because of the focus on fertility. Kraemer analyzes recent feminist readings of the myths and festivals as evidence of women's religion. Kraemer concludes that "the *Hymn to Demeter* and many festivals to the goddess express the realities of Greek women's lives in ritual and myth." See 25.
29. Garland, *Introducing New Gods*, 112.
30. Adi Ophir, *Plato's Invisible Cities: Discourse and Power in the Republic* (Savage, Md.: Barnes and Noble, 1991), 112.
31. Arendt, *The Human Condition*, 30–32.
32. Spretnak, *Lost Goddesses of Early Greece*, 19–20.
33. Kore means daughter, or the Goddess in her maiden form. Persephone is the name given to Kore after her emergence from the underworld as the wife of Hades.
34. Irigaray, *Speculum of the Other Woman*, 243.
35. Irigaray, *Speculum of the Other Woman* introduces a series of quotations from Plato's *Republic* with this comment (p. 157). Italicized words are Irigaray's emphasis.
36, Ibid., 161.
37. Spretnak, *Lost Goddesses of Early Greece*, 107.
38. Kraemer, *Her Share of the Blessings*, 27.
39. Chrys Caragounis makes reference to the complex of buildings are revealed by archaeology together with the two caves. See his *The Ephesian Mysterion*, 19.
40. Ibid., 15.
41. Irigaray, *Speculum of the Other Woman*, 243.
42. Wasson states:

> Each year the new candidates for initiation would walk that Sacred Road, people of all classes, emperors and prostitutes, slaves and freemen, an annual celebration that was to last for upwards of a millennium and a half, until the pagan religion finally succumbed to the intense hatred and rivalry of a newer sect, the recently legitimized Christians in the fourth century of our era.

R. Gordon Wasson, et al. *The Road to Eleusis: Unveiling the Secret of the Mysteries* (New York: Harcourt, Brace, Jovanovich, 1978), 35–36.
43. John C. Engelsman, *The Feminine Dimension of the Divine* (Philadelphia: Westminster Press, 1979), 53.
44. Wasson, *The Road to Eleusis*, 78–79.
45. Engelsman, *The Feminine Dimension of the Divine*, 53.
46. Irigaray, *Speculum of the Other Woman*, 263.
47. Ibid., 275.
48. Ibid., 295.
49. Ophir, *Plato's Invisible Cities*, 100.
50. Foley quotes from a fragment of Euripides' lost work entitled *Hypsipyle*, which Foley thinks might clarify the mysterious moment of insight in the Eleusinian Mysteries. See Helene P. Foley, ed., *The Homeric Hymn to Demeter* (Princeton, N.J.: Princeton University Press, 1994), 69.

ANSELM'S PROOF:
THE ART OF CONCEIVING

PHILOSOPHY HAS BEGUN. THE Greeks were in love with her, but she was soon old enough to be sold into marriage to another patriarch, the Christian God. There her relation with *mythos* was soon forgotten because *mythos* had ceased to be, replaced by revelation. Myths were stories told by the heathen, other people, but not by Christians. Biblical narratives differ in that they were so cut off from their origins that it was as if God himself had told them. Myth was, and still is, relegated to the pagan past. The unconquered Sun/Son has triumphed over the dark womb of earth, and it appears that women's mysteries have been erased. Plato won a place in the church fathers' memory but only by special dispensation as a pagan foreshadowing of the ultimate male truth. The neoplatonists, with their hierarchy of emanations of God, provided a much better foundation for the fathers of the church.

For a time, even *philo-sophia* gave way to *theo-logic*: the love of wisdom was replaced by the logic of God. The European Middle Ages are recorded as the time in the tradition of men's thought in which logic served well the church of the fathers. Anselm creates his proof for the existence of God in the context of the emerging triumph of the hierarchical Catholic Church. The proof both participates in the triumph and creates the conditions of that triumph. That is, the proof not only proves the existence of God but also proves the ontological reality of hierarchies as essential to the full understanding of God.

The eleventh century marked an important point of transition. The context of Anselm's writing was the assumption that Christianity was without rival. Only fools doubted. This confidence was reflected in the Crusades as well as in Anselm's writing. The Turks captured Jerusalem in the 1050s. The Christians, who rose in righteous anger and with the bold assurance of God's total support, proposed to prove militarily the superiority of Christianity to all sources of opposition. In 1095, the first crusade aimed at liberating Jerusalem; and by 1099, the crusaders, without discipline or mercy, had sacked Jerusalem in the name of God. Anselm did not support the Crusades, having in mind a different struggle. Marjorie Rowling cites Anselm's response to a young man who asked Anselm's advice on whether he should join the Crusades:

> I advise you, I counsel you, I pray and beseech you, as one who is dear to me, to abandon that Jerusalem which is now not a vision of peace, but of tribulation, to leave aside the treasures of Constantinople and Babylon, which are to be seized on with hands soaked in blood, and to set out on the road to the heavenly Jerusalem which is a vision of peace, where you will find treasures which only those who despise these [earthly] ones can receive.[1]

Anselm had in mind a heavenly crusade and felt no need to support unquestioningly the powers of his time, neither pope nor king. Anselm's independence of thought has left his reputation untarnished in spite of all the challenges to Christianity that took place both during and after his lifetime. It would not be long before the cracks within the edifice of Christian hegemony would show. Before long, the crusaders would be retreating from the more powerful and disciplined Muslim armies. As they withdrew, they brought with them competing ideas that would threaten the dominion of Christian rationality. Western Christianity continued to find itself at odds with Eastern Orthodoxy as well, until in 1054 the final schism broke down relations between the two branches of Christianity. The pope and the patriarch of Constantinople mutually excommunicated each other, with much effect on earth but with little apparent effect on heaven.

There is a modern debate concerning how much Anselm was impacted by the turbulent political affairs that swirled around him. The traditional approach to Anselm as reflected in Eadmer's original biography[2] and in R. W. Southern's more recent portrait,[3] is to emphasize his saintly and apolitical characteristics. The alternative approach (as represented by Sally Vaughn[4]) involves a reanalysis of the texts of the monastics, especially Anselm, in light of his clear political acumen in charting a careful course between church and state. Whatever Anselm's intentions or personal contribution and investment as archbishop of Canterbury might have been, his texts set forth a foundation for the formal structure of Christian authority and power. Our own approach takes the text as in some sense independent of the author and his intentions. Instead, what we propose to examine is how the ideas within the texts serve either to support or criticize current political, social, and economic structures. However saintly or politically adept Anselm might have been, his texts participate in the legitimation of the hierarchical structures within the church, within the state, and within the conception of God himself. Anselm's texts, as well as his life and career, reflected the broader currents of political, social, and religious change and constancy.

The archbishopric of Canterbury was officially independent of both papal and state authority. It was Anselm's job as archbishop to chart a course between these great powers in England. This task not only was made difficult by the Crusades and the great schism but also by changes in the monarchy in England. The death of Edward the Confessor in 1066 left a vacuum in imperial rule, because there was no direct heir to the throne. The invasion of the Normans and the ascendancy of William the Conqueror to the English throne centralized the feudal monarchy in England. William the Conqueror brought with him a monk named Lanfranc, who supported the goals of the Norman monarchy and became archbishop of Canterbury just before Anselm. Together, William and Lanfranc exercised tight control over the clergy and abbots of England and consolidated their authority over the churches and monasteries of England.

Anselm succeeded Lanfranc as archbishop in 1089. Anselm, while affirming the independence of the church from Rome, went one step farther. Anselm insisted on the independence of the church from control by the monarchy, and this brought him into conflict with William's successors. This struggle culminated in the controversy over investitures. The controversy revolved around lay investiture, the practice of secular rulers performing religious rites in which they granted bishops and abbots the symbols of ecclesiastical power. He who has power to grant power has the higher power. The issue for Anselm was one of the ranking of authorities. His thought demanded an absolute hierarchy. There could be a sharing of power, a yoking together of church and state, as long as both recognized an order of ultimate authority, namely God. The greatest value resides in that which lies closest to the ultimate authority. Anselm's political adeptness came directly from the clarity of his vision of the hierarchy of value. There may have been two bulls in Anselm's metaphor of the yoked team, but only one master.

Anselm stands on the eve of a greater change, a change from within the social order. The change is a change in the nature of human relations, which, shortly after his death, will alter the dynamics of male-female relations. In the twelfth century, aristocratic women began to participate in society in new ways. From once having been chattel, they were transformed into objects of veneration. Chivalry and courtly love meant that occasionally a woman's personhood was taken seriously. For example, women like Heloise could engage competitively in male realms. For the most part, Heloise's contribution has been reduced to the status of lover of Peter Abelard; but in her own time, she carved out a sphere of power.[5]

Anselm foreshadows something of the romantic mood of the century to follow, especially in his correspondence. Whether one classifies him as a lover of men or a lover of mankind, the centrality of love and love imagery in his letters hints at the potential of a new evaluation of the sensual and hence of human relations.

Into this tradition of male friendship, the newly idealized vision of romantic love between men and women began to find ever more elaborate
and passionate forms of expression about a generation after Anselm's death.[6]

Love of God sets as important a context for the proof for the existence of
God as does his commitment to hierarchy. Anselm's proof stands as much
in the category of love letter as it belongs to the history of logic. Anselm is
matchmaker between *philo-sophia* and *theo-logia*. Soon *Sophia* will reappear on the scene as the Queen of Heaven, the Virgin Mary, whose cult
seemed to spell a new era of language about the divine. The possibility of
feminine images of the divine was just over the horizon, in the songs to be
sung by the troubadours and poetry to be dedicated to the Virgin Mary.

Images of the divine feminine occur in some of Anselm's own letters and
poetry, and in this way he foreshadows and introduces the flowering of love
poetry in the next century.[7] Yet he also helped set the terms by which the
Catholic Church was able to restrain and contain the potentially explosive
nature of honoring the feminine.

The love that courtly poetry encourages and celebrates is altogether different
in spirit from the love of the Virgin. But one striking resemblance does
emerge, and it is the bond of unity, the means through which the Church
was able to achieve a remarkable syncretism. Courtly love, as its name
describes, took place in courts: it is steeped in social distinctions of rank
and class. As we have seen, in the early and medieval Christian view,
heaven or the other world was also a court, where Christ ruled with his
mother as Queen of Heaven beside him. Surprisingly, it is through this
active and vigorous metaphor that the Virgin was able to assume so much
of the character and functions of the original beloved of Languedoc poetry and to rob it and its many descendants of its dangerous hedonism
and permissiveness. Courtly poets addressed ladies of higher rank and
posed as their vassals, because that was a common social situation of the
times; prayerful Christians followed the model but subverted its content.[8]

Love, like political action and the structure of both the secular and heavenly
realms, must be brought into subjugation to the hierarchies imposed by men.
Within those structures women could be regarded with veneration, because
the restrictions the hierarchy implied carried within them the means by which
they might as easily be burned as witches or raped, if she happened to be of
the wrong social order. Anselm joins love and hierarchy together, a fusion
that will shape the triumph of the church through the ages. Yet there is an
explosive potential at the heart of his synthesis.

Anselm was a busy man, for his rank as archbishop and as a man of God
demanded service to his monastic order. Nonetheless, he found time to craft
a proof for the existence of God. He brought his thought, as he brings his
life, into service to God, the top of all hierarchies. His proof is designed to

draw thought into the impossible tangle of being, the maze which leads inevitably to its pinnacle, the Being of God. It is a beautiful proof, simple enough for beginners yet profound enough to allow thinkers to return to it over and over again. A hundred times refuted, but always by misunderstanding, it resembles the weave of the emperor's new clothes: what one sees tells more about the seer than about the object. The proof is thus magical, self-reflecting, itself an image for the image of God. It deserves reflection, being essentially a reflective surface upon which meaning may be spun.

The proof has its own context, besides the context of historical events. Prior to the *Proslogium* is the *Monologium*, a soliloquy of a man who is searching for God.

> After I had published, at the solicitous entreaties of certain brethren, a brief work (the *Monologium*) as an example of meditation on the grounds of faith, in the person of one who investigates, in a course of silent reasoning with himself, matters of which he is ignorant; considering that this book was knit together by the linking of many arguments, I began to ask myself whether there might be found a single argument which would require no other for its proof than itself alone.[9]

The *Monologium* was the original weaving from which the *Proslogium* emerged. From the weaving, or rather the knitting "together by the linking of many arguments," Anselm sought a single argument as independent as God himself. The proof he desired, and found, must have no dependency on the outside world or inside prejudice. It must be whole, complete, unitary, indubitable. Anselm desired an argument in the image of God by which the image of God that was man may become one with the uncreated Creator. The argument stands alone, and alone it will be in the history of philosophy, a proof that needs nothing but logic to disclose its truth, a proof that compels assent without further ado.

The proof, like the Sun in Plato's myth, tends to blind its viewers to all else. We will thus walk around it many times without daring to look at it, lest we also be blinded. Having grasped it, one is locked into an embrace that requires response but also predetermines the nature of that answer. For this reason, the proof almost invariably shows up truncated in anthologies of philosophy, sometimes as a mere couple of paragraphs, never as more than a few pages. The proof has long since done away with Anselm, a mere mortal whose name is but a title of the proof. The proof, by its completeness, its wholeness, isolates itself. One is tempted to swallow it in one piece, and those who spit it out also spit it out all in one piece. It is shiny and slippery, mirrorlike, giving back to the viewer whatever the viewer gives to it. In some sense, it is the crown jewel of rationality, what all philosophy aspires to be and to do. It is the essence of men's thought, being so totally abstract that it is related to everything equally and in relationship with nothing. All

great philosophy pays homage to it—by rejecting it, of course. It is necessary for great men to compete with each other, and each philosopher stands
upon the shoulders of the man before and refutes him. The greatest testimony to the power of Anselm's proof is how often it has been refuted and
yet remains to be refuted again.

To refute it again would, therefore, serve no purpose. Instead we would
like to seek some way into the proof, through the proof, or perhaps merely
some way to walk with the proof. The proof, after all, is in a book entitled
Proslogium, that is, *A Discourse*. Moreover, the proof is preceded and followed by other ideas, as if it had a way in and a way beyond. How does
one speak within a discourse? One does not begin with the proof, but approaches it cautiously, being careful not to look at it before one's eyes have
become accustomed to its light. Take small steps, baby steps, drag one's
feet, insist on looking around first.

The text offers a way toward the proof, a way "up" even.

> Up now, slight man! flee, for a little while, thy occupations; hide thyself,
> for a time, from thy disturbing thoughts. (*Proslogium* I, 49)

Here it is not a cave one leaves behind, but "disturbing thoughts" from
which one is instructed to flee. What is the disturbance? Whatever it is, it
disturbs our relation with God, this being the aim of our reflections. Thought
is both a pathway to God and a path away from God. The introduction to
the proof hints at two ways, two thoughts. The proof stands in relation to
another way, even though that way is to be resisted. The unified nature of
rationality, upon which the proof depends, begins with a hint of disturbance.

> Cast aside, now, thy burdensome cares, and put away thy toilsome busi-
> ness. Yield room for some little time to God; and rest for a little time in
> him. Enter the inner chamber of thy mind; shut out all thoughts save that
> of God, and such as can aid thee in seeking him; close thy door and seek
> him. (*Proslogium* I, 49)

The disturbing thoughts are associated with burdens, care, toil, busy-ness,
all the stuff of the day to day. They are the world, which is apart from God,
and must be left behind to come close to God. The labors of the world, its
burdens and cares, the interrelationships of human worth and busy-ness, are
a distraction, a disturbance, but also another way of thought. To avoid such
a thinking, one must shut off and close the door, so that one thinks only
within oneself and therefore in relation to God. This is a restful activity, a
leisure activity. It is possible to take such rest because another labors, and,
indeed, the distinction between prayer and labor is built into society and
forms the basis of its hierarchy.

The feudal society which prevailed in western Europe was permeated with privilege and caste. It was a tripartite society composed of three orders (comprising two classes), commonly named the "*bellatores*" the "*oratores*" and the "*laboratores*." The *bellatores*, (those who fought) and the *oratores*, (those who prayed) belonged to the upper class: the *laboratores*, (those who worked) belonged to the lower class.[10]

Even so, it is not to the laboring class that the text refers, and certainly not to the labors of women, who are still invisible, still lower than the castes described. These women, of all classes, are inferior to men and labor for men, that each caste of men might feel some superiority. The text does not invite them to take a little time, for they have no time; laboring defines their essence. They have not even the time to learn to read, and the Discourse is, therefore, not with them. Instead the text laments that the laboring classes have not fully freed the *oratores*, who must flee the occupations that still intrude upon the time to rest, to shut the door, and then to find God.

The way of thought that leads to God is different from the other way of thought, the thought that is connected with toil. The monks to whom it is addressed must also toil, but they must find the way of thought that honors God, not toil. This introduction to the proof for the existence of God begins with a recognition that thought also may either labor or pray. To pray it must be shut off, closed, taken away from the manifold, those other thoughts that disturb, and turned toward the One. Then, with a whole heart, one no longer disturbed, the one who prays seeks the One, seeks his face, addresses him apart from labor, seeking rest. The seeker looks for God, which implies a where, but the text quickly points the seeker back to the question of ways of seeking. It is not where one may seek God and find him, for Anselm was committed to an active monastic system which did not permit the total removal of the seeker from society, nor even from labor.

God is everywhere, which allows his monks to be actively involved everywhere.

> Lord, if thou art not here, where shall I seek thee, being absent? But if thou art everywhere, why do I not see thee present? Truly thou dwellest in unapproachable light. (*Proslogium* I, 49–50)

God is that which is not absent. However there is a way that finds God and a way that does not, a way of looking and a way of looking at the Sun and a way that cares for the world. The looking of the faithful seeks the "unapproachable light," but here the Sun is not easily seen. Perhaps one is still in the cave?

The language of the searching is the language of the lover. He is "anxious in love," "pants," "longs," "desires," but the object of love is not to be seen.

> What shall thy servant do, anxious in his love of thee, and cast out afar from thy face? He pants to see thee, and thy face is too far from him. He longs to come to thee, and thy dwelling-place is inaccessible. He is eager to find thee, and knows not thy place. He desires to seek thee, and does not know thy face. (*Proslogium* I, 50)

But this is not the burdensome love, the caring that is toil; this is the love that is higher, that leads away from the world and into leisure. In leading away from the world the thought that seeks God seeks its origin, and sees in its origin its end. There is a circularity, a way of thought which can be traced in the small room of the self, to the exercise of thinking about God. The Creator creates the created for the purpose of seeing the Creator.

> Finally, I was created to see thee, and not yet have I done that for which I was made. (*Proslogium* I, 50)

Yet there is a distraction, which is the creation. The Creator is undefined, except that it is the alternative of what is given as world. One flees the world, and because one is fleeing the world, one knows that one is coming into the realm of God. The turning away, the contrast, is the way of knowing, is the only definition one can find for God. Always the alternative way, the way into the world, is sketched, and always it is rejected, because it is only by this rejection that the God is found.

The further definition requires the further rejection. What precisely is being rejected? The undefined is the source of happiness, the "bread of angels." The alternative that defines this angelic bread is the bread that is mortality.

> Man once did eat the bread of angels, for which he hungers now; he eateth now the bread of sorrows, of which he knew not then. Alas! for the mourning of all mankind, for the universal lamentation of the sons of Hades! (*Proslogium* I, 50)

Hades, the bread of sorrows, is that which must be escaped, must be fled; this is the burden, the toil, the care. The problem that drives men, the old dead white men, to God, is the painful inevitability of death.

> Why did he not keep for us, when he could so easily, that whose lack we should feel so heavily? Why did he shut us away from the light, and cover us over with darkness? With what purpose did he rob us of life, and inflict death upon us? Wretches that we are, whence have we been driven out; whither are we driven on? Whence hurled? Whither consigned to ruin? From a native country into exile, from the vision of God into our present blindness, from the joy of immortality into the bitterness and horror of death. Miserable exchange of how great a good, for how great an evil! Heavy loss, heavy grief, heavy all our fate! (*Proslogium* I, 51)

The tomb, the womb, the dark cave, still haunts. Somehow they have not escaped it. They flee, but find no way out, no rest. They are still looking, looking now also perhaps for proof that the way out exists. The darkness is more total; the fire appears to have gone out.

> But alas! wretched that I am, one of the sons of Eve, far removed from God! (*Proslogium* I, 51)

Men have not yet escaped death, because they have not yet escaped woman. The relationship to woman, which symbolizes the ties to the earth, are like the chains of the prisoner. Man is removed from God, from the light. The question is whether one can escape the cave, whether one can escape the womb, whether one can escape the labor of birth. The goal is to escape birth by a woman to be reborn in the male God and thus be prepared for immortality. One leaves the cave and comes to the Sun/Son.

In that problem there is also a hint of another way. For they are both driven by death and are drawn by some alternative way of thinking. Death is mortality, is birth, and is labor. In trying to escape these, disturbing thoughts arise that lead into, rather than away from, what must be escaped. Hence death is not just a problem posed to thought; it is a problem in thought. One is tempted. The horror of death also hides a temptation, to thought even as it does to being. Thinking God is hard, therefore one needs a proof, needs a way to lock thought into the proper mode.

> What have I undertaken? What have I accomplished? Whither was I striving? How far have I come? To what did I aspire? Amid what thoughts am I sighing? I sought blessings, and lo! confusion. I strove toward God, and I stumbled on myself. I sought calm in privacy, and I found tribulation and grief, in my inmost thoughts. I wished to smile in the joy of my mind, and I am compelled to frown by the sorrow of my heart. Gladness was hoped for, and lo! a source of frequent sighs! (*Proslogium* I, 51)

The opposition here is not between death and rationality or mind and body. Instead the problem is that for the sons of Eve there is an alternative way of thought. This alternative constantly interrupts the movement away from birth to man's origin as man in the uncreated Creator. Anselm must constantly resist the way of thinking that ties him to grief. He dares not explore mortality, but he also cannot escape it as a possibility of thought and being. The task of the proof is to provide a way to avoid another thought, another way of thinking. It must be foolproof, so that thinking does not once more turn away from the One to contemplate some other pathway, a pathway the sons of Eve might otherwise sometimes wish to take.

> Be it mine to look up to thy light, even from afar, from the depths. Teach me to seek thee, and reveal thyself to me, when I seek thee, for I cannot

seek thee, except thou teach me, nor find thee, except thou reveal thyself. Let me seek thee in longing, let me long for thee in seeking; let me find thee in love, and love thee in finding. (*Proslogium* I, 52)

The depths of thought must be countered by the light. The danger is always that one's eyes might not be sufficiently blinded by the light, that one might still catch some reflection of the shadows. The disturbing thoughts, the cares for the world, are also wrongdoing, vices that cloud the image of the divine, make it hard to conceive of the uncreated One.

Lord, I acknowledge and I thank thee that thou hast created me in this thine image, in order that I may be mindful of thee, may conceive of thee, and love thee; but that image has been so consumed and wasted away by vices, and obscured by the smoke of wrongdoing, that it cannot achieve that for which it was made, except thou renew it, and create it anew. (*Proslogium* I, 52)

This is the strange relationship between God and man! God creates man, that man might conceive of God. The birth order is inverted. God does not give birth to man, but creates man in his own image, and then man returns the favor by giving birth to the idea of God (conceiving). The conception, in thought, follows the making. The conception provides the purpose for why man was created. For Anselm, man is created in the image of God, and then man conceives of that which is larger, greater, more. The Supreme form, the Original from which the image comes, must be conceived. The Original must be beyond mortality if there is to be assurance that the image is beyond mortality. Man must be reborn in his own image as rationality, pure and undefiled by existence, uncontaminated by the memory of the womb. But the thought of mortality always intervenes.

The burdens of caring, the evils of being contaminated by the base stuff of the world, make it difficult to think purely enough to conceive of God. One must first close off the door that leads elsewhere, to the other self, the other one, one's self related to another. One must even believe that there is such a closed-off way of thinking, believe that what one is about to conceive exists prior to its conception. For this, belief is necessary. Thought is an insufficient beginning place. It must be forced out of the cave and into the light.

I do not endeavor, O Lord, to penetrate thy sublimity, for in no wise do I compare my understanding with that; but I long to understand in some degree thy truth, which my heart believes and loves. For I do not seek to understand that I may believe, but I believe in order to understand. For this also I believe,—that unless I believed, I should not understand. (*Proslogium* I, 52–53)

The man in the biblical story who did not believe posited the same beginning, "I believe, help my unbelief" (Mk 9:24). Belief is the space within which one may begin with nothing. With belief one simply starts. The problem is, what is it that one believes? If this is defined, then thought has preceded belief. If it is undefined then it is unclear, and even open, what one believes.

Anselm begins the proof by shutting the door, by placing himself away from the openness of the world, in a space already defined: himself as the image of the Creator. The man must turn away from what is other, what is out there, what is laboring, what is world, what is woman, to claim a closed-in space within himself which is created, not born. The division between self and other, man and woman, interior spirit and exterior world, is the first separation, and parallels God's separation of the firmaments as the first act of creation. This separation must be done first, so that the thinker has decided the directionality of the thought based on what is to be excluded. Only then can Anselm dare to open out the space within belief, can dare to seek understanding.

But is he safe? Is it safe in this belief to undertake understanding? Is it safe to open the question of God and to open God to question? The path of thought that Anselm opens leads to an unknown destination. What is it that one believes? Approached from the *Monologium*, the Soliloquy, the space of belief is defined. Anselm knew precisely what God it is that one believes in, what the proof is about. The proof is going to prove the existence of the Christian God, the one God in whose image is man, God the Father/Son/Sun/Holy Spirit/Wholly Thought/The Word/The Creator-from-nothing. This we know from the Soliloquy, from man shut into himself who thinks safely by himself.

But now there is the Discourse, the *Proslogium*, and a new danger. The *Proslogium* is in conversation with some undefined other, by virtue of its being a discourse. Soon that other will be defined as the fool, someone not to be taken seriously. Yet that other possibility was serious enough so that another monk (Guanilon) felt it worth his while to defend the fool and his position. The *Proslogium*, in its nature as discourse, invites other objections and possibilities. Anselm's attempt to nail down a single understanding by means of his prior belief is fraught with danger. The *Proslogium* opens itself into a conversation with another and into an understanding that can never be totally under the control of Anselm's text.

And so, Lord, do thou, who dost give understanding to faith, give me, so far as thou knowest it to be profitable, to understand that thou art as we believe; and that thou art that which we believe. (*Proslogium* II, 53)

There are two parts to the proof, that God is, and that the proper God is the one who is—that thou art that which we believe. Anselm's thought has a clarity that acknowledges that there are two problems to be addressed: the question of whether God is and the question of whether God is that which we wish to worship. Of course, everyone assumes that the God to be understood is the Christian God. Anselm assumes that, too, but there is an underlying anxiety implicit in the shutting out of the world in the cloistered monastic setting of meditation. To discover that anxiety requires subversion of Anselm's simple faith. Such subversion perhaps stands as a blasphemy to the original intentionality of the text, for it suggests that Anselm's proof might prove the existence of some unintended God.

Suppose one were to prove the existence of God and then find that that God is some other: perhaps Krishna, or a two-headed snake god from the wrong side of the river. The proof opens itself up for thought, for questions about the "who" of God. Of course, we all know to whom Anselm refers his proof. This is why excerpts from the *Proslogium* in standard anthologies have no need for more than the one paragraph of quotation from Anselm. If there is a God, it must be the God given by the Bible, or our church, or whatever authorities we assign the duty of telling us what to believe. For we also believe, therefore we understand. Only the fool has doubted.

Who then is it that Anselm is about to prove exists? To answer that question would require the proof. On the one hand, the identity precedes the proof, is the precondition of the proof. On the other hand, the proof will also be a definition. There are two ways to approach the proof. There is only one correct way, of course, and that is to begin with the assumption that it is the Christian God to be proved. This was, most certainly, Anselm's intention, and the only appropriate acknowledgment of the context of the text. This is a text for "certain brethren." Suppose, however, one does not begin with Anselm's brothers, with the assumption that it is the Christian God that one wishes to prove. For this purpose, the text at hand must be assumed to be a hostile witness. This is an inverted relationship to take to the text; one that turns the text against its overtly stated orientation.

> And, indeed, we believe that thou art a being than which nothing greater can be conceived. (*Proslogium* II, 53)

The definition and the proof interpenetrate. This is the beauty of Anselm's proof. It offers itself as whole and simple and indubitable. Does the proof disassociate itself with those who do not assume that the God to be proved is God the Father? It cannot. It is open in its simplicity. All the proof offers is a definition of a being which, once thought, cannot be thought not to exist.

> For, it is one thing for an object to be in the understanding, and another to understand that the object exists. (*Proslogium* II, 53)

The relationship between being and thought, existence and thought, is, of course, a problematic one in the history of philosophy. Many thinkers have thought they have unwound the puzzle of Anselm's thought by providing one or another statement of the difference between thought and existence. Yet Anselm's proof is too simple for such profound distinctions and counterdistinctions to get a hold upon it. All that Anselm's proof requires is that there be *some* relationship between thought and existence. The fact of having thought of something does not imply its necessary existence. But it does imply a relationship of the thought to the possibility of existence. The thought always implies a relationship to a possible existence, though that relationship may or may not be explicit. One thinks of an elephant and thinks that this elephant is an elephant at the zoo one visited yesterday. Or perhaps that elephant is merely a pink elephant in the imagination. In either case, one carries with the thought a possible relationship between the thought and the elephant's existence. The fact that one makes a distinction between real elephants and pink elephants is an indication that the distinction between real and imagined elephants is a distinction within thought, though it has implications, presumably, for something outside of thought. One can think of a real elephant, and one can think of an imaginary elephant, and one can think the difference.

Reality and imagination are not identical. The distinguishing feature of reality is that it impinges on thought. It comes from elsewhere; it objects. That is what makes something an objective reality: it objects. The pink elephant is subject to our complete control and hence is reducible to thought. It has no objective reality. Like the world, the toils, the burdensome cares, reality imposes itself upon us, calls us out of ourselves.

The relationship between what objects (the objectiveness of objects), and thought about those objects, takes place in thought. We think that our thought about the elephant has some relationship to the elephant. Sometimes that relationship is negative. It is the realization that the pink elephant is not real after all. And when the elephant steps on my toe, and impinges on my thought and my toe, I proclaim this to be a real, existing elephant. The relationship (not the object, but the relationship) exists in my thought and posits the overlap between thinking and being. There must be a point of contact between thought and existence.

As existence impinges its objectivity upon thought, so also thought impinges upon reality. The painter conceives of a painting.

> When a painter first conceives of what he will afterwards perform, he has it in his understanding, but he does not yet understand it to be, because he has not yet performed it. But after he has made the painting, he both has it in his understanding, and he understands that it exists, because he has made it. (*Proslogium* II, 53)

The painting is in thought, but the thought objectives itself in the painting. The painting appears by hard work—and magic! Of course, there are hands and brushes involved, but these merely cover over the mystery, for it is not clear how thought could affect these objective realities. And many is the time when a painter has in mind a great painting, yet produces only messes. To conceive of an idea, and bring what one conceives into reality, is a mystery, a crossing over from thought to reality that is more difficult than it appears.

The existing reality that interrupts and redefines thought, and the thought that interrupts and redefines reality, both assume a difference and a point of contact. Anselm grounds that point of contact in the relationship of thought and existence, just as the painter discovers it. He claims that if thought and existence are to be related, there must be some point at which the relationship is present both in thought and in existence, some point of relationship, some point of overlap, and that this point is assumed in thought. This is the a priori condition of thinking about things that exist. The painter must so perfectly conceive the idea that it can be executed in reality.

"God" is the mere formal statement that thought must posit a relationship between that which is merely in thought and that which is in thought and existence. At this point in the argument, of course, "God" is but a place-holder, a holding that there is, necessarily and by virtue of the nature of the distinction and the relationship, a point of connection between thought and the thought of that which is actually in existence. "God" is also a conception, as the painter conceives of that which will come into reality. The more concretely, the more perfectly, the painter conceives of the painting, the more likely it will come into existence. The act of conceiving already brings thought into relationship to reality. There must be a connection, for thought has conceived of reality, both in the sense of having encountered the objectivity of the other in the thought of it and in the sense of having constructed it. It has thought of the other, of that which is not thought, of that which is. And this thought posits that at some point thought and being must touch.

Anselm's proof may be important to theoreticians and logicians, but this was not his intended audience. Anselm meditates upon the proof as an artist might meditate upon an idea. Anselm's proof is very much a work of art. The artist makes a picture, but before making the picture, the artist conceives of an idea, as perfectly as possible. The act of painting is an act of conceiving. The two are only theoretically separated. But the act of conceiving is also an act of seeking after that way that most perfectly embodies/makes real the thought. Anselm's proof is a conceiving like this, a way of looking for the idea so great that its existence is assumed within the act of conception. The conceiving commits one to looking for that which must be, because its greatness assumes its necessity.

The proof is not a disputation on being, but begins a way of thinking. Anselm has stumbled upon a footprint in the sand, a fragment of a pathway that promises "than which nothing greater can be conceived." The value of the "greater" draws one beyond mere imagining to look for that which it promises in existence, as an artist is drawn into the act of painting with passion and clarity of thought. The end of the search cannot be seen. It merely posits a way to go about thinking, a way that hints beyond thought, or at least knows something about the nature of the edge of thought, to the place where that than which nothing greater can be conceived must dwell. To examine the path will not be sufficient to prove that such a being exists, but to walk the path is to be drawn on by the value of the conception itself. The path leads on, by the nature of its longing toward the greater, and cannot be concluded short of the end of thought itself, which is existence.

A way of thinking, likewise, proposes a way of going on. Any conclusion is related to the way of thinking as a curve in the road is related to a path; the conclusion is that which one cannot see beyond. Anselm does not propose in the *Proslogium* to defend the path, the way of thinking that is his definition. He proposes to follow it. This is why his book is only barely begun when he spots the proof. The value in the way is how it leads one. Only when Guanilon has misunderstood the path does he attempt to defend the proof, and he does it no better than future philosophers will do. The substance of the book, as it would follow from the definition, would be a description of what's along the way.

Yet this was, for Anselm, a dangerous path to walk, for it implicitly opens up the question of the "who" of God. Anselm truncates the search, turns the path into a dead-end, which merely appears to be moving while in fact leading the searcher always back to where he began. Anselm's real commitment is to the pinnacle of the hierarchy in which he participates. There is an escape route implicit in the openness of seeking the greater. If God is that than which nothing greater can be conceived, then the closed nature of the hierarchy cannot hold it. Hierarchies require that there be a top, but the nature of the "greater" opens the top to reexamination. The "greater than" asks a question: Is this God indeed greater, or might there be more value implicit in naming God in another fashion? Anselm's proof submits God to cross-examination.

Anselm is committed to the Christian God as defined by liturgy and dogma. Anselm does not ask whether it is possible that this is not the greater conception of God. Anselm does not open the way to those who might ask questions not already answered by the church. Instead, he attempts to reconcile the Christian God with the conception of the greater, and this is the essential substance of the *Proslogium*.

We will walk Anselm's path, but even then, not as Anselm perhaps would have wanted. Always our walking will keep Anselm's path in sight, as our guide in tracing the countryside. We will walk off the path, in relationship to the path as path, but not as Anselm's trail guides would suggest. Or perhaps we will not stop where Anselm would have us stop, but find other conclusions, other boundaries, other possible meanings to this God-being to which we are drawn by the longing of our own hearts. Or perhaps we will merely walk in another direction on the same path.

God is a being that than which nothing greater can be conceived. We begin with a conception, a thought, a place to begin. This path begins wherever there is that which is a being. Guanilon begins with an island.

> Now if some one should tell me that there is such an island, I should easily understand his words, in which there is no difficulty. But suppose that he went on to say, as if by logical inference: "You can no longer doubt that this island which is more excellent than all lands exists somewhere, since you have no doubt that it is in your understanding. And since it is more excellent not to be in the understanding alone, but to exist both in the understanding and in reality, for this reason it must exist. For if it does not exist, any land which really exists will be more excellent than it; and so the island already understood by you to be more excellent will not be more excellent."[11]

One could just as easily begin with a star, an elephant, or a pizza. One enters the path at any point; because the path traces the relationship of thought and being, it has many entrances.

The distinction between thought and being takes place in thought, and the thought of the possibility of crossing over from the one to the other likewise takes place in thought. Guanilon begins by thinking about an island; Anselm begins with a painting. Perhaps this makes a difference. The painter, lured by the greater value implicit in that which is made beautiful in thought and in being, paints. There is a relationship between thought and being that happens, dynamically and magically, but also in a quite ordinary fashion. Even the fool can see that. So the fool sets foot on the path.

> Hence, even the fool is convinced that something exists in the understanding, at least, than which nothing greater can be conceived. For, when he hears of this, he understands it. And whatever is understood, exists in the understanding. And assuredly that, than which nothing greater can be conceived, cannot exist in the understanding alone. (*Proslogium* II, 54)

This is really quite an exercise in thought for our poor fool. The fool must now pursue the thought as high as possible. That's a long walk from our simple painting! The painter conceives of a painting If at this point the painter should paint the picture, the boundary is crossed, and thought is put aside in the execution, the birthing of the conception. This fool is after a bigger game; he wants to paint a greater picture, a masterpiece. This is hard to conceive, but our fool is up to it. If at this point our fool should paint the picture, the boundary is again crossed; thought is put aside; the painting exists in both thought and reality. What is interesting is that we are somehow closer to God, for this painting is greater. This is not to say that the relationship to God has been made clear, or even that we have as yet conceived of a God, but the greater conception is here.

But surely even our fool can conceive of an even greater painting, a masterpiece that is greater than all other masterpieces. This is a more difficult boundary to cross, but there must surely have been painters who attempted it. Guanilon found a shortcut to this greatest of all paintings, by conceiving of that which he did not have to perform. He conceived of a perfect island, indeed, the most perfect island ever conceived.

> For example: it is said that somewhere in the ocean is an island, which, because of the difficulty, or rather the impossibility, of discovering what does not exist, is called the lost island. And they say that this island has an inestimable wealth of all manner of riches and delicacies in greater abundance than is told of the Islands of the Blest; and that having no owner or inhabitant, it is more excellent than all other countries, which are inhabited by mankind, in the abundance with which it is stored.[12]

Because the island was natural, it need only be found, not made. Unfortunately, he had no intention of going and looking for it. He merely conceived it in thought, like our fool who imagines creating the greatest of all masterpieces. Both thought they found the task easy, which shows they did not even know how to conceive of such a thing. There was no content to their thought, it was merely the most perfect, the greatest.

A child is more honest in conceiving. Children love to contest with each other to conceive of the greatest possible this or that. Perhaps they might argue for the greatest possible unicorn, or giant, or snail. Perhaps you have heard them, as we have, whiling away the hours of a long car ride by conceiving of greater and greater monstrosities. "My unicorn is bigger than Daddy. My unicorn is bigger than this car. My unicorn is SO big that its hoof is the size of this car. My unicorn is bigger than the world. My unicorn fills the universe. My unicorn is SO big the universe is a speck in its eye! My unicorn fills everything and is everywhere, even here, even where your unicorn is. My unicorn is the greatest of all. My unicorn is greater even than that." Children know that to conceive of the greater requires effort, requires some sense of scale.

Has Guanilon even thought of his perfect island? Has he asked himself whether there are palm trees and clear sweet springs, or whether in fact there are pine trees with mountain streams tumbling from snow-topped peaks?

Has he bothered to think what to look for if he should set out to find this perfect island? Or has he treated thought peremptorily and conceived a thought without having conceived it? One may start the meditation which is the essence of the proof at any point, even a point of land. There is a prayerful urgency as one follows the "greater" good through discussions of the qualities of islands, whether the greater island has or has not palm trees, whether there are or are not natives, and whether the hummingbirds on this island sing like nightingales. Guanilon is seduced by the nature of hierarchy into stopping with a "greatest" island. The greatest island is a product of a single linear thought which, reaching its conclusion, must stop. Guanilon's island is only partially imagined, and, being only partially imagined, is unable to subsume existence within its definition.

To conceive of a masterpiece is not something to be done in a second. Many a master would quake at the thought of having to conceive of such a painting, and think the performance simple in comparison to the process of conception. Now if we ask the painter to conceive of a painting greater than any other paintings, one that will be the final masterpiece for that age, or perhaps even for the rest of art history, it is doubtful that the painter will take our commission for that task! The fool imagines that he has conceived of such a painting, and now he imagines walking away with the praise of all the world. Such a conception takes little effort (for the fool), but it is not the kind of conception that leads to a god.

There is, however, a more serious fool than this one, more serious even than Guanilon, who, having heard that there might be such an island, is determined to find it. There is a painter who wishes quite seriously to paint the final painting, the one toward which all paintings point. Both are fools, but these fools are set to conceive of something than which nothing greater can be conceived. Let it be paintings or islands or unicorns (it makes no difference); this is the path that leads to the boundary. The painter stares at the easel, which is still blank. Which color should be placed upon the canvas? Which color is that color than which no greater color can be conceived? No colors? All colors? This is where the task begins.

Perhaps our poor fool is a bit simple, in which case he settles for a blue picture, liking blue better than all other colors. Then this is God, as close as one may come, if only until a better color comes along. The path turns with the ability of the walker. But it is dependent on an honest walker, one willing to walk each step along the way. This is a mystical journey, which sets as its object to find the perfect island. Or perhaps it was a certain grail that was sought. The simpleton finds an old tin cup and sees the grail. Who is to say that it is not?

The perfect island exists, but it cannot be this island, or this, or this, though the simpleton may see through the distinctions to the recognition that the island may stand in a relationship to that than which no greater can be conceived. That than which nothing greater can be conceived may begin as an island, but the island may take some strange turns, because the key term slips away from the identification of any single thing, even the island with which it started. The greater island traces the longing for more than islands can give. Better an island without limits than an island within the restrictions of real islands. But then the greater island must not be an island, not even the island at the top of the hierarchy. Instead the island comes to be a responsive, loving island and more, reaching out beyond the confines of the idea of islands toward something else.

What else is there? There surely is "god." There is that which every island, everything in existence, points toward as the greater. And here philosophy tends to stop. Insofar as God is defined as "that than which nothing greater can be conceived," the tradition has a real live proof for the existence that that definition must also contain. However, like Guanilon, perhaps Anselm wishes to close the definition within the structure of a meaning to which he has committed himself ahead of time. Anselm does not wish to prove the existence of God, as a search for a value that might escape Christianity. He does not want to follow the lure of meaning; instead he wishes to ensure the foundations of a hierarchical patriarchal religion.

The structure of the proof is a pathway of meditation. It operates as a guide and a motivation. Anselm puts that meditation to work on a system of dogmatic theology, but the proof fits the foundations poorly. The openness of the nature of value (the greater) ensures the proof and ensures that the proof will not hold still. The longing to follow the greater haunts Anselm's *Proslogium*, no matter how carefully Anselm tacks it down. He adds characteristics on to God, thus piling on attributes that substitute for the possibility of following the greater beyond the confines of the hierarchy, beyond Christianity.

Within each characteristic, Anselm seeks the "better" quality to add to God. Yet the necessity of reinforcing patriarchy limits his examination. The best he can manage is a "greatest," a frozen vision of the greater. His is a closed system of value, even when it rests upon a proof that only works if it is allowed to be open.

The act of going and looking for the greater commits one to the task of conceiving. The act of conceiving is not the same as merely thinking that one has already got the idea in hand. Few are the people who can think clearly enough even to have conceived a thought, giving it nuance and life! This is but the beginning of the journey, for now the pathway leads on beyond the initial conception to something greater. With whatever one begins, one then must seek that which is beyond the one thought. The beyond in thought lures one, the boundary that draws one into creation, into the painting of pictures, into the longing for the truer picture. Truer to what? The standard is not available for dissection but exists in the critical dreaming of that which would be better. No one outside will set the criteria, but only a question: "Could it not be still better?" If one would follow it, without pause nor the impatience of a thought that would posit as done what has only appeared as a hint, the end result (always the proximate end) is God.

This is a meditation, an act of prayer, an act much like the painting of a picture. The words both come from one and point ahead of where one is as yet situated. The path disappears into mystery, but there is a smell of violets. The path is the promise of destination, for it is itself the proof of the power of conception. To conceive the better is not really to conceive unless it conceives of the better in reality. Whatever "island" is better (after one has overcome the limitation of islands as merely possible, that is, possibly with white sand beaches and quiet seas, or dark rocks and wild fascinating waves) is more than any ordinary island. It must be so much more that it soon resembles "islands" not at all. The island, even one's favorite island, is but a vista on the path; there is that which exceeds "island" in greatness, even for those who like islands. Having begun with islands, one is ready for more, for that which is greater. Where does the path turn here? Who can say but the fool who is willing to search for the island, willing to understand the limitations of islands, willing to dream beyond?

Only once we are beyond all those things, those attributes, which are good only in moderation (as an island that gets too big ceases to be an island) do we begin to conceive of that which is divine. The simple fool sees in the island that which is more and therefore worships the island. The island gives sustenance and security; this constitutes its claim on divinity. Worshipping the island posits the island as pointing beyond, to that which is greater than what appears. All language, when valuing, engages in such a pointing, such a self-conscious willingness to engage in hints and symbolism. Anselm is teaching a way to let language follow its own inwardness, to bring thought in service to that toward which it points.

At this point "being" is reintroduced as value. The painter conceives of the picture and longs to be able to paint it just so. Having posited worth, the longing is to see that conception give birth to reality. There is that in the dream which draws toward reality. Surely it would be better if that which is greater existed in reality! The value of a thought draws thought toward being. Socrates also understood the lure of value. His dialogues turn on the movement of the heart as much as of the mind. We desire that which is of the highest value, even though that value is as yet conceived only as an abstract beyond our reach. Socrates and Anselm share a conviction that at the top of the hierarchy of value there is One Thing. The drawing of worth, which motivates all that desires to go beyond, is posited as a pyramid of meaning, so reminiscent of the pyramids of human beings ranked by their worth. The way becomes a climb, each value trivialized by the value beyond. The search for worth also presumes that which is worth-less.

> And it assuredly exists so truly, that it cannot be conceived not to exist. For, it is possible to conceive of a being which cannot be conceived not to exist; and this is greater than one which can be conceived not to exist. (*Proslogium* III, 54)

God is that than which nothing greater can be conceived. "Greater" is a multipurpose word. Greater is a larger pile of coins. Greater is a higher mountain. Greater than the woman is the man. Greater than the serf is the lord. Greater than the lord is the king. Greater than the king is the king that need not die. The limit upon all earthly hierarchies is that they end. The end hints at the potential for nonbeing, which is implicit in all being. The king has no more claim on being than has the slave. All things can be or not be, that is the limit on their climb to and claim on power.

For Anselm, there is a hierarchy of being. At the bottom is nonbeing, that which is not, is worth the least. At the next level is that which has a possible being, that which might be, that which has a potentiality for being. At the next higher level is being, that which exists, but that which also may fall out of existence. At the highest level is necessary being, existence that must always be and can never not be. This hierarchy of being is inherited from the neoplatonists via Augustine and shapes much of Western metaphysics. Power and value is vested in that which comes closest to necessary being. Just as it takes more being to be in reality than to be in possibility, so it would take more being to be in necessity than in possibility. Here it would seem that being itself were a quantity, capable of being added to until one reaches necessity.

Yet isn't this a curious kind of "greater"? Do things gain value by being posited as necessarily existing? Is the end of the road better than the middle? Certain theorems in mathematics are necessarily true. Are they greater, because we cannot think the opposite without contradiction? Here the heart is not so sure. Somehow we cannot rest easily in a proof whereby God becomes necessary. No matter how many times the philosophers prove the existence of God, those who follow seek only to find the holes in the argument. There is that in the heart that is drawn to value but also that in the heart that rejects proofs. Somehow the heart rebels at this Good, this God, which cannot be conceived not to exist. Is that which cannot be conceived not to exist greater than that which exists? Is that which necessarily exists greater than which exists? Is necessity greater than possibility? Does necessity add to existence? Does the hierarchy work?

There is a passionate resistance of the heart to the idea of that which is not capable of being conceived not to exist. There is a resistance to conceiving of the necessary existence of God. Conceiving of the heart longs toward existence but turns in horror from all necessity. If Anselm should show that the alternative to God's necessity is contradictory, that will not end the longing. Contradiction is, for the heart, not the limit, but the intensification of longing to go beyond, to continue the conceiving, to seek that which is greater. Somehow what we most desire, that which is greater than all that we came to before, is not necessity. God's necessity defines God as that than which no being is more powerful, but is this the greater that the heart desires? That which necessarily exists is not the heart's desire but is the power of all absolute monarchs. The necessity of God rests, not upon an understanding of conception, but upon that hierarchy of being which has equated existence with power over other beings, even over existence itself. There is much of the Crusader in Anselm also, much of the king maker, much of the need to accumulate power.

Anselm's participation in the power struggles of his time is reflected in his meditations. Vaughn is right to see in Anselm's rise to power a commitment to the exercise of power as a value in itself.

> This portrait of Anselm [by R. W. Southern in his *Saint Anselm: Portrait of a Landscape*], sketched with consummate skill by one of the most sensitive and astute historians of the present generation, is now generally accepted. But there are grounds—some of which are suggested by Southern himself—for doubting that Anselm was quite so politically naive.[13]

Southern emphasizes Anselm's commitment to the heavenly order, to contemplation, as opposed to the secular order and political ambition. Vaughn's case rests on Anselm's actions and his clear expertise and involvement in the political life of his day, both at the monastery at Bec and at the archbishopric at Canterbury. Southern's case rests on Anselm's own protestations against political involvement.

> Everything depends on the sincerity of Anselm's protestations, for which we have not only Eadmer's vivid account, but also Anselm's own repeated statements. If we believe him, we shall think that the whole prospect was abhorrent to him. If we do not believe him, and think that his words were a calculated reaction to a situation which in his heart he welcomed, then we must think that, with whatever mitigation, he persistently mis-stated the truth. There is really no half-way house between these two positions, for we do not rely only on Eadmer's account of events; we have Anselm's own solemn and repeated declarations to the monks of Bec, to the bishops of Evreux and Beauvais, and finally to the pope.[14]

The debate between Vaughn and Southern rests largely upon Anselm's words and his actions. Both are correct. Southern is right that Anselm's words must be taken seriously as what Anselm himself thought he was doing. But Vaughn is right that Anselm's words must be seen as supporting an astute political agenda. The link between the two lies not in his letters nor in the accusations of his contemporaries but rather in the theoretical roots in his theological reflections. The goal for Anselm, in every aspect of his thought, actions, and writings, is to crown God as absolute king. Anselm participates adeptly in the hierarchies of his day, because his thought is so deeply infused with the centrality of hierarchy to heaven. Anselm wishes to crown God king by force of thought. Underlying Anselm's proof for the existence of God is a deeply ingrained political metaphor. Anselm's thought and his action are governed by a sorting out and a ranking of loyalties. God clearly must rank at the top, but beyond that the ranking is not immediately obvious, and thus many of Anselm's protestations emerge from his struggle to determine and to act upon his own place in the ranking. The very centrality of the necessity of ranking to his entire system committed and suited him for active political participation.

Prior to the third chapter of the *Proslogium*, God was conceived as existing in both thought and reality, as a promise that the road of conception does in fact stand in relation to both thought and being. The fool was drawn into a search, confident that what was thought and dreamed some where stands in relation to that which exists. The relation was formal, undefined. Any particular conception of that than which nothing greater can be conceived was always relative to a greater, as yet unconceived. That there is that which is both in thought and in reality was promised by the nature of thought, which always refers to reality as that which it wishes to enter by the value of its conception.

The necessity of God in Anselm's argument in the third chapter of the *Proslogium* is different from the argument for the existence of God. Now, however, Anselm wants more for his God. Reality is to be turned into a theorem, subjected to thought. A necessary God turns the act of conception into an assent to be filled by the thought of another. Such a God is already all thought out, completed, needing nothing from the fool in which he is conceived. The conception that desires reality as its own birth into newness, into the unanticipated, is now preordained and predetermined. There is no point in going on; one merely submits to the reasoning as one would submit to a mathematical formula.

> So truly, therefore, dost thou exist, O Lord, my God, that thou canst not be conceived not to exist; and rightly. For, if a mind could conceive of a being better than thee, the creature would rise above the Creator; and this is most absurd. And, indeed, whatever else there is, except thee alone, can be conceived not to exist. To thee alone, therefore, it belongs to exist more truly than all other beings, and hence in a higher degree than all

others. For, whatever else exists does not exist so truly, and hence in a less degree it belongs to it to exist. Why, then, has the fool said in his heart, there is no God (Psalms xiv.1), since it is so evident, to a rational mind, that thou dost exist in the highest degree of all? Why, except that he is dull and a fool? (*Proslogium* III, 55)

Like the absolute dictator, God's existence demands that others' existence be more tentative than his. The argument that God is necessary, that he cannot not be conceived, does not welcome the fool, but turns him dull and foolish. The words become mere words, hard to follow and leading nowhere. If one were to follow them, it would be to attempt to conceive of a world without God. Would it be better if God did not exist? Perhaps. It depends on the nature of the God one is negating. Is the God who cannot be conceived not to exist greater? It depends on what one means by greater. Such a God is beyond influence, more powerful. If one judges power to be of value simply for its own sake, then the God with the most power and the most immunity is truly greater, as a monarch who can kill without being in danger of death is greater.

The whole enterprise of proof-making is tied into the political and social enterprises of hierarchy and power. Transcendence is the theological claim to ultimate superiority and power. God cannot feel, for to feel is to be touched by those without power.

But how art thou compassionate, and, at the same time passionless? For, if thou art passionless, thou dost not feel sympathy; and if thou dost not feel sympathy, thy heart is not wretched from sympathy for the wretched; but this is to be compassionate. But if thou art not compassionate, whence cometh so great consolation to the wretched? (*Proslogium* VIII, 59)

Anselm places God beyond feeling, because to feel is to be dependent on those to whom He is related. To be all powerful is therefore to be beyond all feeling. Yet as Charles Hartshorne points out, a God who does not feel cannot be a God worthy of worship.

What we ask above all is the chance to *contribute* to the being of others. This ultimate generosity of aspiration is stifled by the doctrine that in the supreme relation in which we stand it is only ourselves, not the other, that has anything to receive from the relation. "To love," it has been said, "is to wish to give rather than to receive"; but in loving God we are, according to Anselm and thousands of other orthodox divines, forbidden to give; for God, they say, is a totally impassive, nonreceptive, non-relative being.[15]

Hartshorne sensed the inadequacy of proclaiming as highest that which has no relation to what is below, but the issue for Anselm is one of power, not value. This is the tension in Anselm's enterprise. The heart of the proof is what is greater. But greater can mean an interpretation of the accumulation of power, or greater can mean that which is of more value. If God can feel, God is affected. If God is affected, then those who hurt have power over God in their pain. The king throws coins to the poor but does not feel their hunger. The God throws mercy but feels nothing of the wretchedness of those he saves. Is such a God worthy of worship?

The God of Anselm's pathway has greatness as a king has greatness. The historical precedent and image for transcendence is autocratic sovereignty. Transcendence is the ultimate claim to superiority. The historical precedent and image for transcendence is the autocratic sovereignty and hierarchical infrastructure of monarchy. Patriarchal religion conceived a heavenly host of angels, archangels, saints, popes, bishops, and priests. Each step on the hierarchical ladder derives its authority from the next higher step. The very principle of hierarchy demands that there always be some higher source of authority. The transcendent deity allows for no rivals at the top. Religions that worship a transcendent deity are logically and practically authoritarian in structure.

As images of the God evolve, the terms "goodness" and "justice" become increasingly important but also increasingly empty of all content. Far from supporting a system of fairness, the just God becomes the legitimating force behind a popular morality based on social mechanisms of control. Human laws become irrefutable once identified with the laws of God. The goodness of God protects the interests of his followers. As his followers become the dominant culture, the religious alternatives are depicted as the evil, the immoral, and the demonic.

Theodicy is the great hurdle that Anselm has built for himself. God's existence is dependent on his being better than that which one also conceives. Or rather, the existence of this particular God, this patriarchal God of Anselm's fathers in Christ, is dependent on his ability to find room in heaven for the hell of human wretchedness. Surely we can conceive of a better God than the one who creates the injustice that shapes the world we know! But if it is this God which must exist, because it is better that such a God exist than not exist, then we are confronted with the same problem as Guanilon's island. A better God would create a better world. Why then, is the world not better?

> If God is good, he is not great.
> If God is great, he is not good.

The old folk rhyme of theodicy twists the path of the proof. With Anselm's proof, the quandary of theodicy is placed at the very heart of the question of God.

The answer cannot be given in the abstract clarity of a definition. Rather the definition poses the issue. God is that than which nothing greater can be conceived. What then is God? The painter conceives of a picture, but the picture is not yet in reality. Already there is a relationship between the picture and reality. The quality of the conception, the dream of the picture, will lead the picture into reality. Conceive, therefore, of a picture than which you cannot conceive a better. The act is birthed from the conception, from the lure, from the promise in the value of the conception. The drawing seeks that which it will only partially embody, so the painter paints again and again. The art of painting is the art of conception which sets itself upon a path that longs beyond what is given. Here there is no point of conclusion, no necessity but the necessity of commitment to the path that seeks the greater. God is just around the corner. The painter, the fool, catches a glimpse, and conceives. The picture is painted; a step is taken. The picture stands in relation to that which is greater, is drawn toward it. The proof for God is in the act of conceiving which is drawn forth by that which the conceiving conceives, but which is also a promise beyond the concrete substance of conception, the promise of more. God is a god of painters, of actors who bring God into existence in the search for God.

Anselm constructs his proof in a way that points away from, not toward, the God he has inherited from his father's fathers. The entire set of works is filled with images of sexuality and birth. Yet the centrality of these images also creates a tension. This is a vision of birth that denies a woman's role in conception. It is greater to be the ruler of a divine empire, beyond mortality, beyond corruption, beyond woman.

> Therefore, O Lord, our God, the more truly art thou omnipotent, since thou art capable of nothing through impotence, and nothing has power against thee. (*Proslogium* VII, 59)

Impotence is weakness. The God must escape weakness. He must be good and he must be strong. But it is strength that is the given, and then the task is to reconcile goodness to power. Here is the essence of legitimation of all those in power: to justify their might. And always the apology for God, as the legitimation of the tyrant, ends up justifying things the way they are. The lure of the good founders on the need to justify God in his absolute power.

The dynamics of the argument are present before they coalesced in Anselm's single proof for the existence of God as that than which nothing greater can be conceived. In the *Monologium,* Anselm even considers the possibility that God might be, in some sense, a Mother.

> I should certainly be glad, and perhaps able, now to reach the conclusion, that he is most truly the Father, while this Word is most truly his Son. But I think that even this question should not be neglected: whether it is

more fitting to call them Father and Son, than mother and daughter, since in them there is no distinction of sex. (*Monologium* XLII, 150–51)

God is a progenitor. God begets (and is begotten). The central act of divinity is not the creating of the universe, but the begetting of a child. This is the greatest miracle, the miracle that introduces us to all the wonder of the world. For we also are begotten, we also enter the world by a miracle. The nature of the miracle is hidden from us. We cannot understand it, can only stand waiting by the womb in anticipation of a miracle. Creation from nothing is worthless beside this, that God begets and is begotten. An ancient truth is waiting to be discovered in the abstract conundrum of trinity. The mystery precedes the creation, is nested in the nature of God, or perhaps more accurately, in the memory of her who begets.

Anselm is honest enough to wonder a bit about this trinitarian miracle. Fathers don't usually give birth to anyone. The stolen language of birth and conception haunts the understanding of theologians in phrases like "begotten." To abandon the language would make it more difficult to trace the lost memory of the Goddess, but it also would be to give away the power still echoing in the images. If God makes his Son as a potter makes a pot, then the Father may be more, but the Son is less. The fathers desire the strongest possible link between the Father and the Son. God could have excreted the Son, have imagined the Son, have dreamed the Son, have found the Son. All these images would have distanced man from the images of woman that haunt his highest longings, but none of them have the power to relate the two persons in value and in mystery.

Yet to hold to the language of birth and begetting is to hold open the possibility of worshipping a Goddess. The Mother will not do, however, for never would she fit the trappings of men's conceptions of power. The superiority of men over women is the only basis for the persistence of the images of God the Father, for there is no distinction of sex in the divinity.

> For, if it is consistent with the nature of the one to be the Father, and of his offspring to be the Son, because both are Spirit (*Spiritus*, masculine); why is it not, with equal reason, consistent with the nature of the one to be the mother, and the other the daughter, since both are truth and wisdom (*veritas et sapientia*, feminine)? Or, is it because in these natures that have a difference of sex, it belongs to the superior sex to be father or son, and to the inferior to be mother or daughter? (*Monologium* XLII, 151)

The superiority of might underlies the hierarchies of men's political systems. If one turns to nature with this expectation, it would seem that father and son are superior to mother and daughter. Nature, however, offers contrary examples as well, even of size and strength. For in some instances, "as among certain kinds of birds, among which the female is always larger and stronger, while the male is smaller and weaker." (*Monologium* XLII, 151). God could remain in the image of father only if father remained in the image of God. The denial of the mother as divine required the denial of the mother as the "cause" of birth.

> At any rate, it is more consistent to call the supreme Spirit father than mother, for this reason, that the first and principle cause of offspring is always in the father. For, if the maternal cause is ever in some way preceded by the paternal, it is exceedingly inconsistent that the name *mother* should be attached to that parent with which, for the generation of offspring, no other cause is associated, and which no other precedes. (*Monologium* XLII, 151)

Anselm's assertion of the father as the true progenitor, the first and principal cause of the child, reflects, of course, the dated nature of his biology. It no longer requires refutation but only tolerant acknowledgment of the limitations of his day. Yet if the image is reversed, so is the argument that rests upon it. If the father's seed is not the first and principal cause of the child, then neither is the Father the one who begets, or the Son the one who is begotten. Like a turning in the path that is no longer in common passage, the possibility hints at another way to follow this proof for the existence of God.

What would it mean to follow Anselm's path along the way that speaks of value without speaking in terms of hierarchies of power? Anselm's proof plays upon the dual meanings of great, so that a great man may be either noble or one with control over others. In this short passage, Anselm attempts to ground the Father in the natural assumptions of male superiority and cannot. If this is true, all modern uses of the argument must at this point reverse theology. Of course, very few modern theologians have read the *Monologium* in its essential relation to the *Proslogium*. Few have seen that the proof itself rests upon the qualities attributed to God. Anselm must show it is possible to conceive of a God who is greater, who is more worthy of conceiving. The argument turns, not on existence as a predicate of God, but on value as a predicate of God. God is an idea waiting to be realized, to be drawn so clearly and beautifully that even the fool can conceive of it. Anselm must produce a conception of God so beautiful, so valuable, so great, that the fool is drawn into the search by the conviction that such a being must indeed underlie all that is.

The lure of the divine is the lure of the reality of value. Anselm sets up the path by means of his definition and follows it with an attempt to make the Christian God fit. To suggest any other deity as greater than God the Father, Son, Holy Ghost, would fill him with the most profound dismay. He is ready for the fool who rejects God but not for some so foolish that they might follow Anselm, the fool that is enamored by some other divine image. The choice of how one depicts God has the potential to make a profound difference in determining whether a description of God is in fact a description of that than which nothing greater can be conceived. Anselm's discussion has the potential to intersect contemporary discourse about God-language.

In Anselm's own time, a reevaluation of the feminine was just beneath the surface. Anselm explicitly rejects feminine imagery of God in his discursive works.

> As the evidence demonstrates, when Anselm uses his reflection alone he reaches first a view of God as beyond all sexual distinction; and when he incorporates available theories of the philosophy of science into his reflection, he draws conclusions about the nature of God that imply a completely masculine identity.[16]

However, as Allen points out, when

> Anselm expresses his own intimate relation with God through the use of intuition, passion and the emotions, the Divine Nature is experienced as strongly feminine.[17]

Anselm discovers in his own life times and situations in which it seems more appropriate to describe divinity as feminine. His use of feminine imagery does not propose an alternative to the Father God but rather likens the intercessory aspects of Christ's relationship to the world as inherently feminine.

> And you, Jesus, are you not also a mother?
>   Are you not the mother who, like a hen,
>   gathers her chickens under her wings?
> Truly, Lord, you are a mother;
>   for both they who are in labour
>   and they who are brought forth
>   are accepted by you.
> You have died more than they, that they may labour to bear.
>   It is by your death that they have been born,
>   for if you had not been in labour,
>   you could not have borne death;
> and if you had not died, you would not have brought forth.
>   For, longing to bear sons into life,
>   you tasted of death,
>   and by dying you begot them.
> You did this in your own self, . . .
>   So you, Lord God, are the great mother.[18]

The hierarchical relationship between father and mother is still implicit. It is Christ as crucified who brings forth everlasting life. The relationship between birth and death becomes twisted. On the one hand, birth and feminine imagery are honored by being linked with the person of Christ. On the other hand, this image of birth ephasizes its link with death and its need to be overcome in Christ. Nonetheless, Anselm's comfort with feminine imagery of God anticipates openness regarding the divine character.

> A thing to be wondered at—
> at what a height do I behold the place of Mary!
>   Nothing equals Mary,
>   nothing but God is greater than Mary . . .
> All nature is created by God and God is born of Mary.
> God created all things, and Mary gave birth to God . . .[19]

Anselm's prayers and meditations foreshadow the cult of the Virgin Mary. The rapidity of the spread of the cult of the Virgin Mary mere decades after Anselm's time, as well as secular explorations of language of veneration of ladies of the court, suggests that the images were not buried very far beneath the surface of Anselm's world. His own language foreshadows the coming ascendancy of romantic discourse, which at least offered a moment's respite in the history of the oppression of women.

As a man of his time, Anselm participates in and supports a hierarchy that is based on domination and oppression. His texts likewise refer to doctrines that act to reinforce the power of the fathers. Yet the texts contain hints of alternative verses, alternative ways of thinking. They do this by virtue of their historicity, the way in which a text contains within itself echoes of the old and hints of the new. Anselm's texts point, by virtue of the structure of the argument for the proof for the existence of God, at liberating possibilities. The descriptions of that than which nothing greater can be conceived are intrinsically open. The texts overtly refer and reinforce the oppressive dogma of the Father God, ruler of heaven and hell, most absolute of all monarchs. Insofar as the *Proslogium* attempts to prove the existence of that God by seeking that than which nothing greater can be conceived, the text opens up the possibility that there might be some other deity worthy of worship, beyond the truncated affirmation of the Lord God.

Anselm himself was caught in this dilemma by the language of begetting which he inherited from the church councils centuries before him. The creedal language of begetting and begotten echoes and legitimates the patriarchal preemption of the birth process. The erasure of mothers in the ancestral lists of lineage in the Hebrew Bible and the New Testament was the prerequisite of the deletion of the divine Mother in the "begetting" of the divine child. The birth relationship implicit in all procreative language suggests a Mother God, even a Goddess. It carries remnants of the memory of the ancient worship of the divine Mother. In Anselm, the question of the priority of mother or father in procreation becomes a question of which is a greater, more valuable, image of divinity. Yet in a patriarchal system, the question of whether the mother might not be a greater image of divinity than father is blasphemy. It is perhaps a greater blasphemy in our own age than it was in Anselm's, for Anselm foreshadows an age of exploration of the divine feminine. Anselm's conclusion, that the father has biological priority, was even from his standpoint a tentative conclusion. Anselm was dependent on an analysis of biology unique to the patriarchs. It is easy to laugh now at this peculiar assumption that a man's seed initiates procreation, as if his seed were a miniature human being waiting only to be sown in the fertile field of the woman's womb. Biology operated as a legitimating tool of the father oppressors, mutually reinforced by theology and the father confessors.

The question arises again for us. Is the image of mother as God a more appropriate, a greater, conception than the image of father? Anselm's image not only rests on a faulty conception of procreation. Rather, the biology and the theology share a common orientation toward a hierarchical structure of existence. An application of "greater," whether it be in biology or in theology, is rooted in superiority in strength, or power, or status in the patriarchal state. The application rests, therefore, on the hierarchical construction of the patriarchal worldview.

In the world as we live it, which in its patriarchal underpinnings is not so different from Anselm's, the father still holds the might. But we could, nonetheless, in the longing of our hearts, conceive of the possibility that God might, just because all power still rests with the fathers, choose to conceive of mother as greatest. For to stand against that which is oppressive is better, is greater, than to participate in the bloody acquisition of power over others. Even within Christianity, the tension between the God as absolute in power and might and the God who identifies with the downtrodden and the oppressed continually pulls at theology. The Christian resolution has been to isolate the transcendent God and then build hierarchies of intercession, a move also echoed in Anselm in his feminine images of Christ and in his elevation of Mary. How much greater might the conception of divinity be that roots its value in something other than hierarchies? How much more valuable might a conception of divinity be that chooses those metaphors that lead us beyond the status quo to conceive of that which might be better? Perhaps the Goddess is the metaphor that can lead us toward a conception of divinity that is greater than the bloody history of Christendom. The Goddess has sons and daughters too precious to waste on the Crusades. She who has birthed us, does not see us as pots to be smashed at the will of the potter, but as the children of her womb to which we will return when growing is done.

Is an omnipotent deity greater in the sense of better or merely more powerful? The Goddess is powerful not in the sense of a hierarchical transcendence, but rather as the center of the mighty circle of mortality and transformation. The Goddess, as that than which we have not yet conceived a greater, affirms the value of mortality. That we are born and live and die are all of a piece. Is it not better to seek that conception of greater that values the meaning within mortality, rather than promising heavens of immortality for those who die—and kill—in the Lamb's War? Perhaps the image of woman, whose changes are both cyclical and of vast importance to the human experience, is the better image of the divine. Perhaps the God who is affected, who cries and bleeds and gives her breast to her young, is the better image.

The God who is Anselm's greater good has trouble reconciling mercy and justice. His success requires a society that places God's judgments beyond all meaningful inquiries. God's power justifies his right to judge all humans on the basis of a sin, the meaning of which theologians must continually redefine, for it is not obvious except to those who have already decided to condemn. The images of God Anselm provides rest on such terms as 'goodness' and 'justice'—terms that seem to become increasingly empty of all content. Far from supporting a system of fairness, the "just" God becomes the legitimating force behind a popular morality based on social mechanisms of control. Human laws become irrefutable once identified with the laws of God. The goodness of God protects the interests of his followers. As his followers become the dominant culture, the religious alternatives are depicted as the evil, the immoral, and the demonic.

The question of God implicit in Anselm's proof places value as the crucial criteria of all depictions of God. It dares us to dream higher, rather than justifying God at the expense of those who suffer. This is a vision of "greater" that is not divorced from Christian notions of value, which are in sympathy with those who are weak. God must be defined in terms of those who are in need. The God who stands with the oppressed is colored and gendered and poor. The God who feels nothing excludes the victims of oppression from divinity. As it is, the omnipresent God is not helpful for those who would struggle against oppression. The pain of the oppressed stands in naked contradiction to his claim of absolute goodness. Worse yet, those on the fringe of the dominant society are labeled as "evil" on the basis of their deviance from the norm. The jealous God must maintain the purity of absolute goodness to sustain the claim to absolute superiority. Absolute goodness and absolute superiority are also absolute removal. The victim is left alone in meaningless suffering when divinity is divorced from pain and suffering. An absolutely good God is of benefit only to the oppressor. An absolutely good God always leaves the oppressed caught in the tangled twists of theodicy

Yet it is the screams of victims that cry aloud to heaven. In the midst of rational arguments about the existence of God, theodicy is theophany. The more carefully scholarly arguments proceed proving the existence of God, the more there is the temptation to minimize and ignore the problem of evil. Yet the problem of evil broods as the unspoken voice in the monologue that constitutes proofs. The impossibility of silencing the voice of pain is the living proof for the existence of a religious dimension of experience that cannot be contained in the truncated deity of patriarchal rationality.

Our longing for that which is greater than what we now conceive leads us along a path, the end of which cannot be seen. The desire itself points the way to something we almost remember, the possibility that humans do not have to settle for the constant repetition of leaders and husbands and fathers and doctors that seek to be godlike, on the top of some pyramid. The ones at the top need those on the bottom to ensure their superiority. This can only be done by maintaining and enforcing the inferiority of all those countless others. These others are the source of diversity, of the richly colored hues of differences in traditions, religions, cultures, languages, and so forth. The alternative is a notion of that than which nothing greater can be conceived as being inclusive and nonhierarchical. That which is greater must stand with that which is more diverse, with the wonder of multiplicity and with the playfulness of reality, which will never settle for One when many will do.

The exclusion of the Goddess' voice from the tradition requires the rejection of multivocity. The jealous male God does not wish the competition that she represents. The Goddess was erased, and the nature of rational discourse was shaped by an investment in univocal truth. The structure of thought was reformed into a monolithic search for a single, unquestionable truth. It became no longer even possible to think of a world grounded in the creative activity of plurality called the Goddess. When the Goddess could no longer be conceived, the structure of thought was itself changed. Rational discourse was shaped by an absolute investment in univocal truth. Plurality was restricted to the realm of fantasy, fairy tale, and dream.

Even now, hidden within the history of patriarchal rationality and its discussion of the transcendent authoritative God, one can detect the blurred image of another. In some of Anselm's prayers and poems, the shadow of the mother lurks. Anselm's proof for the existence of God has the potential to raise the question of alternative conceptions of the divine. In raising this question, the proof runs counter even to Anselm's own religious commitment. The task to which Anselm's path unintentionally leads us might well be to bring that possibility of the Goddess into the midst of erudite philosophical discussion. The issue continues to turn upon the question: What is that than which nothing greater can be conceived?

At our gates waits the Goddess, *theotokos*, the mother of god. Never quite lost, though preserved mostly in the bizarre dreams of Gnostics, witches, pagans, and lovers, there has been a haunting. Her greatness rests on her being not one, but many. She is not the female counterpart to the jealous

God Yahweh. She has many names. She is related in the midst of her divinity to her consort, her daughter, her brother, her lover. She is Demeter, Kore, Diana, Cybele, Inanna, Isis, Ishtar, Asherah, Aphrodite, Astarte. She is neither monotheistic nor polytheistic. She is the heart and soul of multivocity, giving birth and joining with the multitude voices of divinity. So essential to her being is relatedness that she cannot be conceived in monotheistic isolation. Yet her multivocity is not that of a polytheistic pantheon, consisting of distinct individual deities. The Goddess is to be conceived "matritheistically." She is the one who constantly calls to mind and to existence the others. She is the one who has not forgotten her lovers. Her greatness calls others into greatness.

She is that than which nothing greater can be conceived, because she will not be separated from her creation. The matritheistic Goddess is interwoven with her creation. She is at home in her world. She is the one who is related, albeit silently, to the ones who would exclude and silence her. Her blood calls passionately to the jealous God, but the jealous God has outgrown the passion even of his own jealousy. Divorced from all relatedness, safe in his absolute transcendence, sovereignty, and benevolence, today he attempts to escape and deny even his own gender. All that is left is the frigid air of disembodied spirit, and the world is left devoid of divinity.

The affirmation of the Goddess is an affirmation of gender as a valuable embodiment of the concrete reality of the world. The attempt by apologists to solve the problem of language about God by asserting that God is above gender fits the pattern of Anselm's approach to greatness. Though the whole tradition and structure of the conception of God is filled with language that puts down woman and elevates man, theologians claim that God is above all that. The genderless God is allowed to keep all the prerogatives of maleness that oppressed women, but now he is above all that also. Next men model themselves on God, claiming that their superiority and mastery is a burden, a service to all for the good of all. If they see any value attached to any subordinate creature, they claim that also. This replays the original mechanism by which men elevated themselves above women and all other oppressed peoples. Men did not see themselves as male animals, but as the "rational" animal, whereas woman remains only as woman.

The God produced by these rationalizing attempts to transcend the issue of gender is not better, but greater in terms of the same tired old formulas of alienation and distance. The God produced by these rationalizing attempts to transcend the issue of gender is greater insofar as he is untouched and untouchable. However, God is not better because he is out of touch with our need to be reconciled to ourselves and to each other. A better God is not "above all that," but is one who is "gendered" and thereby stands with those who have suffered and survived, with those who are the least of these.

The inversion of gender valuations in the divine she changes both the understanding of divinity and the understanding of gender.[20] It asks whether woman, so long identified with mortality and body, might not be a better image of that than which nothing greater can be conceived. Perhaps, the spirit itself would be better if it had a body. If it is better for God to exist than not to exist, is it not better that God should exist as a body than as that which cannot be touched, hugged, or loved except as an idea? A personal relationship with God was important enough for God to become a man, only to be resurrected and return to 'idea' status.

Against the disembodied, genderless "It" of theological speculation, might not it be better if God were that Mother from whom and to whom we come? The Gaia hypothesis and deep ecological feminism provide a new scientific formulation of the ancient equation of Goddess with the earth. Here is a conception of the divine that is sensible and responsive, deserving of love and returning love with the right to walk with dignity upon her all the days of our lives. The fool, with Guanilon to urge him on, went looking for the perfect island. Many natives worship islands precisely as the embodiment of the divine, the divine Mother who feeds and clothes and welcomes her children. Perhaps if Guanilon had set sail beyond his monastery, he would have found that this island, even England, was the embodied presence of that than which nothing greater can be conceived.

The island's perfection, of course, was not of the kind that Guanilon sought, for he described the perfect island abstractly. Indeed, his purpose was to show the ridiculous nature of Anselm's argument, that is, one cannot simply add existence to the idea of a perfect island. The simple existence of islands is surely not the question. Both Guanilon and Anselm see the abstract as superior to the concrete. The alternative is to see in the wonder of the concrete that which is beyond every conception, that than which nothing greater can be conceived. If Anselm's proof points us toward that which is in existence, as that which is greater than what we can conceive, then perhaps the existence of the real objects in the world is the divine waiting to be conceived in thought.

The reality of the world, its textures, its infinite patterns, its surprises is a mystery beyond even the word games of theologians. This is not pantheism, which conceives of the world as a whole, in which all the manifold is again reduced to unity. Such abstractions overlook the unique orneriness of each and every particular in their manifold ways of relating to each other. The reality of the world is closer to animism, the conviction that what is, is alive. Let us experiment with the conception that the world itself is that than which nothing greater can be conceived. What could be greater than the world, in all its wondrous variety, than that in the world which magically answers back to us when we call?

The real is our measure, our criteria, our test of theory. The real stands over and against our thought. To blur the distinction between thought and existing reality is what we fear Anselm has done in his proof. This is what we resist most in his proof. Positing an existent reality from the seclusion of one's monastic study is offensive on some deep, emotive level. Why are we so offended? We know that we cannot manufacture the real; we cannot fabricate existence. The real is that which keeps us from getting lost in thought and imagination. The real keeps us sane. The real is greater than thought.

The real is the objective, that which is other than us and that which is other than all our thought. "Objectivity" is a relational term. It is whatever "objects" to thought. It causes the thinker to stumble and to reassess the conclusions reached by thought. The words "object" and "objective" are derived from the Latin *objectum*, which means "to throw before" or "to present against the mind or thought." Our sense that reality cannot be "added onto" thought as a predicate is rooted in our sense that the objective is a qualitatively different realm from thought. The realm of the real sets the limits upon thought, even as it lures thought to itself.

Now, in the modern world, the objective world acts as the divine court of last resort in all questions of truth. One may doubt whether something is in truth a fact, but to doubt the veracity of fact, the possibility of objective verification, is to reject the very grounds of our confidence in truth. Though philosophers and critics may argue with great cogency and coherence that no objectivity is possible, our confidence in the possibility of objective truth is unshaken. Somehow we feel a sense of assurance in the existence of that "out there" which is prior to our understanding. Our relation to the real is a faith that precedes understanding and that makes understanding possible.

The natural world confronts us with an otherness that both supports and challenges our thought. Surely the natural world is greater than we are. The realm of life and death is beyond even the greatest of human powers. No thought or tool of human contrivance is able to stand against the power of natural disasters. Even the dictator, even the philosopher, even the scientist cannot rival this power. Clearly reality can stand on its own against thought—and thinkers.

Yet the natural world of things is a model for divinity which challenges our equation of "greatness" with power over others. The power of the natural world is a power in which we participate. The power of the otherness of reality is one that seems to welcome human involvement. We act on the world even as the world acts on us. The model of power is one of reciprocity. Though we have no power over death as such, we do have the power to respond over much of the process that ends in death. We may either be overwhelmed by that in-breaking of otherness in our lives, or we may respond with prediction or limited acts of control or acceptance. That which is stands over and against us, but not absolutely.

The natural world of things is that than which nothing greater can be conceived. To understand the world is to be surprised by the world, for the world always goes beyond our expectations. The natural world is a good model of divinity above all because of its irrepressible character of surprise. The natural world continuously resists human efforts to interpret by confronting the human world with newness. The result is a dialogue between the human world and the natural environment which humans cannot suppress. Human thought perpetually stumbles over the reality of the world. It is precisely the world's refusal to be absorbed wholesale into human meaning that identifies it as object, that which is other than human project.

Objectivity is always that which is in the process of being absorbed into human thought. Objects disappear in appropriation. Yet new "objections" constantly reappear, throwing into question what appears to have been finalized. This quality of object transience protects the objective world from being consumed by human appropriation and limits the extent to which humans can claim to control the whole world by their interpretations. Transience guards the objective world by throwing ever new "objections" in human paths of interpretation. The thing itself is that which remains not-yet appropriated into human thought. The first, last, and constant task of being human is to be in dialogue with the objective world.

In that dialogue the object is an active participant. Objects are not passive, unmoving lumps which litter our environment. The world is material, matter, *mater*, mother. We have treated woman as mere objects for man's appropriation, but now woman returns to man with an objection. And the world is changed. So also has all the world been the blank slate upon which men have attempted to etch themselves and their projects. Men have seen matter as passive stuff to be molded and shaped by their scientific experimentation and disposal—and we are reaping the environmental costs of that underestimation of the world in which we live. The earth objects to the treatment she has received. We are encountering the active presence of resistance in our dealings with the world. Each time a problem appears to be solved, a new "objection" arises. This interference with human intentions, which spoils our innate desire for completion, is not something that occurs merely occasionally or that might finally be overcome. Rather, it represents the truth that we exist in a world that is as alive as we are, and from which our aliveness originates. Human activity always brings about an unexpected response from the world, a response we can predict or control only partially. This active responsiveness of the world acts as a limitation on all human endeavors. This limit posed by objectivity guarantees that all human projects move within the dialogical framework of human interaction with the world.

The providential character of accidental intervention of the objective world opens up the possible religious implications of the encounter with the otherness of the world. The world is greater than we are, yet it has a place for us. We relate to what is, as children relate to their mother. The world is our playground and our limit. It is other than us and as familiar as our family. The Mother can be linked with the ancient notions of providence to invoke the heritage of the active presence of the divine in history and in nature.

Yet there are also dangers in reawakening the notion of providence. The temptation has always been to describe divine activity in terms of preordained plans and purposes. Providence has become intimately linked with predestination. If providence is tied to predestination, the critical conversation between human projects and the living presence within the world is reduced once again to dogmatic monologue, in which humans guess what the preordained will of a transcendent God is. The God who predestines is greater because he has power over all human activity. This conception of God assumes that power means the power to control and that divine power must be absolute, beyond human participation. Such a God lessens human beings by his very existence.

The meaning of the her who might be a better conception of the world with whom we speak is that of ineffable mystery which undergirds the perpetual irruption of nonmeaning into the human project of meaning. Such a Mother can neither be described as benevolent nor malevolent. The grace-filled response and the resistance of the objective are what call forth human creativity. All that human experience testifies to is the active presence of nonmeaning that always "objects" to human interpretations and meanings. This conception of providence interprets objectivity as the active infusion of nonmeaning into the human enterprise of making sense. This is a promise of reply. Even silence is a reply, when that silence occurs in the active silence of a mountain meadow or a summer storm. They are the assurance that the objective world is there with us and that we will never be left alone with the finitude of our own conclusions. The ultimate promise is that all closure will be opened up and that human beings do not have the last word. There is that which is greater than we, in which we are called to participate. This is that than which nothing greater can be conceived.

That than which nothing greater can be conceived is a call to conception, a call to artistry. It requires of us images of greatness, and great images. It calls for Michelangelo's David and for performance theater. It calls for a cure for cancer, and a way into acceptance of death. It calls for giving birth and for loving that which walks away from the mother. It even calls for philosophy, for the love of *Sophia*, for thinkers who dream of a greater God, who might even be a Goddess.

That than which nothing greater can be conceived rests upon the image of the painter who understands the act of conceiving and understands what it means to perform the conception. The painter approaches existence as that which lures the painter to paint. The conception approaches reality, seeks to accomplish it in thought. The greater the picture, the greater the conception, the closer the conception comes to touching the real. All works of art seek to conceive that than which nothing greater can be conceived; that is the call to the heart of art. All works of art, of imagining, of conceiving give birth into reality; that is, they cross over from thought to reality and thus posit the two as in relationship. All works of conception follow the path of thought along its boundary with reality. There is a story of an artist who created something so real, that it came alive, alive to be loved and lost. All acts of conception are acts of giving birth to that which is real. All acts of conception are an echo of the mother's giving birth. All acts of conception are a longing for living masterpieces.

The act of conceiving of that than which nothing greater can be conceived is a performance, an act, an art, of moving into relationship with that which is, and thus ascribing existence to that than which nothing greater can be conceived. And indeed, existence comes to meet the conception. What is calls us, and objects to us, and always, always suggests that which is greater than we conceive. The real is beyond thought. It is too wonderful for designation even as a single deity. That which is, is greater than conception, but draws our conceptions into reality. Our conceptions are called into birth—and then turn upon us as a new being, beyond our conceiving. That which we have created is greater than we anticipated, because it is real, but it also objects to our conception. Every work of art takes on a life of its own. That which we have conceived proposes that we might create again; it objects to what we thought we knew, turns on us, shows that we never really conceived that than which nothing greater can be conceived. The realization of art is thus beyond the conceiving of art but also is always inadequate to the conception. The real performance leaves something to be desired. Beyond the conception is the greater conception that lures us into birth, into the real, and on into dreaming.

Perhaps the Goddess is a greater conception than the God, because the God is too tied into hierarchies of power and force, too bloodied with Crusades and doctrine. Perhaps we should dream for a while of the Goddess. We will give birth in her name and in her image. We will draw pictures of the divine feminine and seek to emulate ways of peace and tolerance and mothering. We will honor the Earth who is our Mother, the living otherness with whom we are in dialogue and who is our home and our closest relative. We will heal her, because her needing us is the better way of living and being and of conceiving. But if this image can be bettered, we will seek to draw that one also, for the greater is not a competition but a pathway, a way to conceive, a way to walk artistically upon the earth.

We were created to create and thus to worship God. We were birthed to give birth and thus to honor the Mother. The proof for the existence of God offers an alternative to its own hierarchies of power and superiority. Greater than hierarchies is the wonder of encountering divinity in its manifold presence in the world.

NOTES

1. Marjorie Rowling, *Everyday Life in Medieval Times* (New York: G. P. Putnam's Sons, 1968), 106.
2. Eadmer was a monk in Canterbury and Anselm's constant companion during his career as archbishop. Eadmer's two works on Anselm are the *Vita Anselmi* and the *Historia Novorum in Anglia*. The *Vita Anselmi* can be found in R. W. Southern's translation, *The Life of St. Anselm: Archbishop of Canterbury* (Oxford: Clarendon Press, 1972). The *Historia Novorum in Anglia* was translated by Geoffrey Bosanquet (London: Cresset, 1964). Southern provides an extensive commentary on Eadmer in the second part of his book, *Saint Anselm and His Biographer: A Study of Monastic Life and Thought* (Cambridge: Cambridge University Press, 1963).
3. Southern's *Saint Anselm: A Portrait in a Landscape* (Cambridge: Cambridge University Press, 1990) is considered the authoritative biography. See also Southern's *Saint Anselm and His Biographer* (Cambridge: Cambridge University Press, 1963).
4. Vaughn's *Anselm of Bec and Robert of Meulan: The Innocence of the Dove and the Wisdom of the Serpent* (Berkeley: University of California Press, 1987) is her definitive work. See also Vaughn's *The Abbey of Bec and the Anglo-Norman State 1034–1136* (Suffolk: Boydell Press, 1981) and her article "Anselm: Saint and Statesman" in *Albion* 20, no. 2 (Summer 1988), 205–20.
5. Elizabeth Mary McNamer, *The Education of Heloise: Methods, Content, and Purpose of Learning in the Twelfth-Century* (Lewiston: Edwin Mellen Press, 1992), 2.
6. R. W. Southern, *Saint Anselm: A Portrait in a Landscape*, 142.
7. Prudence Allen, *The Concept of Woman: The Aristotelian Revolution* (Montreal: Eden Press, 1985), 267.
8. Marina Warner, *Alone of All Her Sex: The Myth and the Cult of the Virgin Mary* (New York: Vintage, 1983), 135.
9. St. Anselm in the *Proslogium* (preface), *Basic Writings*, trans. S. N. Deane (LaSalle, Ill.: Open Court, 1962), 47. All subsequent references to Anselm's *Monologium* or *Proslogium* will be quoted from this translation and will be indicated in the text.
10. McNamer, *The Education of Heloise*, 11.
11. Guanilon argues "In Behalf of the Fool" (appendix to Anselm's *Basic Writings*), 309.
12. Guanilon argues "In Behalf of the Fool" (appendix to Anselm's *Basic Writings*), 308–9.
13. Vaughn, *Anselm of Bec and Robert of Meulan*, 4.

14. Southern, *Saint Anselm: Portrait in a Landscape*, 190.
15. Charles Hartshorne, *The Divine Relativity: A Social Conception of God* (New Haven: Yale University Press, 1948), 55.
16. Allen, *The Concept of Woman*, 264.
17. Ibid., 264–65.
18. Anselm from his "Prayer to St. Paul" in *The Prayers and Meditations of St. Anselm*, trans. Benedicta Ward (New York: Penguin, 1973), 153–54.
19. Anselm in the "Prayer to Mary," *The Prayers and Meditations of St. Anselm*, 120.
20. Even those patriarchal traditions that include Goddesses, the ultimate reality, that than which nothing greater can be conceived, is conceived as beyond gender, genderless. Yet in the popular imagination, the transcendent reality is still best referred to as 'he.' In Hinduism, for example, there is a curious relationship between *Brahmins* (the caste), *Brahma* (the male-gendered creator god), and *Brahman* (the supreme reality). Here there is a parallel relationship between hierarchy, maleness, and transcendence.

KIERKEGAARD'S DIALECTIC: THE ABYSS ON THE WAY TO MT. MORIAH

PHILOSOPHY IS A DIALOGUE, a speaking among thinkers. Is *Sophia* present? *Sophia* is the lure, the longing that draws the thinker into the dialogue. What is it that the thinker seeks, and why is the thinker seeking a dialogue? The thinker seeks Truth. Truth both is and is not present in the dialogue. Truth is posited as a possibility within the seeking. The author claims a relationship to the truth that will be provided in the text. This truth claim initiates and orients a conversation. The author's claim upon truth begins the text and a conversation with the reader. The authority of the authorship sets the stage for the search for truth by the claim that here indeed is truth. Yet the author's claim on truth is also a distraction from the seeking, for why seek what has already been found? The reader seeks to get truth by reading the text, as if truth could be bought in the marketplace, or something that could be held between the covers of a book.

The authority of authorship feeds into the reader's desire for an effortless appropriation of the truth. The author promises to tell the reader what the truth is. There is a laziness in being a reader, a desire to be a passive recipient of truth, which is simply handed over by the author, who is an authority in the field. Such a reader might be tempted to gain the truth by reaching behind the author and claiming what the author already presumably has. In this case, the truth is not found—only the authority. The more discerning reader attempts to judge the truth that is in the text but still fails to see that the reader is a participant in the event of truth being created in the discourse with the text. The reader who fails to enter into a reciprocal, participatory dialogue with the text is tempted away from the truth by accepting the authority of the author.

If the author wishes to introduce the reader to a truth that can only belong to those who search, the first task must be to get the author and the authority out of the way. What such an author desires is to awaken in the heart of the reader the longing that is the living presence of truth, of *Sophia*, to be an active participant in the search. The author must dodge the flattery and dishonest love of the reader, so that the reader may begin the internal dialogue which is potential within the text as text. This requires a special kind of authorship, that is self-conscious about the temptations of authorship and which, therefore, is capable of deflecting the infatuation of the reader.

Such an author is Søren Kierkegaard. Perhaps more than any other author, he is aware of the interaction of authorship with the text and the potential of the text to break loose from the author. Only when the text has broken loose from the author is the text available to the reader as participant and seeker after truth. Reading a text by Kierkegaard is both like speaking with another and like self-reflection, a possible conversation with oneself. It is here, in the self-reflexive quality of the text, that transformation is possible. The truth that is appropriate to Kierkegaard's texts is a living, participatory truth, the truth that cannot be possessed but that lures those who have begun to speak with their own hearts.

To turn the reader inward, into self-reflection and the inward search, Kierkegaard constructs his texts so that he becomes a problematic presence within his own work. Each time the reader attempts to get hold of the truth, which Kierkegaard as the author is assumed to possess, Kierkegaard has disappeared behind the masks of the pseudonyms. Kierkegaard, lover of truth, is also the master of deception. He states that "all true communication of truth must always begin with an untruth."[1] The truth that Kierkegaard puts forward is placed in relation to a truth that cannot be appropriated through the author. The untruth, the tricks that make Kierkegaard both a fascinating and a frustrating author, always lead inward into a relation with a truth that can only be appropriated within a life. One must choose, and the choice stands in relationship to a truth that is never possessed but that reflects one back upon oneself.

Kierkegaard is as much magician as thinker. There is a sympathetic relationship between Kierkegaard's use of dialectic and a magician's hat trick. Kierkegaard moves his arguments by a sleight of hand. The reader is bewitched, bedazzled, sometimes confused, but always a participant by virtue of an illusory act, the act of choice manufactured by an author himself in the act of disappearing. Kierkegaard plays with the reader's essential gullibility in wanting to be told the truth, by telling a truth that cannot be appropriated by the reader. This magician's truth, this dialectical possibility, is a truth in two hands. The question before the reader is, "Which is truth?" The judgment the reader is called to make is a judgment of the reader's own relationship to the truth provided by the dialectician.

Dialectic as a rhetorical method works by playing one side off against another. The "trick" by which Kierkegaard's dialectic works requires drawing the reader into a choice between the two sides he creates. Yet there is even here another level of trickery. The skill in Kierkegaard's sleight of hand is the way in which Kierkegaard has subtly weighted the direction of the choice. Dialectic, as Kierkegaard employs it, requires a lightness of touch and flexibility of mind to maintain the viability of the two alternatives so that the reader truly participates in the argument, and yet, also to produce the conclusion in such a way that the reader must see it as the reader's own. Once the reader has claimed the truth, the reader then is confronted with the necessity of self-judgment in relation to the standard implicit in the truth the reader has claimed.

Kierkegaard's focus on the individual (who is his reader) locates the argument in the space between author and audience. To get the individual reader to participate in the dialectic, Kierkegaard must separate himself from his own argument. To succeed, the argument must become the reader's. Kierkegaard the author has chosen, dialectically, to emphasize the distinction between the putative author and his own personal story. The pseudonyms are but one way that Kierkegaard creates choices in such a way as to make the conclusions the reader's rather than his.

Kierkegaard has removed himself from the choice by the construction of magical, imaginary alternative authors. The reader confronts the truth through the thin illusion of Kierkegaard's pseudonymous authorship. The author is unavailable to decide for the reader who speaks the truth. The reader must therefore decide independently of the author. The reader cannot ever be sure how seriously Kierkegaard means what he has put forward, for this book is both by Kierkegaard and not by Kierkegaard. The reader must guess which hand holds the truth. Yet the text nevertheless carries and must carry the mark of authorship. The text holds together in the promise of truth, which is the author's claim upon the reader; otherwise there is no text, only confusion. There is a magician, though he wears many masks. The author, Kierkegaard, participates in the conversation. His participation is misleading, deceptive, and beguiling. One can never be too careful when dealing with magicians.

Within the text there is an author who defines the context of the truth. Kierkegaard does not give up control of the text by placing a choice at its heart. Indeed, few writers are so carefully in control of their authorship as Kierkegaard. Not only the text, but also the reader, belong to Kierkegaard. The reader is *his* reader.

> And here for the first time comes in the category 'that *individual* whom with joy and gratitude I call *my* reader', a stereotyped formula which was repeated in the Preface to every collection of Edifying Discourses.[2]

There is an understanding between Kierkegaard and the reader. The reader's choice is shaped by his identity as given and held open within the text. The nature of the authorship is hidden, but the nature of the readership is determined. The reader Kierkegaard assumes has a wife and a male pronoun. One may broaden the audience of the works by substituting generic word choices. One may even return to the sentimental possibility that Regina (his fiancée whom he loved in the name of the ethical and abandoned in the name of the religious) was in some sense his audience. But even if Regina was his audience, she was not his reader. The authorship attempts to explain Kierkegaard to Regina, not Regina to Regina.

There are many comments by Kierkegaard about women and womanly behavior, and many of them are derogatory. Kierkegaard assumes his reader has a wife (or at least a fiancée) and a male pronoun. One might try to broaden the audience by substituting sex-inclusive language, but to accomplish this, one must turn a blind eye to the tenor of the frequent comments Kierkegaard makes about women. Kierkegaard speaks of women only to describe their voices as hysterical,[3] their nagging as being like the dripping rain,[4] and woman's place as keeping silence in relation to a world of superior men (just as a man must keep silence before his superior, God).

> In a revival it is not assumed that the man awakened in an extraordinary way should go out and proclaim this to men; on the contrary, this may remain precisely the secret of the awakened man with God, it may precisely be humble to keep silence about this in a womanly way.[5]

It is not enough simply to "fix" Kierkegaard (even assuming one has the right to do so). Rather, one must address the ways in which the patriarchal culture of which Kierkegaard is a part informs his entire project.

It would take quite a trick to bring Søren Kierkegaard to discuss in sympathetic fashion the issues relating to feminism in the twentieth century, given the record of his reaction to the "modern womanish whims"[6] of his own time. It is only reasonable to assume that he would have nothing to add to further current feminist self-analysis.

> The Kierkegaardian world view rejects the other and suppresses difference in order to sustain the single-minded duty-bound commitment to the patriarchal order of universal truth. In this construct, there is no room at the inn for the 'other' who is constituted as woman. Kierkegaard, after all, rejects the aesthetic mode, which he defines by a variety of characteristics that have traditionally, under the power of the law of the father, been descriptive of the woman's experience.[7]

This discussion will be a trick: to pull a possible Kierkegaard out of his works, a Kierkegaard who is capable of entering into sympathetic dialogue with a feminist. This trick assumes that one cannot simply bracket off Kierkegaard's comments about women and his clear rejection of women's attempts at social change.

The trick is possible given the dialectical structure of his works. Dialectic, like politics, can bring about the strangest bedfellows, for it is rooted in dialogue. One need only find a dialogue within the Kierkegaardian corpus into which women might enter and still retain their own claim upon truth, without too much straining of the concepts. If we can do this, Kierkegaard's personal views become solely of historical interest. The text becomes a truly autonomous text; the author becomes a possible author; and the focus rests on the reader, who might well be Kierkegaard's own solitary individual. One might say that the result is the construction of a text which is authored by a possible Kierkegaard, even a "Kierkegaard" who might be a pseudonym for another author or authors.

Dialectic as a method of indirect communication works by creating autonomous positions, positions independent of the author, which play off of one another. As Kierkegaard says, "Every idea consistently carried through has *eo ipso* the power to require the contrary to become manifest."[8] The "trick" of indirect communication is that it places the reader in the decisive position of choosing between the alternatives presented, and yet the order of presentation moves the reader decisively in a single direction. Kierkegaard is a master of creating viable categories, which each hold validity and yet which cannot be reconciled, drawing the reader into a choice between the two sides he creates. Kierkegaard loads the dice in the direction the reader is to go. Dialectic, as Kierkegaard employs it, must provide a real choice but must also lure the reader toward the higher, more difficult choice. Having once entered into Kierkegaard's web, few escape.

It might be possible for a feminist to engage in discussion with Kierkegaard's text, because the nature of Kierkegaard's dialectic gives the text a life of its own. Kierkegaard's focus on the individual, who is his own reader, places the focus of the argument in the space between author and audience. To get the individual reader to participate in the dialectic, Kierkegaard must separate himself from his own argument. To succeed, the argument must become the reader's. Kierkegaard the author has chosen, dialectically, to emphasize the distinction between the author and the man. The Kierkegaardian corpus includes a large number of pseudonymous works. The pseudonyms are but one way that Kierkegaard creates his autonomous texts. Pseudonyms render the relationship between author and text problematic; the author disappears as soon as the reader attempts to rely on the author's intentions. Kierkegaard anticipates the modern analysis of texts as inevitably separate from their authors, who all become, in some sense, possible authors.

> Inscription becomes synonymous with the semantic autonomy of the text, which results from the disconnection of the mental intention of the author from the verbal meaning of the text, of what the author meant and what the text means. The text's career escapes the finite horizon lived by its

author. What the text means now matters more than what the author meant when he wrote it.[9]

Kierkegaard's texts are in some sense without author, standing in a dialectical relationship to his own continual self-reflection. Throughout his authorship, Kierkegaard explores many possible relationships that an author might take toward a text. For example, in the little book, *On Authority and Revelation: The Book on Adler, or a Cycle of Ethico-Religious Essays,*[10] Kierkegaard changed his mind on several occasions on whether he was author, editor, or merely mouthpiece to the argument. The history of the text and its revisions is itself a discussion of the meaning of the Kierkegaardian authorship. He listed several pseudonyms that he considered publishing it under, including Johannes Climacus, Petrus Minor, Thomas Minor, Vincentius Minor, Ataraxius Minor, and H.H. Ultimately part was pseudonymously published, yet when the whole was published it was given his name.

The discussion of why Kierkegaard used pseudonyms is a part of the tradition carried on by devout Kierkegaard scholars, all of whom must come to some conclusion on what Kierkegaard the real author meant by all these possible names he assigns to the texts (which we know he really wrote). In doing such an analysis, they set themselves at odds with Kierkegaard's own understanding of what it means to author a text. Kierkegaard discusses this very issue in a text, *The Point of View for My Work as An Author: A Report to History*, in which he attempts to explain what he really meant to say, that is, that he really is a religious author.

> It might seem that a mere protestation to this effect on the part of the author himself would be more than enough; for surely he knows best what is meant. For my part, however, I have little confidence in protestations with respect to literary productions and am inclined to take an objective view of my own works. If as a third person, in the role of a reader, I cannot substantiate the fact that what I affirm is so, and that it could not but be so, it would not occur to me to wish to win a cause which I regard as lost. If I were to begin *qua* author to protest, I might easily bring to confusion the whole work, which from first to last is dialectical.[11]

What a curious claim! Kierkegaard the author must attempt to interpret his own works as if he were no more than a reader.

Such a loosening of the relationship of author to text gives tremendous power to interpreters, even the perversity of a feminist interpretation. The power of interpretation over the text was something Kierkegaard knew and feared. The text belongs not only to the reader but to interpreters, the creators of other texts. How do we as interpreters approach Kierkegaard's texts, which are so self-conscious about the nature of interpretation? In this perverse interpretation, we approach the text by means of an untruth, that is, we reverse the manifest meaning of his works. We seek an interpretation that is intentionally aimed elsewhere than toward that religious purpose which guides the whole of Kierkegaard's work as an author. Our right to stand in relationship to Kierkegaard's texts is not based on a commonality of purpose but on a shared willingness to participate in his dialectic. Our purpose is more dialectical than explicative, and perhaps more illegitimate. Because we wish to engage in a conversation, the multiplicity of authors, even the ambiguity in the identity of the author in any particular work, is more important than the fact that Kierkegaard really wrote them.

There is no longer a Kierkegaard, and the fact that there once was a Kierkegaard is of merely historical interest. Instead there are the texts in their various assertions of authorship, the possible authors, existing inside as well as on the front page of each book. And, because there are more than one possible authors, we may claim for our own an author, a minority possibility within the text, who is willing to engage in a conversation with a woman. Only in this sense is there a Kierkegaard willing seriously, or at least ironically, to entertain the legitimacy of a feminist critique of religion.

The possible Kierkegaard with whom we will speak, whom we shall call H.H., authored a book once entitled *On Authority and Revelation: The Book on Adler, or a Cycle of Ethico-Religious Essays.* In that book he constructed a dialectic between two categories: the genius (who generates a change in the existing order)[12] and the apostle (who generates a change in the heart of the faithful). Genius in our own age has become a matter of intelligence to be quantified. It has lost its qualitative meaning as that which generates the new. "Genius," "genesis," and "generate" share the same Greek root (*gignesthai*, which means "to be born, to come into being"); they all echo the power to create. Likewise, we think of apostles as characters in the Bible. For these apostles, God was someone they knew well, and the only problem was trying to stay alive without being crucified or thrown to the lions. As H.H. uses the term, the apostle is one who is sent on an errand; the apostle is a messenger. H.H. (our pseudonymous authority) examines both the genius and the apostle insofar as they are harbingers of change. The genius introduces change by creating or originating something new, something generated by the genius' own ingeniousness. The apostle introduces something new, but only as a bearer of a message from outside. H.H. is interested in the difference in the source of the change and nature of the change that each introduces.

The dialectic between genius and apostle is like a dialogue in which the two alternatives serve to deepen and clarify each other by their conversation with each other. H.H.'s genius introduces change by the power to come up with a new, revolutionary idea, but a new idea is not a revelation. Though both come through the individual, the one originates in the individual and the other originates in God. The subject of the work is the individual who is reading the book and who may be confused about his (or possibly her? probably *not* her) relationship to the changes that are demanded of the time. The work sets up the two categories, genius and apostle, as ways of understanding one's relationship to the possibility of divine intervention in time.

The quality of a dialectical argument is directly dependent on the strength and flexibility of the categories created. There must be room in the categories for the reader to move about, to find sufficient meaning with which to identify, and once inside the category there must be no escape into some Hegelian synthesis. The subject of *On Authority and Revelation: The Book on Adler* is the relationship of immanence and transcendence as they play themselves out in the public sphere, the sphere of history. The purpose of the book is to require the reader to choose against immanence, and for transcendence, to choose the God who is present in history only as a command that leads out of history into the eternal. By H.H.'s sleight of hand, the apostle is dialectically the lesser category because the apostle does not originate the message. Yet the apostle exceeds the genius dialectically because the apostle's revolution is eternal, whereas the genius is but another word for a world-historical individual.

Magister Adler, a contemporary of Kierkegaard and the apparent subject for this book, was only of peripheral interest to H.H. Adler was an unfortunate and over-wrought clergyman of rural Denmark. H.H. chides Adler for Adler's confusion over the two categories, genius and apostle, and this provides the excuse to clarify the reader's choice between immanence and transcendence, between the ethical and the religious. Adler (so H.H. tells us) thought he had had a revelation, though on reflection Adler wasn't so sure. Adler proceeded to publish a great deal in an attempt to understand himself, books that now exist only insofar as Kierkegaard the editor referenced them. His publishing raised for H.H. the issue of publicly speaking out of the religious sphere. This question of religious externality remained a subject largely untouched in Kierkegaard's other works, yet it is crucial because it raises the issue of the content of faith.

Faith is a central concern for Kierkegaard throughout his works. To be an individual in faith is to commit oneself to a truth that is found in inwardness. The external world poses the problem of its own meaning, which the individual must decide by a choice made alone and without reference. Faith is not a content, but a direction, a projection of relationship beyond the world to the God who constitutes the whole meaning beyond. Faith is an interpretative act that constantly turns the individual back toward inwardness, the irreducible privacy of the choice of meaning.

The meaning of faith is in some sense given, because Kierkegaard has in mind the one set of meanings given by Christian dogma. However, the relationship that the individual takes to those meanings, the value the individual assigns to the meanings given, belongs to the individual alone. Faith is the inwardness of the individual standing before God. The religious is to be understood only in the depths of inwardness, as the whole relationship of the self, as the source of the relatedness of the self, and as its choice of the meaning of the whole. Faith is the self in its inward relation to the whole as constituted by God.

But if faith is inwardness, how does one understand the fact of revelation itself? Revelation is necessarily external. The apostle is the messenger and thus relates both as inwardness and as the external bearer of the message. There is a tension throughout Kierkegaard's works between the inward event of faith and the content of faith as determined in some way by the church. The fact of revelation, which the individual appropriates in faith or rejects in offense, is crucial. But the fact of revelation carries with it all kinds of confusing and perhaps even irrelevant content. The revelation happens as an event in the world. So how does one recognize a new revelation, one not certified by time and tradition? A new revelation must be possible, for this is a historical faith in the eruption of the eternal into history. Discerning properly the qualitatively different in its guise as the historical is difficult.

This is the awesome responsibility of the apostle, to claim and make known what faith will rest upon. Once the revelation is given, all later responses must take place in inwardness. The revelation alone is an outward as well as inward event. It is this dual nature of revelation that poses the problem. God's living presence in the world means that a revelation could occur at any time. How would one know? How would even the one to whom the revelation was given be sure? The apostle must exist as an ordinary individual, a mere messenger, but then also must carry the responsibility for the eternal in time. The genius knows, and is responsible for the new, but a newness that lacks the problematic dimension of the question of the origin faced by the apostle.

The discussion of the external nature of revelation which occurs in *On Authority and Revelation: The Book on Adler* may be unusual among Kierkegaard's texts, but it does not defeat Kierkegaard's basic purpose of turning all arguments back upon the reader as individual. As with all Kierkegaard's works, the apparent focus is a cover for pointing the individual back toward self-reflection. By directing the eye of the reader toward Adler and toward the categories of genius and apostle, the reader is unaware that in fact the magician/author is about to pull the coin out of the reader's own ear. The categories of genius and apostle both draw the reader into identification with possible ways of relating to the world. The inner dialogue provided to the reader seems to suggest that one might indeed be a genius, or perhaps instead an apostle, if one only knew how to understand the categories. The identification is, of course, fictional. The author cannot know whether the reader is a genius or an apostle, or merely an ordinary human being. The author allows the reader to suspend reality to explore the reader's own inwardness by means of the costume of possibility. One might be the genius or one might be an apostle, in possibility. By the possibility, by the act of pretense, the reader reveals a relationship to the categories that mirrors that truth toward which the reader turns. The identification serves the structure of the Kierkegaardian works by making the analysis an internal event of possibility, produced by the illusion of identification, even while one pursues intellectually the two alternatives of genius and apostle. In this way, *On Authority and Revelation: The Book on Adler* fits quite naturally into the authorship as a whole, as a dialectical discussion of the ordinary and the extraordinary in terms of the inwardness of the individual.

"Truth is subjectivity." But this does not mean that everyone is free to create truth. Rather, Kierkegaard's Truth is given eternally by God in a revelation, to be appropriated subjectively by each individual. There is a distinction between the one who receives the revelation directly from God for public disclosure and the one who relates to God by means of the revelation. Adler confused the two. Touched by the experience of Truth, he thought he had been given a direct revelation. So Adler published his faith experience, without having understood the nature of authority implicit in revelation.

Unlike the silent and passionate internality of the solitary individual, revelation is a social and historical act, and therefore appears to be subject to the ambiguity of all external events. It lacks the purity and ideality of the individual's silent transparency before God. H.H.'s problem is to find a way to retain the inwardness of the religious even in the messiness of the historical fact of revelation. Because Adler's revelation was very messy because of the confusion of the age (so H.H. suspects), it made an excellent foil for the dialectical analysis of revelation itself. Revelation is an event that remains historical, except for the individual of faith, for whom it mediates the eternal.

H.H. must find a way to distinguish the revelation of the true apostle from the revelation that Adler claimed to have had. But he cannot do so on the basis of any external criteria of what ought to be in a revelation, because all human criteria are already negated by the claim of the revelation to come from God. The distinction must come from within, from inwardness. Adler's confusion makes possible a dialectical discussion of the relation between the inward and the external as it might occur in the apostle. The dialectic sets two categories of inwardness and outwardness into conversation, the categories of genius and apostle.

What makes the distinction of interest to us in this context, is that the genius, whatever its role in H.H.'s discussion, also echoes a curious revolutionary possibility. Our discussion explores H.H.'s argument as an event, much as H.H. explores the event of Adler's revelation. Just so, our discussion stands in a dialectical relationship to H.H.'s own truth claims. H.H. invents the category of the genius to get at the category of the apostle. We will leave the category of the apostle to H.H.'s own formulation; our trick will be to place that category in dialectical conversation with a feminist as agent (genius) of social change. The genius and the apostle are united by their necessary social dynamic. Each stands in relationship to the existing order, to the status quo. Their relationship is a negative one, but nonetheless it is definitive. Both are *extraordinarius*, that is extra-ordinary.

The "ordinary" has the double meaning of the status quo and its ideality as the ethical. It is the practical business of marriage and family and school. The existing order is the-way-things-are. It is also the ethos of the time. The possibility of living out one's proper relationship to the ideal informs and transforms communal reality and gives meaning to the relative universality of any existing society. The everyday holds hidden within it the ideal, the Kantian universal. The notion of the ordinary in H.H. is one of his most powerful ideas, an idea that emerges out of the "practical" side of Kant's categorical imperative. To live ordinarily is to live universally. The life of the ordinary is a rich and powerful action by which that in the culture which deserves to be universalized is brought into practical employment. This is the duty set before every concrete individual as the embodiment of a culture. It requires reflection and care and offers in return the possibility of bringing into being that which makes cultural norms a form of truth.

> To this extent, therefore, it is a mere idea, though at the same time a practical idea, which really can have, as it also ought to have, an influence upon the sensible world, to bring that world, so far as may be possible, into conformity with the idea.[13]

One stands in relationship not just to society but to the implicit meaning that is the universal possibility that gives life to the particularity of one's historical situation.

Faith, as Kierkegaard develops it in his other works, already stands in a peculiar relationship to the ordinary. Faith absolutely relativizes social norms and external relationships. However, because faith relativizes *absolutely*, it also leaves the ordinary intact, except perhaps for a halo that glows around everything from donkeys to dinner. Faith negates everything and hence transforms it into pure possibility. The impossible becomes possible. Faith makes ordinary life transparent to the divine—an experience both terrifying and ecstatic. This is Johannes de Silentio's (pseudonymous author of *Fear and Trembling*) marvelous formulation of the knight of faith.

> But if I knew where a knight of faith lived, I would travel on foot to him, for this marvel occupies me absolutely. I would not leave him for a second,

I would watch him every minute to see how he made the movements. . . . Here he is. The acquaintance is made, I am introduced to him. The instant I first lay eyes on him, I set him apart at once; I jump back, clap my hands, and say half aloud, "Good Lord, is this the man, is this really the one—he looks just like a tax collector!" . . . Encountering him on Strandveien, one would take him for a mercantile soul enjoying himself. He finds pleasure in his way, for he is not a poet. . . . Toward evening, he goes home, and his gait is as steady as a postman's. On the way, he thinks that his wife surely will have a special hot meal for him when he comes home—for example, roast lamb's head with vegetables.[14]

However wonderful this is internally, it pays to remember that externally this means that faith leaves the status quo just as it was, so much so that the knight of faith might well work for the IRS. The individual is transformed, but in a patriarchal world he still comes home expecting dinner. He no longer complains about what is served for dinner—being transformed makes everything taste equally good—but dinner is still served by his wife from the kitchen. He may even, in a wonderful awareness of the meaninglessness of all earthly distinctions, offer to wash dishes. But the meaninglessness of all earthly distinctions makes it unnecessary to reconsider the structure of earthly distinctions, or to rethink who should wash the dishes. The status quo remains untouched, precisely because it has been revealed as absolute relativity. The individual's transformation changes everything so completely that it is as if nothing were changed. All relative change is meaningless and all external change is relative. Only the individual can change absolutely and that is because only the individual can stand in relationship to an eternally valid measure. If the individual should try to change the world in light of his experience of blessedness, he makes the same mistake as Adler. He takes the inward experience of transformation and confuses it with an external revelation.

Kierkegaard's works take the status quo, the social order, as a given. Kierkegaard is a conservative by virtue of the radical transformation he wishes to make available to every individual. Precisely because he wishes to stress the absolute nature and absolute justice of the spiritual realm, he has no interest in changing or examining the merely relative justice of the existing order. Faith does not require social change, because all orders merely pose the problem, all are relative. However, revelation is both a relative and an absolute event. One cannot move from an analysis of faith to an analysis of revelation because faith takes revelation as its foundation. Its relationship is direct and not dialectical. The dialectical tension can only be created by introducing a category that equates the existing order with the ethical, following the same pattern as the earlier relationship between the ethical and the religious.

The apostle comes into being by fact of a revelation. An apostle is a category of being human that already holds some difficulty for H.H. because an apostle speaks out of inwardness into the public realm. Unlike the absolute inwardness of the individual in the religious category of faith, the apostle *must* speak. The speaking ties the apostle irretrievably to the external. By speaking, the apostle changes the world. Is then everyone who changes the world an apostle? No. Most change is as relative as the world is and is grounded in the capacity of individuals to begin again. This is a remarkable possibility but is still a human possibility. This is the category of the genius.

Our ordinary lives have a momentum of their own that resist change. Social orders do not change in any decisive fashion under ordinary circumstances. Typically, the meaning foundations have sufficient flexibility for a society or an individual to change without altering the metaphorical structures, the ideality that underlies it. The existing order is given as a set of meanings by which one may act in the world. Most of the time, change is a gradual exploration of the potential meanings inherent in the ethos of an existing order. There is much flexibility in the foundational meanings, essentially the value meanings, of an ethos. Take the ways in which a foundational document like the Declaration of Independence has served both to justify the status quo and, on occasion, to change the order. We understand justice by reference to a document, but in the process we may begin a whole new era of civil rights. This is possible because the existing order always makes ideal claims, universal claims, to which the society must refer to legitimate its order. These same claims, however, also serve to judge the status quo and serve as a basis for change as the individuals within the society seek to tie the reality closer to the universal implications.

Most of the time, the meaning foundations have sufficient flexibility for a society to move within. However, in the process of reflecting out of the foundational claims, sometimes it may happen that an individual begins to reflect directly on the claims themselves. If they reach deep enough, through need or foolhardiness, they are in danger of bringing the foundation itself into question. Because an existing order is a set of meanings, it is always vulnerable to exposure of the meanings itself, a process that is potentially deadly. The point may be reached in which the individual (however many individuals may reach this point, it is always as an individual that they must face the implications) no longer can rest within the taken-for-granted values of their own ethos. This is the point of genius.

The transformation of the basic structures of a society require a different kind of reflection. We understand the possibility of extraordinary because we witness the reversals that crack the status quo. We can observe the current possibility of a new point of departure in the paradigm shifts of history. Social orders resist change in any decisive fashion under ordinary circumstances. The existing order is given as a set of meanings by which one may understand whatever one wishes to examine. It is the starting point of reflection, of being human. To change the social order requires more than the Hegelian announcement that change will occur. In fact, the announcement of change is often the signal for much ado about nothing. One may even get tenure for such an announcement—proof that nothing has happened of a qualitative sort. Real change requires lifting one's own history by its bootstraps. We use the image all the time, without hearing the difficulty implicit in the task of finding a point to begin when one has begun by negating where one is standing. One cannot stand without standing *on* something. One has not understood change (except in retrospect) unless one finds oneself surprised. Of course, in retrospect everyone can see the fall of communism. But who would dare anticipate and predict the fall of capitalism? This has not yet happened, and therefore it is not inevitable. The rise and fall of empires is certain only in the abstract.

How could change, real change, occur? Every thought must depend on the presuppositions that are already embedded in the social order. Real change alters the presuppositions. Change requires that there be those who relate to the order as *extraordinarius*. They stand in relationship to the existing order as its negation. Change occurs by virtue of the genius, that is, by that individual who constitutes a new point of departure.

It is remarkable that such change ever happens. Real change requires a point of departure at odds with its own presuppositions. The existing order is our foundation. One needs an Archimedean point outside the existing order from which to transform it radically.

> All movement presupposes (as anybody will be convinced who thinks the dialectic of this situation) a point, a firm point outside. And so the true *extraordinarius* is the point outside, he stands upon the Archimedean point outside the world—a firm point *extra ordinem—et terram movebit.*[15]

Revolution requires that there be those who relate to the order as *extraordinarius*. They stand in relationship to the existing order as its negation. The genius (or the apostle in another sense) is the Archimedean point. The genius is the fulcrum that can move a world. External, relative change occurs by virtue of the genius; that is, by virtue of that individual who constitutes a new point of departure.

It is always tempting to say when one is explicating the great thinkers of the past that this thinker, even this Kierkegaard, was a genius. This is not an appropriate compliment for one who so carefully attempted to secure the meanings of his order against the tumult of his day. Better to say that his was a refusal of genius, a tormented attempt to focus his tremendous powers of reflection on the salvation already provided within his own culture.

Genius is the pathway of turning the world upside down; it is the way of anarchists and nihilists. Radical change shows the relativity of meaning without the hope of absolutes. Revolution turns away from eternity and faces the abyss.

To understand this category of genius requires a concrete illustration, even if only in thought. What would it mean to turn upside down the patriarchal culture that Kierkegaard takes for granted? We propose a thought experiment, which is surely appropriate in conversation with Kierkegaard. Let us suppose our age stands on the brink of a new point of departure. Let us even suppose that a feminist is the genius, the herald of a postpatriarchal age. Let us suppose that it is possible to reverse the fundamental presuppositions of patriarchy. This is the supposition, the thought experiment, which grounds this project.

Having supposed a feminist might represent a new point of departure requires an explanation of how she comes to depart from the existing order. Reading H.H. presents an example of the very forces that push women to the abyss from which the genius might emerge. The woman who is drawn into H.H.'s dialectic is offered a hope, but a hope that is not ultimately meant for her. H.H. addresses those issues of the social order which are closest to her own experience (marriage, family, relationships), yet H.H. ignores the reality of women's experiences in these lived social realities. She is but a bit player in her own life's drama. Nowhere is woman more present, yet more ignored, than in H.H.'s discussions of marriage. Perhaps this is because of the dangers inherent in a woman's reflection on marriage.

> In case a marriage were to reflect upon the reality of marriage, it would become *eo ipso* a pretty poor marriage; for the powers that ought to be employed for the realization of the tasks of married life are employed by reflection to eat away the foundation.[16]

The destruction of marriage is unlikely as long as the one who reflects on marriage is male, even when that male is H.H. The institution remains rooted and secure, and questioning remains in the domain of exploration of alternative ways of choosing to marry or not to marry. But H.H. never considers how it might change the discussion for a woman to reflect deeply upon marriage. A woman's being in a patriarchal culture is subsumed under her relationship to marriage. Whereas a man might wonder whether to marry or not to marry, a woman *is* married or unmarried, miss or mistress. To attempt to understand what it means to be a woman requires genius, because she has no meaning in the existing order except as a subset and attachment to Man. To reflect on Woman as such is to step out of humanity, for humanity is but another name for Mankind. This is a revolutionary realization, an extraordinary realization, a not knowing of something so simple as her species and straightforward that it is a kind of insanity to wonder about it. The first revolutionary act is a realization of the roots of the meaning of the established order by uncovering one's own disrelationship to that meaning.

There is a dialogue in Kierkegaard that is as yet submerged. To uncover this dialogue, this sub-verse, one must take seriously the possibility that the pronouns and the stories speak truth and that his dialectic addresses everyone, but not women. Curious, to everyone, but not to women. Or perhaps, to everyone, and to women insofar as they are included in an "everyone." This is the double message inherent in generic terms such as "individual" which sometimes includes women and sometimes doesn't. One must not, of course, make too much of such peripheral issues as the gender identity of pronouns in analyzing an author of Kierkegaard's stature. First of all, one's audience is likely to become restless and uneasy. Surely potshots at a work that is not about women, claims no expertise on women, and is simply a product of its own cultural presuppositions are out of place in real analysis. Rather, one must address the ways in which the patriarchal culture of which he is a part informs his entire project. One must take seriously the possibility that the pronouns do tell us something about the nature of his project.

This experience of reading Kierkegaard duplicates the experience of women in the culture at large. The feminist as genius (and clearly we are speaking here of feminist as an idea, as a possibility, not to be confused with any particular feminist) marks a new point of departure for understanding the individual's participation in mankind. One becomes a feminist, whether one wills to or not, the first time one no longer unconsciously reads oneself into the various cultural uses of the generic "Man." Boys and girls, men and women, do not start out wondering about what their culture means by these terms. Woman lives the ambiguity of inclusiveness. Until one day, she cannot. She cannot hear the inclusiveness any more. She starts to hear and see and feel differently. To no longer be a man is to experience the vertigo of being unable to participate in the structures of meaning that inform our cultural life.

Strangely enough, other people, even other women, go right on assuming the cultural meanings. Increasingly she feels as if she is living in another reality. Yet (and here H.H.'s category of the genius is very helpful) one does not simply jump to another meaning. Instead one dwells in the void of past meanings. The coming to consciousness as a woman constitutes a negative relationship to existing meanings taken on as a way of being. She is not-a-man. The individual is now *extraordinarius*, out of order. She continues to relate to a world that, by being conscious of, she at the same time negates. To become a feminist (and one does not become a feminist in this sense by joining an organization) is to take on the risk of defining a new world by redefining the self. It is to exist outside the world of meanings by which she was defined. In the genius, the internal and the external intersect. The answer she comes to she must hold at her own risk and at the risk of being responsible for the downfall of a world. And perhaps she will be present at the birthing of a new world.

Between the end of the old and the birth of the new is a death. To avoid the vertigo of meaninglessness, one might immerse oneself in transitional organizations or major political activity. A lot of activity can cover for the lack of a new meaning upon which to build a world. There is a void between the old and the new, a void in which one can see what has been lost, but nothing new has yet appeared. Or perhaps one can find a way to stretch the word "man" a bit wider, so that one can run for political office and find a way to return to the ethical possibility of change within the existing order. Surely this is much better! The genius must face the loss of meaning head-on when as yet nothing new has appeared. Genius is a termination of the relationships that give meaning to being human.

Anyone who thinks such a collapse of meaning is desirable has misunderstood the categories. H.H. has a deep sense of the agony implicit in real change. Better to give up the revolution and go home, if one can:

> In case, for example, a son should feel called to introduce a new view of the domestic life (and as a son is bound by filial piety, so shall or ought every individual be bound by piety towards the universal)—would he not then, if there was truth in him, wish precisely that the father might be the strong one who could encounter him with the full power of parental authority?[17]

To be *extraordinarius* means to abandon one's father, to disappoint one's mother, and to destroy one's home. A feminist as genius abandons not just her past, but also her future, her husband, and her children. She cannot simply change the meaning of marriage; she recognizes that her reflections stand to destroy the very foundations of marriage. To be *extraordinarius* means to relate to home, family, authorities as their nemesis. Meanwhile, she has found a nice man and settled down. Life does go on, but she also realizes that if the revolution is to succeed the nice man will also be hurt, will even have the right to feel betrayed. And then, what if no new meaning should emerge? To have destroyed what protections there are for women in marriage and under the law, while leaving them vulnerable to exploitation rests upon the head of any thoughtful feminist. The risk of genius implies responsibility for a future which one can barely imagine and cannot control. What if a feminist were to accomplish her goals?

Even success is bitter. The only triumph one can achieve is merely another existing order. Relative justice does admit of change, but no absolutes. A new postpatriarchal order might emerge, in which patriarchy gives way to the new. In this new order, men remain, but the fathers are no longer in charge. Problems remain, maybe more, maybe less. Moses was probably quite glad, once he glimpsed the promised land, to die before things really got out of hand. To be a genius is to stand knee-deep in negativity. Genius relates dialectically to what it accomplishes, and victories in this world are bittersweet. What one may achieve can never fully make up for the pain of loss of meaning, because never again will one be fully confident in meaning itself. All orders are relative orders, and no one knows better the fragility of human society than those who have changed it. Who can assure the genius that what has been accomplished with so much pain will not be undone in the next generation?

H.H.'s formulation of the *extraordinarius* places the genius in a powerful relationship to the existing order, but the relationship is essentially negative and ultimately limited. The genius is the form of the *extraordinarius* that is relative, with all the implications of the relative. The genius may be insightful and clever, but the relativity of the genius constitutes the untruth in contrast to which H.H. will make manifest the absolute, the apostle. Perhaps Kierkegaard would not mind too much granting the term "genius" to a feminist, as long as absolute truth demands nothing more of the wife of the knight of faith than to stay home preparing roast lamb's head and vegetables. And perhaps, after all her marching and shouting and private doubts, a feminist may be quite happy to come home to her knight.

A feminist may be the paradigmatic genius, but over and against this idea stands an alternative: the choice of eternal meaning. The apostle represents another kind of *extraordinarius*, one with, one might say, more lasting implications. The apostle speaks with the authority of revelation. The nature of the apostle's claim stands in a negative relationship to not just this order, but to every order. The apostle has the power to offer an eternal answer to the world's problems, an answer quite different from that of the genius.

When the apostle speaks, everything is changed. The apostle is in the world and in relationship to the world. Therefore, his pronouncement suffers from all the ambiguity of historical happenstance. Yet the apostle is other than the genius. The genius stands in a negative relationship to *this* order. Should the new order in fact happen, the genius settles down into the universal as a proper ethical agent, a regular citizen. Not so for the apostle. The apostle is just as much at odds with Christendom as with the Pharisees. The apostle relates to the existing order negatively at every point, for his negativity to the order comes from a positive relationship to the eternal. The apostle is an *extraordinarius* of a different order than the genius. The apostle takes no positive relationship to any order but calls on the individual to choose: to obey or not to obey.

When the apostle speaks, everything is changed. Yet the world may never notice. The truth of revelation comes from outside the subject, yet its truth can only be subjective. That is, the subject has no control over the content of the revelation but only over the relationship taken to the revelation. In one sense, the content is irrelevant. To every question about content, the apostle replies by standing on an authority that he will not produce. Only the individual can replicate the authority to which the apostle refers, and he can only do so by a turn from within. As for the apostle, he also stands before the same authority in the absolute sense. In the relative sense, in the world-historical sense, he is at his own risk. No one can say by what means he could be judged, for he provides no criteria but his own willingness to risk all, and his challenge to the individual is to do the same.

So let a feminist change the world. Our possible Kierkegaard has no reason not to allow the category of the genius to apply to a feminist. The world that she may or may not bring into being is as relative to the eternal as is the world she left. Surely, H.H.'s argument stands under no threat. He was even willing to grudge Adler the title of genius.[18] If a feminist is a genius, she, like Adler, may nonetheless be swept into the dustbin of history. Or perhaps the knight of faith will come home some day and cook dinner. It is all the same to the apostle. All transformations of the world are relative, indeed are as nothing, in comparison to the revelation that belongs to the apostle alone.

The relativity of the masculine pronoun in Kierkegaard hints at the structure of the world in its submission to man. History is, therefore, subject to the genius, to the possibility of radical change, even to the reconception of woman. Such a change would threaten Kierkegaard and render his examples problematic. Certainly he would oppose a feminist revolution; he saw it coming even then and despised all it implied about women and himself. Yet the structure of his argument would remain intact even so, and there is a possible Kierkegaard who might even welcome the way in which such a challenge highlights the implications of the whole.

Were it only possible to stop the thought experiment (our imaginary feminist) at this point: to challenge the existing patriarchal order but leave religious faith intact! Many are the women who would like the established order transformed, but not their faith. They have challenged their husbands, left their fathers behind. But the questions about patriarchy turn out to have implications for heaven. How does one stop the revolution before it touches God the Father?

The absolute nature of the revelatory events formally negates challenge. Believe or do not believe. Obey or disobey. Individuals must face this choice at their own risk and in the transparency of a relative relationship in the face of a divine absolute. Kierkegaard has constructed his argument in formal, structural terms. H.H. gives us the categories to analyze the structural argument across the corpus of pseudonymous works. The possibility of the relative negation of the ethical claims of the existing order, which occurs in the genius, suggests dialectically the possibility of an absolute negation of the ethical claims in the apostle. The beauty of the dialectic is that it makes a purely formal claim, immune to questions about content, yet revelation is content. The religious transforms the individual so totally that the individual ceases to care about the relative injustice of the status quo. The teleological suspension of the ethical places the existing order (with its universal ethical duties) and absolute truth in existential tension and forces the individual to sell everything for the single jewel of unchanging Truth.

> Faith is precisely the paradox that the single individual as the single individual is higher than the universal, is justified before it, not as inferior to it but as superior—yet in such a way, please note, that it is the single individual who, after being subordinate as the single individual to the universal, now by means of the universal becomes the single individual who as the single individual is superior, that the single individual as the single individual stands in an absolute relation to the absolute. . . . The story of Abraham contains just such a teleological suspension of the ethical.[19]

In this way the religious becomes de facto, a conservative move. Religion touches the existing order at every point, yet leaves it unchanged. Kierkegaard quite naturally opposes social change as a distraction to absolute change, but his opposition is only relative. The structure allows for change, even deepens the analysis of change. Kierkegaard quite naturally opposes social change as a distraction to absolute change, but his opposition is only relative. The structure allows for change, even deepens the analysis of change. A feminist might well appeal to Kierkegaard to understand herself better, but then she, too, must choose. The more difficult the choice, the more value she must sacrifice, the more powerful the revelation of the absolute against her revolution. Like Abraham before the sacrifice, the more outrageous the claim the more one is thrust back upon oneself. One cannot appeal elsewhere, because all elsewheres are relative to the negation of the relative in the absolute.

There is a point beyond which Kierkegaard cannot be pushed. God's word includes a wide territory of texts and dogma, all in some sense implied by the category of revelation. In securing the formal claim of the apostle's truth to absolute authority and to absolute risk, Kierkegaard has taken for granted the tradition he inherits, without separately undertaking to repeat its content. The apostolic claim is flexible; it can carry as much or as little of the Christian dogma as Kierkegaard wishes. Whatever is credited to the apostle as content must be regarded as a divine challenge: obey or don't obey. The only legitimate criterion is the inward criterion of faith.

Strangely, Christianity is vulnerable at only one point, that is, the point of its world-historical success. No enemy can attack it, but its friends could destroy it. If Christianity should come to be believed because of two thousand years, or because it is reasonable, or because it is regarded as revelation, it loses its tension with the relative, and faith becomes easy. Hence the importance of Kierkegaard's existence to Christianity. He is a John the Baptist in retrospect: crying for some wilderness in fear that God might come and be made to live in a cathedral. Adler is but another symptom of the disease of Christendom, the danger that the outrage might become respectable. The worst thing that could happen to an apostle would be to keep his job within the state church. The only test for authentic revelation is its continuing offensiveness. The apostle who supports the existing order has either been misunderstood or is not an apostle.

The absolute must have no congress with the relative lest the categories be confused. Here Kierkegaard has need of the feminists, for only they can help Kierkegaard disentangle himself from patriarchy. Kierkegaard's texts fall victim to his own conservatism. In addition to his need to clarify Christianity is the less conscious (but nonetheless recognizable) commitment to maintaining the patriarchal system he represents. Kierkegaard wants the established order to stay put, the ethical to be clear and unambiguous, so that his knights of faith can go charging out without wondering who is the dragon and who is the damsel. The ethical is the constant in his equation, the point of departure for the religious. And the religious returns the favor by reinforcing the status quo. Kierkegaard is very close to making his religious system mirror a patriarchal social system which is thereby legitimated by divine sanction.

Our imaginary feminist may be a genius, but she is not an apostle. Yet her venture does touch on a new challenge to Christianity, one that has been in the works for a long time. Kierkegaard gives a clear setting of the initial terms in his battle with Christendom. Christianity has never rested easily since it got into bed with Constantine. Though this political move guaranteed its survival, it also turned Christianity into a civil religion, a transformation that has shaped it ever since but to which it has never reconciled. Christianity was never meant to be a worldly success.

> Faith in divine transcendence, faith in the "absolute paradox" of the transcendent God-become-man, had steadily evaporated, not simply as a matter of doctrine but as it is reflected in the sense of self-identity or in what Kierkegaard likes to call the "life outlook" of these professed Christians, until it had vaporized at last into mere participation in bourgeois Protestant culture. One becomes a "Christian" simply by being born and nurtured into that society.[20]

Christianity was conceived in the breaking of the categories of normalcy for the sake of an absolute duty to God. Its transcendent God could serve the purpose of legitimating the divine right of kings only by losing God's own revolutionary angle, the sheer over-and-against quality of a God who refuses to do what is expected. The story of the man who was also God—the God-man—and the story of the God who hung on a cross, are stories of a God whose claim to transcendence rests in paradox, in man's confrontation with the possibility of paradox, with impossibility.

> Look, there he stands—the god. Where? There. Can you not see him? He is the god, and yet he has no place where he can lay his head, and he does not dare to turn to any person lest that person be offended at him. He is the god, and yet he walks more circumspectly than if angels were carrying him—not to keep him from stumbling, but so that he may not tread in the dust the people who are offended at him. He is the god, and yet his eyes rest with concern on the human race, for the individual's tender shoot can be crushed as readily as a blade of grass. Such a life—sheer love and sheer sorrow. To want to express the unity of love and then not to be understood, to be obliged to fear for everyone's perdition and yet in this way truly to be able to save only one single person—sheer sorrow, while his days and hours are filled with the sorrow of the learner who entrusts himself to him. Thus does the god stand upon the earth, like unto the lowliest through his omnipotent love. He knows that the learner is untruth—what if he made a mistake, what if he became weary and lost his bold confidence! Oh, to sustain heaven and earth by an omnipotent "Let there be," and then, if this were to be absent for one fraction of a second, to have everything collapse—how easy this would be compared with bearing the possibility of the offense of the human race when out of love one became its savior![21]

Kierkegaard is the prophet of Christianity's otherness. His very method attempts the negative task of breaking the Christian loose from every meaning to which he might hold. Kierkegaard attempts to hold open a space for an immediate and direct confrontation with the divine. Where all relative meanings collapse, there the eternal meaning may appear.

> How, then, does the learner become a believer or a follower? When the understanding is discharged and he receives the condition. When does he receive this? In the moment. This condition, what does it condition? His understanding of the eternal. But a condition such as this surely must be an eternal condition. —In the moment, therefore, he receives the eternal condition, and he knows this from his having received it in the moment, for otherwise he merely calls to mind that he had it from eternity. He receives the condition in the moment and receives it from that teacher himself.[22]

But before that can happen, even the ideas about God most precious to the human must collapse. Faith is an encounter with the indissolubly other.

One of the most memorable stories of encounter and confrontation with that in God which does not belong to social meaning is the Johannes de Silentio's story (in *Fear and Trembling*) of Abraham. The story of Abraham is the story of a patriarch who must sacrifice that aspect of his own being which can ensure his immortality in the life space of society. Johannes de Silentio reconceives patriarchy as a duty, the duty of fathers to sons, and a promise, the promise that one will live on in one's sons. The patriarch, Abraham, comes head on into the challenge to both these norms in God's requirement that he sacrifice his son.

> My listener! Many a father has thought himself deprived of every hope for the future when he lost his child, the dearest thing in the world to him; nevertheless, on one was the child of promise in the sense in which Isaac was that to Abraham. Many a father has lost his child, but then it was God, the unchangeable, inscrutable will of the Almighty, it was his hand that took it. Not so with Abraham! A harder test was reserved for him, and Isaac's fate was placed, along with that knife, in Abraham's hand. And there he stood, the old man with his solitary hope. But he did not doubt, he did not look in anguish to the left and to the right, he did not challenge heaven with his prayers. He knew it was God the Almighty who was testing him; he knew it was the hardest sacrifice that could be demanded of him; but he knew also that no sacrifice is too severe when God demands it—and he drew the knife.[23]

Abraham has such trust in God that he can give away everything and has such faith in God that all is returned. What Abraham must give away is his son, the son of his old age, more precious than his own life, the guarantee of his patriarchal status as head of a tribe that can survive his own death, the promise inherent in the very essence of patriarchal society. But this is not all he gives away. Abraham is required by God to himself do the murder. Abraham is called upon to sacrifice what is good and right, to sacrifice duty— to God.

> The absolute duty can lead one to do what ethics would forbid, but it can never lead the knight of faith to stop loving. Abraham demonstrates this. In the moment he is about to sacrifice Isaac, the ethical expression for what he is doing is: he hates Isaac. But if he actually hates Isaac, he can rest assured that God does not demand this of him, for Cain and Abraham are not identical. He must love Isaac with his whole soul. Since God claims Isaac, he must, if possible, love him even more, and only then can he sacrifice him, for it is indeed this love for Isaac that makes his act a sacrifice by its paradoxical contrast to his love for God.[24]

The tension between the ethical and the religious is essential to Johannes de Silentio's project. Without it, the religious collapses into the ethical and the transcendent collapses into the socially sanctioned. Yet Johannes de Silentio is not quite ready to sever the most basic agreement with patriarchal society as such. The issue of faith is both Abraham's willingness to sacrifice his son, as symbol of the highest conception of duty within patriarchy, and his willingness to have faith that God will indeed live up to His promise to make Abraham the father of generations. Though Johannes de Silentio is willing to separate God from any particular social norm, he is not quite able to separate his God from the legitimation of patriarchy itself. Man must have faith in God, as the Father, and as the promise that their systems rest on a divine sanction.

The choice between the ethical and the religious can only occur to one who has not dodged the ethical challenge being generated even now by women. It will be easy to make Kierkegaard's move and try and reinforce patriarchy as a social system so that the leap may be not so large. But, whereas Kierkegaard must then labor to differentiate Christianity from its social clones, those who are willing to hear about justice in gender are then ready to join Abraham and Johannes de Silentio on the mountain. But the mountain now is the challenge to Christianity to decide between the radical transcendence of God and the status of God as primary adherent to man's own historically determined patriarchal social system. Kierkegaard's answer is that God is other but has promised to man the triumph of his own claims to supremacy. God is other *and* God is Father.

What could be better for Christianity, in its absolute apostolic formulation, than a challenge to its own patriarchal relativism? The nature of dialectic demands that the choice be made more difficult, and for this one needs a feminist. Choose. God the Father has conceived a son. God has come to earth as a man. Woman has no divine relevance except as an empty receptacle. Here we stand again on the mountaintop with Abraham, do we not? Christianity is a direct challenge to human decency, to justice, to the wholeness of humanity. For it is unethical and wrong for God to be a patriarch. There can be no justice while God wears a male pronoun, co-opting and negating the value of woman's birth, excluding half of humanity from the affirmation made by his divinity. Such a God is evil, a God who would demand the sacrifice of a child, because he has never really been a mother.

Out of the whirlwind, the God of Abraham replies. He makes no attempt to qualify his names, nor to answer the ethical charge against him. To quote from another patriarch who also wrestled with God's apparent injustice:

> Then the Lord answered Job out of the whirlwind:
> "Gird up your loins like a man;
> I will question you, and you declare to me.
> Will you even put me in the wrong?
> Will you condemn me that you may be justified?"
> (*Job* 40:6–8)

The revolution that feminism seeks is a revolution founded in justice. It thus confronts head-on the limits of the ethical as a basis for ultimate claims. This God of the patriarchs is not to be bound even by His own ethical norms. He breaks out of ethics and demands faith. This is a God who confronts the ethical head-on and says: "Choose!" If there is to be a leap of seventy thousand fathoms from the ethical to the religious, this is it. To understand justice and then to sacrifice it to the absolute is Christianity in all its sternest and most absolute character as faith. That, after having fought through the realization that to be a woman is not to be a subset of man, to then find that God still says he will have a son, that he will send that son to be crucified, and that only by that son may the faithful come to him, is an offense. Can a woman say "yes" to such a God? What would it mean to say "no" to God in such a way that is not merely taking offense at the paradox, that is not merely a return to the relative human claims of justice? The question turns two ways. Christianity must ask which it worships, God or the legitimacy of patriarchy. The feminist, or rather the woman seeking her own encounter with spirit, must ask whether the category of the divine can be reduced to the demands of justice. Their conversation with each other could be the context of just such a reopening to the divine enigma for which Kierkegaard longed.

> By taking away such inadequate views, the stories open up space for a new discovery of God, or, a discovery of a new God. This God is not to be found in the stories directly, but only beyond the traditional options made impossible by the stories. To use Kierkegaard's concepts, one could say that the stories of Abraham and Job provide the absurd by virtue of which a repetition, a new birth, of our view of God can be accomplished.[24]

Christianity can only come into its own when the absolute is not equated with the established order. The religious is in tension with the ethical. All Christians should dialectically work for the triumph of the new order, for the new order will not be Christendom, and that is to its benefit. Then, when God calls from the mountain, it will be possible to distinguish his voice from the professional clergy who sometimes think they understand him better than he does himself. It will be difficult to be a Christian in that order, for these women will claim some new meaning that even reaches and touches the divine. The conflict between ethical duty and the absolute duty to God is essential for every Christian. The Christian needs to hear the claims of God over and above society. To do that he needs a society that is not a mirror image of the absolute patriarch. The Christian needs the diversity and challenge of a revolutionary change in society, to a society in which Christianity really offers a choice.

Can, then, a woman be a Christian? This is another kind of sacrifice, a sacrifice of one's own right to be. Woman's otherness from the patriarchs means that the promise to Abraham is a promise in which she is an object, not the subject. Her sacrifice precedes the trip to Mount Moriah. Will Sarah, in faith, accept staying home (and doing the dishes) while Abraham goes to the mountain? Can the individual-who-is-a-woman come to transparency before the God who was/is/will be the God/Man? The individual who is a man comes to the mountain with Abraham and sacrifices his dearly beloved. He hears the cries of the woman whom God the Father has subordinated. If he has faith, he dares to sacrifice her, knowing that in God all things are possible. And he knows he will have her back, in faith. But how can she come to the mountain? Could Abraham come to the mountain and sacrifice himself? No, the problem is even more serious than merely offering to die at God's hand. Can he come to the mountain and negate himself, acknowledging that there is no call for him, that it was all a mistake, and that it was really another whom God called? Could Abraham accept that God has nothing to say to him simply because of his sex, and still have faith? This will be the dilemma for the woman, who comes to the mountain and is told to go and serve her husband, and is told that by her husband, and not by God. She might still have faith because her very being is relative. After all, God is absolute and therefore everything is possible. Perhaps even this is possible. Or perhaps there is another possibility still waiting to be found in the story of the journey to Mount Moriah, if only we read it from the social location of a woman, who is also an individual.

Johannes de Silentio in *Fear and Trembling* retells the traditional Abraham stories by means of images of a mother weaning her child, borrowed from the practices of mothers of his time and place. The underlying assumption that inform these customs is that the mother must control and initiate the weaning process, with the implicit threat that otherwise the child would never give up the breast.

> When the child is to be weaned, the mother blackens her breast. It would be hard to have the breast look inviting when the child must not have it. So the child believes that the breast has changed, but the mother—she is still the same, her gaze is tender and loving as ever. How fortunate the one who did not need more terrible means to wean the child![26]

These little tidbits of Danish child-rearing serve as the morals for the *Exordium* on Abraham. Each *Exordium* begins with the passage from the biblical story of Abraham's sacrifice of Isaac. The story is then retold in terms of the various possible responses Abraham might make to the other characters in the tale: Isaac, Sarah, and Eliezer, the servant. Johannes de Silentio's retelling of the stories focuses on what Abraham might have been thinking as he brought his son to Mount Moriah. The stories, though they seem to give reality to the other characters, are an internal dialogue in which Abraham is alone in his struggle with himself before God. The point of view of Abraham as the protagonist is summarized and encapsulated with the morals of the story, which are taken from Danish weaning practices. In the morals, God takes the persona of a mother in interaction with a child, who symbolizes the individual before God. In the *Exordium*, the possibility of identifying God as a mother is hinted. However, the images of mother are distorted by the social practices of nineteenth-century patriarchal Denmark. Behind the mother who must wean her child is the father who demands the mother return to his service.

Let us, therefore, play with these elements: the interactions between mother, child, and implied father, as well as the vivid characters of Sarah, Isaac, and Eliezer. The *Exordium* in our retelling continues to be an exploration of the faithful before the mountain of sacrifice, but now the internal struggle that we will examine is that of Sarah. Likewise, our morals will be based on child-rearing practices that honor, rather than seek to dissolve, the bond between mother and child.

I

And God tempted Abraham and said to him, take Isaac, your only son, whom you love, and go to the land of Moriah and offer him there as a burnt offering on a mountain that I shall show you.[27]

"It was early in the morning when Abraham arose, had the asses saddled, and left his tent, taking Isaac with him, but Sarah watched them from the window as they went down the valley—until she could see them no longer."[28] Then she saddled her own donkey and rode after him. When she got to the mountain and saw what Abraham was about to do, she shouted at him and beat on him with a stick, saying: "You old fool, you always think you know everything, even what God wants! Well, you're wrong about everything! Isaac isn't even really your son, your seed. I just told you that so you wouldn't lose your faith in God's promise. You can't sacrifice what doesn't belong to you!" Then she took Isaac, turned from Abraham, and left.

When the child is at the breast, the mother virginally conceals her breast from her husband, lest the husband be jealous of the new love in her life. Fortunate is the woman whose husband can love without possessing!

II

"It was early in the morning when Abraham arose: he embraced Sarah, the bride of his old age, and Sarah kissed Isaac, who took away her disgrace,

Isaac her pride, her hope for all generations to come."[29] The two rode away together, but Abraham came home alone. Abraham told her that he had sacrificed Isaac as commanded by God. Sarah was unable to understand, but her duty to her husband required that she keep silent about what she did not understand. Abraham suggested that there might be more children and was surprised that Sarah had lost interest in having children, preferring disgrace. Then Sarah went and sat by the road to wait for Isaac and, though she was obedient to her husband, she never spoke again.

Some fathers have been known to require the mother after a certain number of months to blacken her breast and wean the child so that she may be available to her husband to bear more babies. There is no duty that can heal a broken heart. How fortunate it is when mothers are not forced to choose between their husbands and their children!

III

"It was early in the morning when Abraham arose: he kissed Sarah, the young mother, and Sarah kissed Isaac, her delight."[30] As he left for the stables Abraham told Sarah what God had said. Sarah said nothing, but while Abraham was out saddling his asses, Sarah took Isaac from his bed and stole away into the wilderness. There she joined Hagar, and they found other Gods to worship, Gods who were not so ready to sacrifice their own children and the children of others.

When a child is born, the mother must choose whether to nurse her child from her own breast or whether to preserve her breasts for the pleasure of her husband. Fortunate indeed is the woman whose God is a Mother!

IV

"It was early in the morning, and everything in Abraham's house was ready for the journey. He took leave of Sarah, and Eliezer, the faithful servant, accompanied him along the road until he turned back again."[31] Sarah followed at a distance. When she saw what Abraham was about to do, she thought of many arguments against him, but had no way of addressing God. So she turned away and went home. In this she was no different from all the other women, but it was counted in her as faith that she kept silent and did not interfere in a man's relationship to God—even at the cost of her own heart.

When a mother nurses a baby, she must realize that the relationship is only temporary and not determinative to her being. Otherwise she will lose both her child and her husband, for the one will grow up and the other will be excluded from her heart. Therefore, from the beginning she must prepare to wean her child. How fortunate the couple whose relationship is strong enough to hold another without being divided between duty and love!

In all these stories, Sarah is presented with a choice. But her choice is different from that of Abraham. Her relationship with God is indirect, mediated through the support of her husband. If her choice is for the God of Abraham, that choice must be through Abraham. Or maybe Sarah and Abraham are interchangeable, and gender is irrelevant to faith. Perhaps women birth children in the same way that men beget them. This would work if being a woman is not decisive and if women's experience of mothering is identical to the father's duty to his son. In other words, the solitary individual might be woman, and this is the easiest solution to the dilemma—if one can stop there.

The interchangeability of male and female in terms of the solitary individual raises the issue of whether the same is true of God. Can one alternate images of God the mother with God the father? This is the great experiment of the last twenty years throughout Christendom. It would seem that God as a transcendent being would have to transcend gender. On the abstract level, this solution is not difficult. However, insofar as Christianity is committed to a concrete historical revelation, God cannot be subject to reformulation by historical revisionists. Not only was Jesus a man, but Jesus calls God his father and is begotten, not birthed, by God. There is a gender-specific element in the very origins of Christianity that cannot be easily dismissed. Can a transcendent religion be subject to the ethical presuppositions of a particular time?

Kierkegaard insists on the priority of the religious over the ethical, even as he affirms the essential historical character of Christianity. Even to say that the Christian God is tainted by relative patriarchal assumptions of human social construction threatens the absolute transcendence of God. Anyone but Kierkegaard can simply dismiss the relativity of the historical revelation of Christianity as a fallible human attempt to understand that which is absolutely beyond human conception. But not Kierkegaard. The danger of denying the absolute nature of Christianity's historical character is that everything, even God, becomes relative and disappears into human projection.

Kierkegaard might well take another tack. The patriarchal content of the revelation represents a challenge to any woman who would be both faithful and a feminist. Here Abraham, or perhaps Sarah, visits Mount Moriah, and is confronted with a choice. By naming himself Father, Father of an Only Begotten Son, the feminist must decide whether to have faith or not. Any route she takes is fraught with anxiety and uncertainty. Who is this God who addresses her? And can she have faith in his goodness even in the midst of his apparent injustice?

Kierkegaard needs feminists, women who will challenge the relativity of the patriarchal content of Christianity. What Christians need is a clear sense of the choice they are making. And no one is better able to intensify that choice than Kierkegaard. But Kierkegaard does not intensify the choice sufficiently, because the Christianity he is trying to elucidate is so thoroughly embedded in the status quo. God the Father acts so much like fathers in patriarchal society that there is nothing surprising in his demands. If patriarchal assumptions are challenged, women and men are presented with a clearer choice: Will you have faith? And who is the one in whom you will have faith? The choice of gender language for God reaches all the way to eternity.

What might it mean to choose against Christianity? There is another option hidden in the heart of the issue of gender language. Might it be possible to walk away from Mount Moriah and find God elsewhere? Sarah might proclaim to that father who demands a sacrifice that "You are not God!" This is also a faith; it is a faith that seeks rather than knows. The woman who in her spirituality seeks God elsewhere needs Kierkegaard to clarify the nature of the search and the choice. A God who can be reconceived is not a transcendent God. Kierkegaard would warn the feminist that there is a danger in creating a God who is just as we wish. The over and againstness of God requires that God be offensive. The accusation that Christianity is nothing more than a legitimation of patriarchy and the status quo turns back on the feminist, who might also one day be the founder of a status quo in need of critique. People who create God in their own image soon find themselves alone with no one to ask the difficult questions. The human turn to God is a longing for an answer in the dark. That which we have made cannot hold us nor comfort us in the midst of our own darkness.

Can one have a God or a Goddess who is over and against, who is other than ourselves, without reverting to the language of transcendence? Can the immanent respond and surprise us, and save us from the tendency to absorb everything into our social construction of meaning? We need more than a mother who says the nice things. Currently, the very conceiving of the Goddess is so new that it challenges and lures us away from the patriarchal context in which we dwell. But we will need her to speak to us even if we succeed in beginning again. And we will need her to be other than ourselves.

Even the feminist needs Kierkegaard to remind us that the religious must stand over and against the ethical. The ethical is the highest statement of ourselves. The ethical will guide us in conceiving of the possibility of an inclusive society that moves beyond patriarchal structures. The aim is justice, a justice we have discovered in the corners of patriarchal society. We dream of a matristic society in which all the structures necessary for the perpetuation of the fathers' claims on their sons have been abandoned. We dream of a matristic society in which sex is sacred. We dream of a matristic society in which the art of peace replaces the technology of war. This old dream has followed us across the centuries. It is not even foreign to Christianity, though we must seek to relearn it from indigenous peoples whose memories are longer than our own. For now, it is enough that there might be a Mother as well as a Father.

We ascribe to the new dream of divinity all the graces that we are missing. But we will someday need more, and perhaps we already do. It is not enough for us simply to leave behind the jealous God. We need a vision of an Other which is as strong as the transcendent Other that stirs our hearts and challenges our thoughts. We cannot invent the Goddess; we must find her. So let our dreams and our imaginings play with that which is. We find the Goddess over and against us, every time we look beyond the surface. The immanent divinity intrudes into even our imagining, for our imagining comes out of dreams we did not request. We create in the context of a natural world, and our dreaming must be answerable to that discernible divinity which lies outside all that is artificial and inside all that is created and born.

Over and against the transcendent deity, the Father God who waits on the mountain, is the mountain itself. The mountain speaks, and the mountain's speaking is as hard and other as the burning bush. We have not yet remembered how to ask what the mountain says. We are learning, however, that all that dwells on the mountain cannot be taken for granted and subsumed into men's projects and profits. The mountain will have its say, and the challenge it offers to us now is to have faith that there is a way even now to make peace with it, if only we will listen.

Nature is as hard a deity as any patriarchal God. Questions of morality grind to a halt in the face of the awesome power of the wind. The images of deity were once taken from nature; we now return those images to their home. This is a dangerous undertaking. The Mother of Gods is Kali, who dances upon the corpse of the God, with baby skulls dangling on a necklace around her neck.

> As the good and terrible mother, she represents, or is, the power of the material world—Mother Nature, in her creative, nurturing, and devouring aspects. These really are not separate aspects, for without eating her children, how could she sustain them at her breast? Every nursing mother needs food. She eats what she has given birth to, for she has given birth to everything and thus there is nothing else to eat.[32]

We return to the pain and sorrow, which is the dark side of ourselves as much as our world. This is a deity who is beyond good and evil, or perhaps is before good and evil. We will dance in the darkness; we will sing songs in the pain. We will call the nighttime our mother. Here is our Mount Moriah, to face the awful awesomeness of nature and still have faith that our puny efforts at justice and peace have meaning.

Whereas Abraham must go to the mountain and keep silence, we go to the mountain and must speak. Abraham cannot speak before God because God is the qualitatively other. God is so far beyond Abraham that there is nothing that he can add to God. Our speaking is a willingness to create songs that the Mother might sing. Reciprocity is at the heart of immanence. Our speaking is grounded in her speaking. Her speaking finds a voice in our singing. She has been silenced for so long that we respond to her vulnerability as well as to her power.

Kierkegaard offers for us a choice, and we return the favor with yet another choice. The time may be coming when no Christian will be a Christian automatically but instead will have to choose. The images of an alternative divinity are already emerging in spite of concerted efforts on the part of patriarchs to suppress them. The challenge comes from within. Women who have always known that their Christian God must be a God of love and compassion, who stands with the weak and oppressed, have begun to reexamine their own tradition. Within the revelation, it may be that *Sophia* speaks next. Deep within the heart of the Christian community, there are those who have dared to reimagine God, calling out to their own scriptures as a child calls out in the night. And *Sophia*, hidden so long beneath the overlay of patriarchal gloss, has answered their cries and revealed her name.

The Christian tradition stands poised to open out into a new horizon, which is both revolutionary and grounded in revelation. These Christians are tested by their community's rejection. But there are other and harder tests ahead. One might be called to leave house and home, tradition and scriptures, to follow a divinity one cannot quite recognize. She walks in the gardens and haunts the ruins of people we do not yet know. She comes before us and behind us, and our hearts are stirred with new longings. But to follow her we must step out of the security of old well-worn paradoxes and parables. The music has been lost for her prayers and hymns, but we are nonetheless called to dance and sing.

There will be those women who will say that those called to follow her are undermining the revolutionary confidence necessary for real social change. For others, the spiritual journey feels like a revolution in itself. The spiritual journey is a narrow path, for it is as easy to tumble into political activism as it is into the addiction of new spiritual experiences.

Political awareness can become a tyranny of its own, not least because it locks us into the issues and perspectives of a particular time. But when we are looking at questions of the sacred, we move beyond time. To create the changes in consciousness needed to transform society at a deep level, we need insights broader than those the issues of the moment can provide.[33]

Patriarchy plays up the distinction between political change and eternal realities. The patriarchs also sense the change in the wind and would suppress the something new that might be ready to give birth. Still the call comes through the night, to dance a new world into being. The dance finds its measure in the awakening of the old earth. There will be hard days ahead, for it may be that the time is not yet right for change. Or, it may be that change will come, and that there will be no one waiting for us on the other side.

Why do women need the Goddess?

> The Goddess awakens in infinite forms and a thousand disguises. She is found where She is least expected, appears out of nowhere and everywhere to illumine the open heart. She is singing, crying, moaning, wailing, shrieking, crooning to us: to be awake, to commit ourselves to life, to be a lover in the world and of the world, to join our voices in the single song of constant change and creation. For Her law is love unto all beings, and She is the cup of the drink of life.[34]

We need the Goddess to answer the longing of our hearts. Kierkegaard's dialectic moves by the longing he awakens in the heart of the reader to overcome the isolation and loneliness of the solitary individual. At each stage (the aesthetic, the ethical, the religious), the individual thinks that that which is hidden in the heart can be named. At each stage, the individual finds another, but another to whom the individual still cannot wholly speak. The solitude of the solitary is not broken by poetry, or marriage, or love. Only in the encounter with God does the heart of the indivisible individual find solace, because only God's hiddenness is great enough to encompass the hiddenness of the individual.

The movement through the stages is hierarchical, a moving up and out of solitude. In the conclusion of the search, one assumes that the repose in faith is possible because God is the last, the final, the highest stage. The Goddess as another is not the termination of a ladder, but a spiraling inward. What is a spiral?

> [A]ll things are swirls of energy, vortexes of moving forces, currents in an ever-changing sea. Underlying the appearance of separateness, of fixed objects within a linear stream of time, reality is a field of energies that congeal, temporarily, into forms. In time, all "fixed" things dissolve, only to coalesce again into new forms, new vehicles.[35]

Immanence locates divinity within the context of what is given. The God called from outside of thought, as the mystery of that which thought cannot think. As another of Kierkegaard's pseudonyms proclaimed, thought is that which collides with its own boundaries and out of that paradox discovers the other.

> But what is this unknown against which the understanding in its para-doxical passion collides and which even disturbs man and his self-knowl-edge? It is the unknown. But it is not a human being, insofar as he knows man, or anything else that he knows. Therefore, let us call this unknown *the god*. It is only a name we give to it.[36]

The otherness of God is what draws thought. By placing God at the limits of our thought, Kierkegaard also posited his transcendence. Yet that which is within each of us is as unknown as that which is farthest away. What we desire is that what we have found to be true not be the final limit. Our heart desires to be stretched beyond what we are able to conceive, to encounter another, and then to love.

Can immanence satisfy the longing in our hearts? This is another kind of test, and the answer cannot be given once and for all. The answer cannot be given by a revolution nor by scriptural tradition. We can discover God only by giving ourselves over into trust. The answer is a statement of faith and of challenge. Perhaps it is not God's greatness, or his superiority, which allows us to find our being in him. Perhaps we seek that which is other than ourselves, that which cannot be dissolved into ourselves, another to take us by the arm and turn us around from our solitude. Perhaps what we seek was never transcendent at all but was to be found in the world to which we have not yet turned.

We have not yet learned to speak with the wind. We were busy waiting for the still small voice, and we forget the fire and the wind and the water. Around us the trees and the soil and the stars may be singing. Will this be enough to bring us out of our solitary individuality? The feminist revolu-tion, if revolution it will turn out to be, can introduce us to our duty to the earth along with our duty to each other. If that is all it does, it will not be enough. We need more than reasons, we need response from something that is more than duty. For those who do not feel it, religion has always reduced to the quality of the content of the answer. But no answer would satisfy those of us who long for the stars. We call out. We stand on mountain tops and demand answers, but it is the voice we want to hear. The answers we bring down the mountainside are never adequate, were never adequate, but the encounter with something beyond our own pale echo of consciousness, if we get it, will be enough—more than enough.

There are differences in the way in which the Goddess answers from the way in which the God answers. We need the Goddess to teach us how to speak with death and to learn to speak with a baby's cry. The Goddess makes no promises of immortality, of answers beyond the veil. She is death, and she is the question. She promises a grave. She promises that she is alive to our questions. She claims from us our answers, proposes problems for our solutions, undoes every theory, taunts us with a mystery just beyond our imaginings. She claims our voice and demands of us our goods and evils. She is the partner for those of us who are and will be the creators of the only answers that can be found. She is the partner in a dance, an Other to match our steps, beyond us and within us and beside us. Will this be enough?

In our choice of Gods we risk everything, for by naming divinity we cast ourselves into the abyss. Kierkegaard will choose, and we will choose. There we will each rest for all of whatever remains of eternity. This is a choice that reaches so far that it risks heaven and hell. Perhaps one does not believe in these ancient symbols for the ultimacy of choice, but they remain symbols for the quality of the risk that one must take in naming a god. If you would abandon God, you abandon God for all eternity. One must choose in the seriousness of those willing to count the cost. If there is a God who judges, will you choose to obey? To refuse is damnation. To choose against God is to suffer the possibility of being wrong all the way into torment. If God should exist, and if you should have to appear before him, would you still say that you choose the Goddess? This is how serious the choice may be. So also for Abraham the choice must reach all the way to the end. If it should turn out that there is another God, a God who is Goddess and does not demand the sacrifice of children, will you still choose this God of yours to love? Abraham perhaps knew of such deities that did not demand such sacrifices, for contrary to patriarchal myth not all pagan cultures have such a tradition. Abraham knew, and Sarah knew, that this was a choice. Only Kierkegaard is too far from such choices as to know the ramifications of the choice between gods. The posing of the choices will not hurt him, but aid him to claim his own meaning as more than the rote answer learned in a required catechism class.

Existence poses the question of God as the question of our own claim upon the whole of meaning, reaching all the way to eternity and back. The question is not whether God exists, but by what meaning we will exist. To be a woman who exists before God as a woman might sometime mean that she dares to say she will have no more of great fathers, and she will do so no matter what Father she must stand before. To be a woman, who exists before herself as a woman, perhaps means she must be willing to follow her tears to the Ground. To be a woman, who exists before the earth as a woman, might mean to look no more to abstract heavens to end her tears. To be a woman, who exists before her own questions as a woman, is to risk letting go of the old, in order that a new might begin. God might be in his heaven, but all is not right on his earth. The time is coming when we will need to ask to whom we sacrifice and when we will refuse to sacrifice anymore.

NOTES

1. Søren Kierkegaard, *On Authority and Revelation: The Book on Adler, or a Cycle of Ethico-Religious Essays*, trans. Walter Lowrie (New York: Harper and Row, 1966), 191.
2. Søren Kierkegaard, *The Point of View of For My Work as an Author: A Report to History*, trans. Walter Lowrie (New York: Harper and Row, 1962), 20.
3. Kierkegaard, *On Authority and Revelation*, 26, 47.
4. Søren Kierkegaard, *Repetition*, ed. and trans. Howard V. Hong and Edna H. Hong (Princeton, N.J.: Princeton University Press, 1983), 170.
5. Kierkegaard, *On Authority and Revelation*, 24.
6. Ibid., 181.
7. Irene Makarushka, "Reflections on the 'Other' in Dinesen, Kierkegaard, and Nietzsche," in *Kierkegaard on Art and Communication*, ed. George Pattison (New York: St. Martin's Press, 1992), 158.
8. Kierkegaard, *On Authority and Revelation*, 125.
9. Paul Ricoeur, *Interpretation Theory: Discourse and the Surplus of Meaning* (Fort Worth: Texas Christian University Press, 1976), 29–30.
10. Translated by Walter Lowrie (New York: Harper and Row, 1966).
11. Kierkegaard, *Point of View*, 15.
12. Kierkegaard's discussion of genius has close parallels to Max Weber's notion of charismatic leadership. The genius breaks lose from existing cultural assumptions and generates ideas that may serve as a new point of departure. See Weber's "The Sociology of Charismatic Authority," in *From Max Weber: Essays in Sociology*, ed. and trans. H. H. Gerth and C. Wright Mills (New York: Oxford University Press, 1975), 245–52. (This selection is from Weber's *Wirtschaft und Gesellschaft*, part III, chapter 9, 753–57.)
13. Immanuel Kant, *Critique of Pure Reason*, trans. Norman Kemp Smith (New York: St. Martin's Press, 1965), 637.
14. Søren Kierkegaard, *Fear and Trembling* [with *Repetition*], ed. and trans. Howard V. Hong and Edna H. Hong (Princeton, N.J.: Princeton University Press, 1983), 38–39.
15. Kierkegaard, *On Authority and Revelation*, 43.
16. Ibid., 30.
17. Ibid., 38.
18. Ibid., 122.
19. Kierkegaard, *Fear and Trembling*, 55–56.
20. Stephen Crites, *In the Twilight of Christendom: Hegel vs. Kierkegaard on Faith and History* (Chambersburg, Penn.: American Academy of Religion, 1972), 59.
21. Søren Kierkegaard, *Philosophical Fragments*, ed. and trans. Howard V. Hong and Edna H. Hong (Princeton: Princeton Univresity Press, 1985), 32.
22. Ibid., 64.
23. Ibid., 21–22.
24. Ibid., 74.
25. Mark Lloyd Taylor, "Ordeal and Repetition in Kierkegaard's Treatment of Abraham and Job," in *Foundations of Kierkegaard's Vision of Community: Religion, Ethics, and Politics in Kierkegaard*, ed. George Connell and C. Stephen Evans (Atlantic Highlands, N.J.: Humanities Press, 1992), 49.
26. Kierkegaard, *Fear and Trembling*, 11.
27. Kierkegaard's translation of Gen. 22:1–2 in *Fear and Trembling*, 10.

28. Kierkegaard, *Fear and Trembling*, 10.
29. Ibid., 12.
30. Ibid., 13.
31. Ibid., 14.
32. C. Mackenzie Brown, "Kali, the Mad Mother," in *The Book of the Goddess: Past and Present: An Introduction to Her Religion*, ed. Carl Olson (New York: Crossroad, 1985), 121.
33. Starhawk, *The Spiral Dance: A Rebirth of the Ancient Religion of the Great Goddess*, rev. ed. (San Francisco: Harper and Row, 1989), 7.
34. Ibid., 212.
35. Ibid., 32.
36. Søren Kierkegaard, *Philosophical Fragments*, 39.

Chapter 4

F o u r

NIETZSCHE'S PROPHECY: THE ETERNAL RETURN OF WHAT COMES BEFORE

Philo-Sophia, the love of wisdom, has lost her heart, but gained truth. In Friedrich Nietzsche, the echo of her old divinity has been replaced by a level of objectivity. Men have now been searching for truth for many generations, dedicating their lives to philosophy, or at least to a search for truth. Truth, by the time of Nietzsche, has an honored history as the "other" to which thought does or does not correspond. Truth is that which man is after. He comes "after" it, in the sense that it is before him, and in the sense that man is "after" it, desires to get it, to have it, to possess it. The truth is the object of knowledge, and philosophy is man's pursuit of truth.

Suppose truth is a woman—what then?[1]

Suppose truth is a woman. Suppose that *Sophia* is now to be regarded as *Veritas*. The change for *Sophia* is one from subject to object, albeit to highest object. Wisdom teaches, is inherently personified, changes, responds to the questioner. Wisdom calls forth the poet, the dreamer and visionary, who can understand with heart more often than mind. Wisdom is the ancient name of divinity that sneaks into even the biblical heritage as the feminine identity of God.

> Wisdom cries aloud in the street;
>   in the markets she raises her voice;
> on the top of the walls she cries out;
>   at the entrance of the city gates she speaks:
> "How long, O simple ones, will you love being simple?
> How long will scoffers delight in their scoffing
>   and fools hate knowledge?
> Give heed to my reproof;
> behold, I will pour out my thought to you;
>   I will make my words known to you.

Because I have called and you refused to listen,
    have stretched out my hand and no one has heeded,
and you have ignored all my counsel
    and would have none of my reproof,
I also will laugh at your calamity;
    I will mock when panic strikes you,
when panic strikes you like a storm,
    and your calamity comes like a whirlwind,
    when distress and anguish come upon you.
Then they will call upon me, but I will not answer;
    they will seek me diligently but will not find me.
Because they hated knowledge
    and did not choose the fear of the Lord,
would have none of my counsel,
    and despised all my reproof,
therefore they shall eat the fruit of their way
    and be sated with their own devices.
For the simple are killed by their turning away,
    and the complacence of fools destroys them;
but he who listens to me will dwell secure
    and will be at ease, without dread of evil."

(Prov. 1:20–33)

The voice of Wisdom was heard, could be heard in the street and in the markets. *Sophia* spoke, and the wise, who were her disciples, listened. Parmenides heard and became a philosopher. The righteous heard and learned how to walk aright. Even the ancient patriarchs heard and listened in their own way. They brought her into servitude to the fear of the Lord, but they heard. The ancient personification of *Sophia* is hinted at in Nietzsche's identification of truth with woman.

Suppose now that truth is a woman. It is kind of Nietzsche to include woman in such complimentary terms, especially desirable because so many of Nietzsche's comments about women are not kind.

Everything about woman is a riddle, and everything about woman has one solution: that is pregnancy. Man is for woman a means: the end is always the child. But what is woman for man?

A real man wants two things: danger and play. Therefore he wants woman as the most dangerous plaything.[2]

But suppose that truth is a woman. Then truth must be a plaything. And then, it must be that Nietzsche does not hate women, that there is hope for him yet, for he has elevated woman to the status of that which all thought seeks, to the status of truth. But if truth is a woman, can she speak? Truth is silent in the modern world, silent not only by choice but by her nature.

Truth is that which is out there and available to man, as his proper object as a seeker and lover after truth. Nietzsche speaks of woman as truth and hints at the relationship of man the lover to the beloved. Truth is a woman, and woman is an object of man's desire.

Suppose that truth is a woman. The metaphor is playful. He calls truth a woman much the way a man might call his boat a woman, or his nation a woman, or his toys. The metaphor is not a serious metaphor; it is a joke between men. It is not a joke that women are supposed to hear. But women who listen change the very nature of the metaphor. It is not truth that Nietzsche addresses in his supposing, and it is certainly not woman. She is not the audience. Rather Nietzsche addresses the men who have, so inexpertly, wooed her. Nietzsche's writing is not a love letter to truth, but a manual for lovers or (better yet) a manual for seduction.

> Supposing truth is a woman—what then? Are there not grounds for the suspicion that all philosophers, insofar as they were dogmatists, have been very inexpert about women? That the gruesome seriousness, the clumsy obtrusiveness with which they have usually approached truth so far have been awkward and very improper methods for winning a woman's heart?[3]

Nietzsche wishes to correct a misunderstanding about how one pursues truth, and he does so by beginning with the supposition that there might be an analogy between woman and truth. He breaks from the tradition that would have begun by going after truth directly, by providing a method or a foundation for the investigation of truth. He begins not by looking for or at truth directly but by addressing those who look for truth and by identifying the problem as being how one looks. "Supposing truth is a woman" allows men to reexamine the problem of truth. The way a philosopher has to approach truth is similar to the way a man has to approach a woman. In both, the way one comes on is everything. Truth, like women, escapes men's direct appropriation.

The metaphor by which Nietzsche makes his supposition works in two directions, commenting on truth and commenting on women. Though he wishes to change the way of approach, his supposition relies upon his audience's knowledge of truth and of women, as set, well-understood, common properties. In supposing truth is a woman, truth is still that same truth that men have sought throughout the history of philosophy since Plato. It is "out there," available for men's appropriation, a thing to be gotten hold of by thought. The object, "truth," is passive, awaiting the qualified man to claim her.

Equally so, woman is supposed to be like truth. Woman is there for man's appropriation: passive, something to be claimed by the man who knows how to approach her. But, as Nietzsche points out, she is not for the clumsy, nor the direct.

What is certain is that she has not allowed herself to be won—and today every kind of dogmatism is left standing dispirited and discouraged. *If* it is left standing at all! For there are scoffers who claim that it has fallen, that all dogmatism lies on the ground—even more, that all dogmatism is dying.[4]

Truth has proved elusive, has refused to be gotten hold of, has escaped. Woman, on the other hand, has not. Man has got woman. Because man has mastered woman, has mastered the art of mastering woman, Nietzsche can use that success to point to how men might also approach truth, supposing truth is a woman.

The simple statement, "Suppose truth is a woman," holds within itself all the ambiguities of Nietzsche's approach to women and to truth. It reveals that the two are intimately related. The nature of woman is at the heart of Nietzsche's philosophy. The nature of woman stands in for "truth," for the object of philosophical inquiry. To understand Nietzsche's question, one begins by supposing truth is a woman. Woman is not, then, something peripheral to the enterprise, and Nietzsche's comments on women cannot be placed in brackets apart from questions of his philosophy "as a whole." Nietzsche represents a break with philosophy as it was traditionally done, and the break is signified by "supposing truth is a woman." By this phrase Nietzsche places at the center of the philosophical enterprise the question of how one might approach truth. If one wishes to study dead butterflies, a pin to stick them onto the board is all that one needs. But if one wishes to study butterflies on the wing, a net and a certain degree of subtlety, of indirection, is essential. Nietzsche is after "truth on the wing," and therefore he supposes that truth is a woman. Nietzsche represents a new approach to the approaching of philosophy.

He arrives not a moment too soon. The dogmatists who have guided philosophy by their careful scrutiny of butterflies pinned with rational discourse to dead pages seem themselves to be dying. They have not caught truth. Therefore one begins again, rethinking what one was after and how one is to go about pinning it to the page. Nietzsche proclaims that it is "we *good Europeans* and free, *very* free spirits"[5] who seek with arrows and bows to pin down truth. And he begins with that which is both elusive, like truth, and yet has been pinned. He begins by supposing truth is a woman.

Nietzsche writes in the time of the triumph of patriarchy. He can suppose about truth using woman as his metaphor because woman is available for appropriation. Supposing truth is a woman carries—and denies—another text, a supposing that woman is Truth. *Sophia* is still behind the scenes, the possible divinity which stands in relationship to Nietzsche's critical analysis of patriarchal divinity. Yet *Sophia* is also still (and for as long as men's memory can reach) reduced to the being of man's appropriation, to the woman of patriarchal triumph. Truth is elusive, still the object of men's arrows but never quite pinned. Woman offers easier access, for she has been domesticated and limited, and hence provides a metaphor for successful appropriation which may be extended to truth.

Nietzsche stands in relationship to patriarchy which is, like everything about his thought, full of twists and turns. He is, in some sense, the last prophet of patriarchy. Like all prophets of the biblical tradition from which he emerges and resists, he both foretells the future and attempts to call that future back to its ancient premise. He recalls the past into the future, attempting to cast his claim beyond the limits of time by a call to a new morality, which is also ancient. He is the prophet of patriarchy. He is a prophet, condemning the slippage of meaning from the ancient values of conquest into contemporary moral decline (into the morality of the antagonist, the woman). He is the prophet of patriarchy, recalling its inner most meaning as a value in itself.

Supposing truth is a woman—what then? The phrase calls toward woman, speaking of her desirability as the metaphor of the longing toward truth. The dogmatists think they have her, yet they have failed. Their failure would suggest a new approach. What then? Perhaps the domestication of truth has weakened philosophy. Dogmatism domesticated truth with marriage, with the proper bedding of woman according to the norms and limits for her freedom established by the men. However, marriage does not quite accomplish its goals. It does not sufficiently possess. Nietzsche calls for, and foretells, and recalls, an alternative, beyond the limits of marriage—beyond the morality of good and evil. Beyond good and evil lies the strength of the conqueror, the will to power, the glory of the hunt. Therefore one must reexamine whether marriage really serves the purpose, whether dogmatism really got the woman, or if, by marriage, the woman got the man.

> The will to truth which will still tempt us to many a venture, that famous truthfulness of which all philosophers so far have spoken with respect—what questions has this will to truth not laid before us! What strange, wicked, questionable questions! That is a long story even now—and yet it seems as if it had scarcely begun. Is it any wonder that we should finally become suspicious, lose patience, and turn away impatiently? That we should finally learn from this Sphinx to ask questions, too? Who is it really that puts questions to us here? What in us really wants "truth"?[6]

Having supposed truth is a woman, the questions she raises are indeed strange and wicked. Where indeed do these mysterious questions arise? Why should we be patient with her queries? Nietzsche now proposes that we ask "about the value of this will. Suppose we want truth: why not rather untruth?"[7] The quotation from *Beyond Good and Evil* establishes a metaphoric link between woman and truth, and then proposes a turn away from truth, as the only way for men to regain charge of the enterprise. The prophet in Nietzsche recognizes that the conquest of values, by which man proclaimed himself master, has not yet succeeded, is even now in grave danger. The truth tempts him to a gentler, a weaker morality, a morality grounded in the desirability of truth and the domestication of woman, supposing truth is a woman. Therefore truth itself must be overthrown, in the name of another morality, another value, a value that belongs to men who will not be bound, even by their own desire. To desire is good, to be bound by that desire to the morality of that which one desires, is to lose the battle. Better to conquer and to take.

> For all the value that the true, the truthful, the selfless may deserve, it would still be possible that a higher and more fundamental value for life might have to be ascribed to deception, selfishness, and lust.[8]

The link implied in the metaphor still holds good. The turning away from truth, that still in the end might be what one is after, is a turning toward deception, selfishness, and lust. One wishes to turn away from the values implicit in the metaphor of truth as woman, while remaining always in relation to that from which one turns away. All this is to be done in the name of that which the prophet proclaims as the new philosophy, the new values, which nonetheless points back to the Greeks and their forefathers.

Nietzsche stands in essential relationship to the patriarchal project. He is dangerous, as dangerous to those for whom he speaks as to those against whom he speaks, because he makes explicit the patriarchal project. This is not the same as saying that Nietzsche is a misogynist, just as one can be a racist, can support and legitimate a racist structure without belonging to the Ku Klux Klan. Nietzsche's statements about women hint at the nature of his prophetic stance but are not the exclusive points of access. Rather, at every point in his philosophy Nietzsche proclaims the threat that women and what they represent pose to the triumph of "manly values." Nietzsche therefore gives access to the meaning of the triumph of patriarchy and suggests that which would be its reversal.

The construction of the image of woman in Nietzsche is subsumed under the social construction of her identity. Woman represents the alternative to patriarchy and to patriarchal values. Woman is not the ontological figure of woman as essence, the unchanging character of woman's self-relationship to her natural endowments. Nor is woman some specific woman borrowed from Nietzsche's personal history—perhaps his mother, his sister, or perhaps his lover. There may be something of each of these in Nietzsche's metaphors of the feminine. However, insofar as these ways of conceiving woman are seen as essential to Nietzsche, the comments on woman remain isolated, contradictory, and misunderstood. It is woman as symbolic as those set of values he wishes to destroy that unify his comments about women and place them at the center of his enterprise. Nietzsche resists all that woman represents historically.

Even now we are not accustomed to thinking of woman as constituting a social force in history. We are barely accustomed to thinking of her as existing in history at all, except as a marginal figure waiting in the wings for the historical action to end. Comments about women in philosophical texts are taken out of context by the philosophers themselves as well as by their interpreters. The dialectical structure of the antagonism between men and women, and how it informs history and the history of thought, is still not understood. Nietzsche understands the antagonism.

> To go wrong on the fundamental problem of "man and woman," to deny the most abysmal antagonism between them and the necessity of an eternally hostile tension, to dream perhaps of equal rights, equal education, equal claims and obligations—that is a typical sign of shallowness, and a thinker who has proved shallow in this dangerous place—shallow in his instinct—may be considered altogether suspicious, even more—betrayed, exposed: probably he will be too "short" for all fundamental questions of life, of the life yet to come, too, and incapable of attaining any depth.[9]

Woman stands for the course of resistance to men's projects that has existed and continued from the first construction of that project. To understand Nietzsche's conception of woman one must understand where he stands in the construction of the patriarchal project and how he saw women in relation to that project.

Our analysis of Nietzsche is thus both indebted and different from the current course of interpretation of Nietzsche's understanding of the feminine. Peter Burgard's collection of essays represents a good sampling of the new kind of thinking being done on the relation of the feminine to Nietzsche.[10] Some interpreters continue to see Nietzsche's misogynist commentary on women as only incidentally interesting. Others see Nietzsche's misogynism as so infusing the works so as to render them obsolete. Of more particular interest are very recent trends in Nietzschean scholarship which have begun to identify the excessive nature of his comments about women as demonstrative of a deeper methodology worthy of investigation.

> Woman is thus inscribed on both sides of an opposition fundamental to the tradition in philosophy that Nietzsche made it his life's work to question and go beyond. Through the association of the figure of woman with both sides of this hierarchically inscribed binary opposition, we might say that woman comes to be a figure of Nietzsche's subversion of that opposition as such. Nietzsche's irreducible ambivalence about woman would thus reinscribe itself as woman's subversive ambi-valence—an ambivalence that is crucial to his philosophical program.[11]

Burgard's term "ambi-valence" first of all suggests that Nietzsche is at least ambivalent about the essential nature of woman. But more than that, Nietzsche ascribes value to woman. But his ascription of value to woman is a subversive move, one that helps Nietzsche to further his attack upon philosophy. The examination of woman's value furthers Nietzsche's project of devaluation and revaluation of all Western values.

It is not that Nietzsche overtly identifies woman as the crucial player in the production of the new philosophy and the transvaluation of a new man. However, Nietzsche's excessive statements and hyperbole about woman provides a peculiar paradigm for transvaluation.

> Woman is inscribed in Nietzsche's first major articulation of the principle of excess—his formulation of the Dionysian principle—by way of the maenads, by way of the relation between Dionysus and Medusa, and perhaps also by way of his notion of woman's barbarity. And woman, variously equated with life, nature, truth, lie, music, wisdom, etc., constitutes the or at least a moment of excessive identity in his philosophy. More significantly, woman, as we saw in the case of truth and lie, can be held to figure the beyond of philosophy that Nietzsche seeks.[12]

Nietzsche's hyperbolic evaluation of woman gives the interpreter access to his way of thinking in general.

Burgard's collection concludes with essays by Bennett and Irigaray. What sets these essays apart from the essays that precede them is the way in which they see Nietzsche's comments about women as decisive both for Nietzsche and for women. Benjamin Bennett's essay "Bridge: Against Nothing" posits Nietzsche's thought as aiming at free revolutionary thought, a kind of revolution in which nothing is accomplished, and hence the most free of all. Revolution can only come from outside the established order. Revolution requires a qualitative break. Nietzsche provides just such a break, but this break goes nowhere; it is literally a "bridge against nothing." Bennett attempts to place Nietzsche's free revolution in conversation with feminist thought as a revolution in progress, or at least a possible revolution.

> For feminist thought is either revolutionary in the fullest sense, or pointless.[13]

The significant question posed by Bennett is whether feminism is capable of escaping its dependency upon the categories provided by the status quo. The question is whether the words of the old dead white men will continue to rule, even now when they are placed in the mouths of women. Because the circle of oppression is also the hermeneutical circle, the circle of meanings, texts, and methods that make thought possible, it would seem that Bennett's thesis must be that there is no hope for a genuine feminist revolution. Yet as Bennett points out, revolutions do indeed take place. There-fore, they must be possible.

Revolution is a kind of Archimedean point. It is a point that can move something that appears to be stationary and secure. In this case, it is the existing order, the status quo, which is to be moved by fundamental revolu-tion. The problem is how one is to begin, how one is to find that point outside the system, with a sufficient connection to the system, to activate the processes of change. The necessary gap between the status quo and the revolution is what makes a beginning unlikely.

> There is no need for revolutionary thought, no impetus, except where a positive value accrues to the degree of sheer differentness of its Else-where, which in turn, however, is exactly the degree to which the exis-tence of a usable bridge becomes improbable, hence the degree to which that Elsewhere, in the judgment of reasonable people, stands revealed as a Nowhere, a utopia.[14]

Because woman is both peripheral and central, she constitutes in Nietzsche's thought the Elsewhere from which might come a new point of departure. Bennett plays with the image of Elsewhere. The Elsewhere in theoretical physics is simply a negative statement, the limit the separates the space-time horizon from that which is beyond, about which nothing can be said. In Bennett's use of the term, the Elsewhere becomes a utopian vision of a future promise, though as yet unconceived. Clearly Nietzsche never intended the woman to play the role of the herald of the beyond, of the Elsewhere. Bennett can credit this possible role to feminists only because Nietzsche's conception of the new beginnings is so ambiguous.

> My point about later Nietzsche is that the text forms a kind of vortex. The qualified (male) reader, by the mere act of understanding, finds him-self irrevocably in a situation offering no possibility whatever of useful historical action or vision. This vortex, this ever inwardly self-gathering structure, is the only "place" defined by the texts. And the place of women (the unlimited room for women's fake but scrupulous use of the text as leverage for being and aiming Elsewhere) is simply everywhere or anywhere "else," everywhere outside of that self-centralizing readerly location.[15]

Women's exclusion from the audience of the text makes her the ideal revolutionary reader. She cannot participate in the structure of the intended argument because she is not a man. But a man cannot go beyond himself, for he is trapped by his own nature by being only man, just prior to that which comes next. His inclusion in the argument is his exclusion from its promise. Like Moses, the most he can achieve is the sight of the promised land. Woman's exclusion from the words of promise place her outside the limits. She is disqualified and therefore may take up her own position relative to Nietzsche's proclamation of revolution.

The intersection between Nietzsche's free revolutionary thought and the potential revolutionary thought of contemporary feminism is, from Bennett's perspective, an interesting point for examination. The problem, of course, is that feminist interpretation of Nietzsche is still interpretation and thus fails the test of radical otherness necessary for the vortex of revolutionary thinking. To be revolutionary, thought must be both interpretation and beyond interpretation. Luce Irigaray comes closest in Bennett's mind to satisfying both requirements. Irigaray does so because she does not attempt to interpret Nietzsche but rather to speak with Nietzsche as one who has already been excluded. Nietzsche's misogynism provides the precondition for Irigaray to become the disqualified revolutionary interpreter.

> Precisely the situation of being a qualified reader, a reader addressed by the text and in a position to understand it, denies one the possibility of making any reasonable historical use of one's understanding. The text therefore becomes useless, except perhaps, paradoxically, from the point of view of the disqualified reader, the reader who is excluded from the text's projected community of understanding, the reader whom the text never speaks to, but only about, which means the (or a) woman. Thus the relation of women to the Nietzschean text occurs at exactly that point where the text develops what I call its free revolutionary leverage.[16]

Irigaray is the disqualified reader because she speaks as a woman rather than as a spokesperson for women. She is the "I" that is excluded from participation in the subjectivity of Nietzsche's audience. Nietzsche's audience is so exclusively and intentionally male that there is no room for her to speak, for her to participate in the community of discourse set up by the text. The fact that she nonetheless speaks sets up an outside that breaks into the circle. This is an essentially revolutionary act. Bennett has a clear sense of the formal conditions of a feminist revolutionary discourse, but he is unable to give such discourse any content, or even to imagine how it might have content. This establishes Bennett's status as a qualified reader, well versed in the structure of revolutionary thought but incapable of conceiving anything beyond the bridge to nothing.

Luce Irigaray is Nietzsche's own, very own, revolutionary. Irigaray claims for herself the disqualification as her point of departure.

> But there it is, I am a woman. And who imagines that a woman is capable of thinking? Isn't this phenomenon beyond the ken of our tradition?[17]

Irigaray reaches out to touch Nietzsche where he chooses to be untouchable, his connection with women. But his connection with woman is hidden, disguised, and distorted by his commentary on women. Far from protecting him from Irigaray, it opens him to his own seduction. Nietzsche constructs his argument as a maze, but a maze designed for men. The twists and turns of the aphorisms are calculated to entangle man in a thicket of ideas and possibilities that forces him to go under himself. Nietzsche's disgust and contempt for the "other," and his need for there to be an "other" from which to turn away, prevents woman qua woman from entering into the maze. Yet his continual fascination with the subject of woman binds him to women and leaves him vulnerable to seduction.

> But of your contempt (I) shall make a thread to find my way back. In what you vomit up, (I) shall seek out what you're giving back to me. By interpreting your contempt, I shall find my skin again. Washing off the disguises of wretchedness.[18]

Irigaray is Nietzsche's marine lover, playing on the love of Zarathustra in the seven seals.

> If I am fond of the sea and of all that is of the sea's kind, and fondest when it angrily contradicts me; if that delight in searching which drives the sails toward the undiscovered is in me, if a seafarer's delight is in my delight; if ever my jubilation cried, "The coast has vanished, now the last chain has fallen from me; the boundless roars around me, far out glisten space and time; be of good cheer, old heart!" Oh, how should I not lust after eternity and after the nuptial ring of rings, the ring of recurrence?
> Never yet have I found the woman from whom I wanted children, unless it be this woman whom I love: for I love you, O eternity.
> *For I love you, O eternity!*[19]

Zarathustra loves that which contradicts him the most. But is that which contradicts him really "eternity"? Nietzsche invokes the feminine imagery, but rejects concrete woman, thereby making woman into something that cannot touch him. Irigaray dares to jump into the foaming sea, hearing the siren song, and becoming the contentious lover of the one who thinks he only wants the abstract love of the eternal.

Irigaray's conversation with Nietzsche violates Nietzsche's intention to exclude woman. Yet this violation of the taboo against woman's speaking is a revolutionary act that opens Nietzsche to a new possibility, one that he cannot conceive of without woman. What Irigaray finds in Nietzsche is the need for self-definition in the face of his denial of her identity. It is the point of exclusion that makes possible the best point of departure. Men who consider themselves sympathetic with women, positive in their evaluation of women in their thought, subsume women in their own thoughts and ideas, and hence render women invisible. Nietzsche, the great revolutionary, forces women to define themselves even against revolution.

So therefore she is unable to talk about herself as he does, without getting lost in the process. Illusion spun by the master to seize hold of her again in what she says. But, as master—and in every sense, non-sense, counter-meaning, double-meaning . . . —he cannot hear her. Can scarcely find anything to talk back to. Which sets things off again, thanks to a negation or denial. To the nth degree. The operation is always the same.[20]

Nietzsche's analysis of woman gives access to men's analysis of women. He reveals the interests of the master in all definitions of woman. In order to be, man negates woman. By negating woman, man creates himself, sui generis. Woman limits man, unless man can walk over and beyond her, can reach that divinity that is also male, also in denial, and must also be destroyed lest it limit man.

Nietzsche is the prophet of man's attempt to overcome himself, but the self he really seeks to overcome is woman. In all of this woman is unknown, except negatively, as limit. This limit self, this boundary, is what Irigaray claims and makes speak. The speaking is still and necessarily in terms of woman as that which Nietzsche has rejected, yet the very act of speaking so close to man opens up the possibility of the boundary as having being. Irigaray gets as close to Nietzsche as skin, removes the finery that hid her nature as the limit, and source, of man. Irigaray takes on the category of skin, of limit as woman in relation to man. As Nietzsche's own skin, she speaks back to him, and therefore uncovers the possibility of woman. This is a revolutionary possibility. It is a learning to speak that bridges the existence of woman as more than the other constructed by man's commentary. Yet it does so within the context of doing nothing more than speaking with a man, within the circle created by men's meanings.

Irigaray's participation in the event of Nietzsche's construction of meaning breaks loose from the silence imposed by men upon woman. A woman speaks. This is no small event! The speaking presents the possibility of woman, as an ontology, a givenness-in-possibility. Nietzsche remains intact, though a possibility that is other than what the text delimited is presented. Irigaray sings a song of the sea, of Nietzsche's lover who both is and is not within the text. She is the revolution in interpretation. She represents feminist interpretation by not speaking for or about feminist interpretation, but as a woman (I) who already preexisted her own speaking in Nietzsche's speaking. The circularity of interpretation is maintained, but with a new player.

The revolution that Irigaray represents is in relation to Nietzsche as a revolutionary thinker. Yet the nature of revolution that he offers remains unexamined and off-limits for appropriation. It is a revolution that might be claimed, but its claiming is always disastrous, as in the nazi appropriation of Nietzsche. Nietzsche's revolution, as Bennett points out, is a revolution to nothing. It does not lead anywhere. The text mimics all the movements of transformation, but it does not transform. Irigaray's interpretation spirals inward on the transformation, in a way that opens the text inward for woman, but here also it is not clear that the bridge can lead anywhere for women. Nor should it. Her exercise is a recognition of the power of women to move into texts that have been closed off from women. This is liberating. It lays down an example that can be followed of woman thinking as woman. But because the subject is Nietzsche, the path cannot lead anywhere, for Nietzsche has constructed his text to lead no where. He is a bridge to no where, and thus all transformation within turns back from the edge of the abyss. The lover of Nietzsche is the abyss, but that abyss is still limit.

It is curious that Bennett terms Nietzsche's text the text of "free revolutionary leverage," for the text in fact acts to turn back revolution. The freedom is also a lack of content that promises everything and begins nothing. The bridge is described as, in a certain sense, done, but no beginning is made. The gap between what is, and what is beyond, remains. We are called beyond, called to abandon an order too limited, but the new never emerges. Perhaps this is because Nietzsche himself is bound like the prophets before him to this side of the promise. Or perhaps, and this, too, is like past prophets, the call is not forward, but back.

Back to what? To understand what is to be recovered, one must first understand what Nietzsche's text proclaims as lost. Europe is asleep, and called to wakefulness.

> Let us not be ungrateful to it, although it must certainly be conceded that the worst, most durable, and most dangerous of all errors so far was a dogmatist's error—namely, Plato's invention of the pure spirit and the good as such. But now that it is overcome, now that Europe is breathing freely again after this nightmare and at least can enjoy a healthier—sleep, we, whose task is wakefulness itself, are the heirs of all that strength which has been fostered by the fight against this error.[21]

Nietzsche's audience, the "we," is called to wakefulness. "We" are called to fight against the error. The identification of the "we" also is the identity of the task and of the error.

Irigaray enters the text as the disqualified "I" of a small note on Nietzsche's "truths" about women. The text identifies itself apart from the other, by the "I" and equally by a "we." To be drawn into Nietzsche's argument is to be drawn into an elite group, the we. We are his audience and his protagonist in the revolution. This we is to be separated from all women and many men. These others, the herd, the mob, the small men—the women being both included in this group and excluded even here—are those who are to be left behind. It is to "us" that the "free" revolution is dedicated.

The "we" relates to the "I" in that both stand in relation to the power to command. The I of Nietzsche's analysis assumes a community, which covers over the duplicity necessary to command. The I wills that someone obey, even if the only someone who is available to be ruled is the same, in some sense, as the ruler.

> That which is termed "freedom of the will" is essentially the affect of superiority in relation to him who must obey: "I am free, 'he' must obey"— this consciousness is inherent in every will; and equally so the straining of the attention, the straight look that fixes itself exclusively on one aim, the unconditional evaluation that "this and nothing else is necessary now," the inward certainty that obedience will be rendered—and whatever else belongs to the position of the commander. A man who wills commands something within himself that renders obedience, or that he believes renders obedience.[22]

Such an analysis identifies above all that which is to be desired in being an "I" with the power to command others. For Nietzsche, the hierarchy has become so internalized that it is the source of identity itself. To be one must be at the top of some heap; there must be that which is under.

The revolution to be proposed is one that is grounded in the perpetuation, or perhaps the return, of the hierarchical order. Usually one assumes that a revolution would be a toppling of an order, a removal of those who are at the top by some group, presumably closer to the bottom. This is a revolution that is to place those at the top on the top. It is no new group that is to be given, or to take power, rather those who are strongest, those who command are called—to command.

This is the revolution of the established order, seeking to establish itself as an order. Such a revolution is not a revolution, but a call to arms in the face of an enemy that is not willing to fight. The real problem is not the "other," but the ones in charge, the ones in power. The powerful have lost their will to fight; they have become soft and meek. Nietzsche calls for a renewed attack on the powerless by the powerful. The powerless pose a threat to all that is most strong. This is what Nietzsche worries about the most, that the essential warlike values that underlie Western culture may be lost. Nietzsche fears that the powerless might win (indeed that they may have already won) without lifting a hand. The powerless may win because the battle may end, and when it ends, there is no place for the strong and no value to strength.

The weak must be destroyed, lest they win. The weak have the capacity to win by the sheer weight of their passivity. Weakness can win by the pity of the strong who stop killing them. But even this is to give the herd too much credit. The powerful lose if the vanquished cease to resist. To be victorious the strong must not lose their fighting edge. They must not lose what has made man great, which is the resistance against the "other."

We opposite men, having opened our eyes and conscience to the question where and how the plant "man" has so far grown most vigorously to a height—we think that this has happened every time under the opposite conditions, that to this end the dangerousness of his situation must first grow to the point of his enormity, his power of invention and simulation (his "spirit") had to develop under prolonged pressure and constraint into refinement and audacity, his life-will had to be enhanced into an unconditional power-will.[23]

The free spirits are called to resist weakness and the complacency that comes with victory. There is no revolution against the established order, but rather a preservation of the established order as the victorious order. The strong stand in danger of being vanquished by their own victory, by the lack of something to conquer. Their victory has removed the "other" from the status of competition. Once removed, there is nothing left to fight. Where there is nothing to fight, the strong cannot win. Where there is nothing to fight, the strong become weak. Nietzsche, the "revolutionary," must by force of will turn the vanquished into an ever-present danger to be subjugated again and again. Nietzsche wants to establish the weak as something strong enough to be worthy of being conquered.

There once was a time when it was possible to conquer and to be victorious. The power of the victors was their capacity to establish the meaning of the good and the noble opposition of evil. These were the self-conscious creators of value, the evaluators, who serve as the paradigm for the will to power.

I found that they all led back to the same conceptual transformation—that everywhere "noble," "aristocratic" in the social sense, is the basic concept from which "good" in the sense of "with aristocratic soul," "noble," "with a soul of a higher order," "with a privileged soul" necessarily developed: a development which always runs parallel with that other in which "common," "plebeian," "low" are finally transformed into the concept "bad."[24]

In former times, the full emphasis was on the strength to win, to come out on top, to be among the nobility. The moral quality of being noble was to be identified with a certain class, as over and against some "other" group. The basic question is this: How is it possible that those who were victorious (the strong) lost the battle of morality? Nietzsche testifies to the inversion of values as a profound threat to all that is noble and good in human affairs.

It was the Jews who, with awe-inspiring consistency, dared to invert the aristocratic value-equation (good = noble = powerful = beautiful = happy = beloved of God) and to hang on to this inversion with their teeth, the teeth of the most abysmal hatred (the hatred of impotence), saying "the wretched alone are the good; the poor, impotent, lowly alone are the good; the suffering, deprived, sick, ugly alone are pious, alone are blessed by God, blessedness is for them alone—and you, the powerful and noble, are on the contrary the evil, the cruel, the lustful, the insatiable, the godless to all eternity; and you shall be in all eternity the unblessed, accursed, and damned!"[25]

Nietzsche's attack on the Jews is infamous and easy to caricature. The question that always remains to be answered is why he chose the Jews as representative of the spirit of revenge. The Jews provide a historical occasion, for their identity as a people is purely accidental to their role in Nietzsche. Nietzsche identifies the Jews as spoilers of the grand battle of culture and value. The Jews are spoilers because their strength is in endurance and not in conquest. They survive; they will not die. Nietzsche's claim is that the noble must have an enemy to retain their fighting spirit. An enemy requires someone easily identifiable and someone whose values can be placed in opposition to one's own. What is so frightening about Nietzsche's choice of an enemy is that he targets those who are most vulnerable, those who are weakest. This is not an ontological statement about the nature of Jews, nor is it a racial statement. Rather, the identification of the Jews is based on historical circumstances that were created by anti-Semitism, expatriation, and the history of oppression. The fact that the Jews are oppressed in Nietzsche necessitates a value judgment, an evaluation of Judaism as such. For Nietzsche, slaves ought to be slaves and the independence of the slave's thought is a slap in the face of the master's morality. This for Nietzsche is what justifies a return to warfare between the two moralities. The goal is not to destroy the Jews but to elevate the master. The battle that was once won on the battlefield has yet to be won in the realm of the spirit.

Here is the horror that Nietzsche poses. It is a horror straight out of the nightmares of the strong. It is the revenge of the little creatures: the ants, the rabbits, the birds. Nietzsche is a genius at identifying the most powerless and reinterpreting their powerlessness as a threat. The threat is that the weak might yet rise and join forces against the strong. The very persistence of the conquered is a threat to the conqueror, and this the Jew symbolizes well. The Jews represent a threat to the mighty because their values have survived, because they do not forget. The strong conquer and conquer and conquer, but eventually they must cease conquering and go home to bed. While they sleep the nightmare begins. They have built a castle on the hill and held it against all comers, but their servants whisper as they serve. The hill itself slides away from beneath the mighty edifice, grain of sand by grain of sand. Like the myth of Sisyphus, the strong can push up their stones and build their castles, only to have the rocks tumble upon the morrow. Only the weak survive.

How could this be? How could it be that the strong, the noble, the aristocratic do not triumph? It is not a battle between might and right, for the mighty define the right. Nietzsche lumps them all together: the Jews, the slaves, the priests, the Christians, the women. Or, sometimes he plays them off against each other, so at one moment the Jews are the focus of his diatribes, while the next moment the Christians are.

> To be sure, whoever is himself merely a meager, tame domestic animal and knows only the needs of domestic animals (like our educated people of today, including the Christians of "educated" Christianity) has no cause for amazement or sorrow among these ruins—the taste for the Old Testament is a touchstone for "great" and "small"—perhaps he will find the New Testament, the book of grace, still rather more after his heart (it contains a lot of the real, tender, musty true-believer and small-soul smell). To have glued this New Testament, a kind of rococo of taste in every respect, to the Old Testament to make one book, as the "Bible," as "the book par excellence"—that is perhaps the greatest audacity and "sin against the spirit" that literary Europe has on its conscience.[26]

The real "sin" of all these oppressed groups is that they persist, and their persistence is a kind of spiritual success. The power of the strong is dissipated in the peace that comes between wars. The will to power cannot show itself nor find itself while at rest. The strong cannot simply survive; they must expend themselves, must will themselves to power against the odds. They need hardness. Without hardness they become soft. By their invisibility and their sheer numbers, the herds of little things of the world continually threaten to overcome the great. Nietzsche wants to make himself afraid of the little squirming things on the edges of his sight. He calls for vigilance. He alone of all the strong has recognized the perpetual cycle of the return of the "other."

Nietzsche's fear is also his cure. By naming and identifying the enemy, he perpetuates the battle and thus can hope to usher in a new era of will. The Jew is but a symbol of all those small men who must become the enemy, so that the strong may reestablish an order based on warfare. This model of warfare is not necessarily a physical call to arms but rather is paradigmatic of the will to power that undergirds all that Nietzsche considers great. What Nietzsche requires is not, in fact, war at all, but rather the constant threat of war and the will to wage that war.

The war takes place in the ambiguity of the victory of the strong. The strong have both won, yet they have also lost. The strong win yet are always in retreat. The weak lose, yet they always survive. Whose world is it? Nietzsche creates a fear of the small. Has not Christianity triumphed with its love of neighbor and pity for suffering? The values of Christianity seem to have won the battle over morality and values. Everywhere lip service is paid to equality of all before God and the triumph of love over hate. The weak, the small, the slaves win the peace that dominates the warlike. Even God falls to the small; the cross is hung in the sanctuary of the small, with nice Sunday smiles and nice Sunday hats. This mediocrity has become the measure of meaning.

Or, has the victory really gone to the crusaders, the militant missionaries, and the generals who offer prayers for victory in battle? The heart of Christianity is the worship of the great man, the man who is God, and the great men who become the fathers of the church, passing on their legacy of the call to greatness. Christianity, with its "family values," subjects all the weak to the father who dispenses justice and mercy as he wills. The morality by which the world operates looks very much like the will to power of the strong, even within the religion that claims love for the weak. The value system to which Nietzsche appeals is the value system that conquered the old world and then the new world. The morality granted to oppressed groups is more often used to keep them in their place, to placate them, and to keep them from gaining any power. The wars are won by the strong. The world is dominated by the strong.

To say the weak have won, or are in danger of winning, is too strong a statement. Even the very phrases that seem to proclaim the leveling implicit in equality come with a rider, the small print of domination. The preamble, "all men are created equal," has stood the test of time to provide the strong with the opportunity to oppress. Likewise, the *polis* has made all free men into masters. The order of the men who dominate has taken men into war, produced great leaders, and has ensured the divine right of those strong enough to hold rule. The two value systems coexist at every point and in every people that Nietzsche examines. The Jews, insofar as they symbolize the jealous God, and battle to establish his reign in a promised land, are worthy of admiration. But the need to justify that victory with a morality that valorizes the widow, the orphan, and the one in need undermines the self-consciousness of greatness which is the inheritance from the Jewish great men, the Jewish patriarchs. These values weakened them. So also for the Christians, the Greeks, the Germans, and so forth.

There is in every value system the values of the oppressor, the values of the great men who will to subjugate others. There is within, close indeed to the heart of the value system, another system of values that limits the extent of victory and contains the seeds for the victor's self-destruction. The winning is a triumph of might which defines the right. The promised land, manifest destiny, the nobility of free men, the gunslinger, the wild west, the last frontier, all honor greatness, all honor the daring who take what they desire. There is no system of values that is not the direct inheritance of the victory of the strong men and that is not centered around the admiration of strength, around the will to power. This is the other side of the truth about values. Nietzsche's call to the strong men, the new men, the men who will be immoral is but the call of all times and all places by the father to his sons. "Go west, young man!" But the young men will only come if there is danger and reward. Where is the enemy? Where is the danger? Where is the reward that will rescue European man from his own sleepiness, will give him something to fight for?

> A new species of philosophers is coming up: I venture to baptize them with a name that is not free of danger. As I unriddle them, insofar as they allow themselves to be unriddled—for it belongs to their nature to want to remain riddles at some point—these philosophers of the future may have a right—it might also be a wrong—to be called attempters. This name itself is in the end a mere attempt and, if you will, a temptation.[27]

To win is to be tempted to establish an order. Somehow the new species must find a way to perpetuate the revolution, to ensure that there is always a battle and that they climb up the hierarchy by means of climbing upon the bodies of their enemies.

For this purpose Nietzsche invents an enemy who cannot disappear, who will always be available for the best to detest. They are those who bend their back before the values of the conquerors, who, having lost nonetheless, are available to be conquered again. He poses them as if they were an opposing power to those who command, yet their "opposition" is the opposition of those who do not command but are commanded. The opposition Nietzsche requires has no power to oppose, yet they are to be commanded to take the role of the opponent. How does one transform these weak and unlikely enemies into something suitable for doing battle with the strongest?

This is the real substance of Nietzsche's will to power: to provide an enemy for the triumphant proponents of Western civilization. The emphasis upon the greatest as greatest in power is not new to Western philosophy. The emphasis on best, as that on top of the hierarchy of the lesser, is likewise not new to Western philosophy. What is new is to see the conquered as deserving to be conquered again. His contribution is to see that those who desire only peace and comfort for all are the genuine threat. And indeed they are, in a peculiar way, for they tempt the great away from greatness.

> What they would like to strive for with all their powers is the universal green-pasture happiness of the herd, with security, lack of danger, comfort, and an easier life for everyone; the two songs and doctrines which they repeat most often are "equality of rights" and "sympathy for all that suffers"— and suffering itself they take for something that must be abolished.[28]

The necessity of times of peace poses its own threat to all warring peoples. To the "attempters" it is disastrous. The revolution that Nietzsche would propose cannot be done (because war is inherently unstable), but must be done, if Western civilization is to survive. The strong always win, but thereby they lose unless there is another frontier. This is the story of civilization.

This is the story of whose civilization? Perhaps there are two stories of two civilizations. There have been many battles, and one would presume that the strong have won them all. Yet of everything they won, nothing remains. History has been written by the strong, and according to all their accounts, the strong have won. But everywhere it is the weak who continue. The Romans conquered and were conquered by their slaves who won the real battle, the spiritual battle, and called it Christianity.

> Modern men, obtuse to all Christian nomenclature, no longer feel the grue-some superlative that struck a classical taste in the paradoxical formula "god on the cross." Never yet and nowhere has there been an equal bold-ness in inversion, anything as horrible, questioning, and questionable as this formula: it promised a revaluation of all the values of antiquity.[29]

Always strength triumphs, if one can bring it to the battlefield, but the strong never win. The grass wins. The graves are covered. The old woman with a broom sweeps her hearth, sweeping away the ashes of the burning villages, putting her house in order again. Who is the winner?

Nietzsche's "new" vision is the same old nostalgia for an age of might, in which strength had some purpose. He proclaims the right of the strong man as above good and evil. More accurately, he identifies the strong man as the spring from which good and evil emerge. The new philosophers are beyond the current morality, depending on who defines it. Nietzsche's new values are the old values of conquest, but where are those who are to be con-quered? Can the weak resist?

What Nietzsche needs is not the arrogant young men who are drawn to him, with their secret fantasies, their coffeehouse prattle, or their SS uni-forms. Always there is a temptation to read Nietzsche directly, to wish to join the militia, to be the new philosophers, to identify with the images of strength and victory, to be the superhero "superman." Nietzsche's images appeal to the intrinsic longing for superiority that is so basic in patriarchal culture, a longing that entices all young men to leave their families, to leave the safety and security of their mothers, and follow him. Irony of ironies, to be a follower of Nietzsche, who desires leaders not followers! Irony of iro-nies, to look to Nietzsche to define the values that shall make them into the new philosophers! Even the nazis think that they have understood Nietzsche, irony of ironies! In the name of being great men, a few of them died and many of them killed. Strangely enough, they all look alike, and none of them is responsible enough to be tragic. How could something so banal, so bureaucratic, and dependent upon clerks be Nietzsche's new strong men?

What Nietzsche needs are those with sufficient strength to withstand him, even him (or perhaps especially him). What he needs are not the new philosophers, but those who are sufficiently strong to stand against what he proposes. Shall we call these the old philosophers? Older even than the order of the sword? Shall we call these the ones who are not yet? What Nietzsche wants and needs is something that will surprise him, that will break open the confines of smallness, even (or perhaps especially) the smallness of great men. Nietzsche needs that which he desires least: the response of the small, the weak, the feminine.

Nietzsche's patriarchal commitment is central to his project. Without taking seriously Nietzsche's antagonism to woman, everyone becomes the potentially new philosopher, even women. Everyone reads themselves into the revolution, and, because the revolution is fundamentally based on the root metaphors of Western civilization, everyone has already accomplished that which Nietzsche found so difficult. For the great to emerge there must be that which it opposes. Who is Nietzsche to oppose? The gods are gone. Who is great enough to provide the bridge, or perhaps the gap, that can make it possible to go to an-other side? Whereas Nietzsche despises a variety of groups for their smallness and weakness, only women are rejected on the basis of any strength they could exhibit. No woman could be Nietzsche's great philosopher!

Nietzsche's praise of women is as misogynist as his attacks against women. Yet his hatred of women, like all strong passions, is subject to reversal. That which Nietzsche hates in women is also what he needs. Only woman can offer the kind of absolute opposition that will not fail Nietzsche in the end. Woman's resistance to that which Nietzsche proposes is dependable. He needs opposition, but he needs opposition that cannot be collapsed into his own analysis. The ones who are to come must not be tainted by Nietzsche's own limitations, even his images of greatness. The new must come from an unexpected direction. Nietzsche's misogynism holds open a place for the entry of the new. Only that which has been excluded can serve as a point of entry for the qualitatively new.

Nietzsche invites reversal. This particular reversal assumes Nietzsche's own analysis but places it in the context of a subverse within the overt intentionality of the text. Nietzsche's misogynist comments on women serve as a clue that can lead into an alternative interpretation of the meaning of smallness, greatness, and the creativity of the new. The analysis and the pursuit of that which opposes any particular value is at the center of Nietzsche's search for the transvaluation of all values. To oppose Nietzsche as deeply and thoroughly as one can is to align oneself with the heart of Nietzsche.

For to join Nietzsche is to seek to overturn everything, even Nietzsche himself. Nietzsche loves his enemies more than his friends. Nietzsche's nihilism requires all values to be inverted, even his own.

What Nietzsche needs is a good woman. Of course, it is not quite clear what a good woman would be. Nietzsche's conventional wisdom about good women requires inversion. Irigaray comes to Nietzsche from behind, or perhaps from within. She emerges out of a metaphor, not the metaphor Nietzsche created and called woman, but a more embracing metaphor, the metaphor of the sea. The metaphor of the sea provides an alternative access to the ontological otherness of woman, which is as close to man as his own skin. Hers is an inverted otherness, enclosing and encompassing man in what is almost himself.

Nietzsche desires woman as the ontological other, and in this way Irigaray answers in her concreteness as woman that is also an ontological reply. She answers him as one, as the one great enough to reply. If ever there was someone with sufficient strength to exhibit the will to power, it would be Irigaray. Her will to power demonstrates her independence from Nietzsche. She masters Nietzsche's text. Irigaray is both woman and the overcoming of woman. She is a new species of woman, perhaps. She is also a new species of great man by virtue of being a woman. Irigaray is both Nietzsche's own and Nietzsche's other.

Irigaray is the disqualified reader. Irigaray is also the lover Nietzsche seeks when he turns to the sea. She is the one who opposes the great man that is Nietzsche and thus comes into identity with the great man that Nietzsche desires. Her ability to satisfy Nietzsche's requirements makes it clear that she is not really the opposition that Nietzsche seeks. Her antagonism is ontological and personal without answering the question of whether feminism or feminists might be the new species, the new philosophers, the way into the as yet unconceived future. She answers the need Nietzsche already has by giving him the sea, a depth capable of addressing his longing, capable of answering back.

A good love affair between Nietzsche and the sea might well solve Nietzsche's problem, but perhaps this is a problem that one might wish to have intensified and inverted rather than resolved. Nietzsche appeals to the lure of the new, of the as yet undreamed future. The terms of the dream are corrupted by old blood. Nietzsche's dream of the new is just as much a nostalgia for the good old days when men were men and women were something to be won from dragons and dragged home by the hair. He wants the new, but he also really wants men to wake up and become real men (who don't eat quiche). Irigaray clearly understands man's antagonism to woman, but she has simply broadened the categories of greatness to include women rather than challenge them. What is needed is a little conversation with the kitchen.

What echoes through Nietzsche is the most ancient of wars, the war hidden in the war between the sexes. Within the hidden history of man's triumph there is an enemy too close to him to be named. This enemy both is, and is not, woman. Woman symbolizes a system of value that might infect men: the effeminate. She is the enemy because she symbolizes and supports all that is small. She is what makes man all-too-human. But woman is also not the final enemy. She is able to duplicate and embody (as Irigaray illustrates) all the same values that a man can. Yet there remains a strange association with the word "woman." She is the one who humanizes man and holds him to the earth.

Nietzsche treats the battle as to the death and as of immediate threat. This is, perhaps, rooted in his own need to create a present danger of sufficient magnitude to draw out the great men. These men sleep and must be awakened. The great men will only come forth if they perceive a threat. Therefore Nietzsche must exaggerate the danger, must create a threat, must make a call to arms. Nietzsche is the prophet and the propagandist of the old warriors who have grown weary and sleepy with the coming of peace. He is the prophet who must bring to anger and response another generation who has forgotten. More than that, he is the prophet who would call forth the last warriors, the ones who can fight the battle on spiritual terms, in terms of values, and win the decisive war that will usher in the new age of man.

Nietzsche has, therefore, attempted to craft an image of danger that is perhaps not quite real. Men's victories continue. There is no ceasing of warfare anywhere in the world. The world continues to measure greatness in terms of the accomplishments of great men, while those "others" remain "anonymous." Everywhere men rule, by might and by force of will. There are exceptions, of course, but the exceptions enforce the rule. Women even sometimes triumph against the odds, but they do so within an establishment dominated and determined by men. They are exceptional, and their status of being exceptional qualifies them as men of a sort. Not surprisingly, their advent seldom means much for women-in-general, or for any of the other "small" men, the minorities created in the wake of man's victories.

Irigaray, breaker of the mold, writes in her own voice; she writes as a woman and lets her womanliness be a voice in her writing. But she does not threaten, in any real sense, the domination of men and "great men." Her uniqueness guarantees no spill over, no change in the existing order of men's speaking. She is quite qualified to be Nietzsche's lover, for she speaks only by virtue of her will which is strong enough to satisfy even Nietzsche. She also fits the pattern of genius, willing so greatly that by her will she can change the meaning of the world. She is that one to whom Nietzsche calls, but in so doing Nietzsche is not yet confronted. The one who is needed is the old woman with the broom.

> There was an old woman tossed in a blanket
>   Seventeen times as high as the moon.
> But where she is going no mortal could tell,
>   For under her arm she carried a broom.
> "Old woman, old woman, old woman," said I.
> "Whither, ah whither, ah whither so high?"
> "To sweep the cobwebs from the sky,
> And I'll be with you by and by."[30]

She has no name. She has no greatness about her at all, for all she knows is the cobwebs in the corner, "and I'll be with you by and by." She sweeps the dust that lies over the graves of the great. She, and those like her, have been raped by the great, borne their sons, even mourned them when their days of greatness are over. To her, however, the fact that they were great is not as important as the attempt to save a story to tell the grandchild. Yet her stories, like her life, are of trivial things. It is nonetheless she who threatens Nietzsche, by the humbleness of her will which persists in powerlessness.

Perhaps Nietzsche has met this old woman, though she must have left her broom at home. Zarathustra spoke to her about women.

> When I went on my way today, alone, at the hour when the sun goes down, I met a little old woman who spoke thus to my soul: "Much has Zarathustra spoken to us women too; but never did he speak to us about woman." And I answered her: "About woman one should speak only to men." Then she said: "Speak to me too of woman; I am old enough to forget it immediately." And I obliged the little old woman and I spoke to her thus . . .[31]

She tempts him into speaking to her about "woman." Zarathustra would rather not. He prefers to speak of woman in locker rooms and board rooms, where women are excluded. There men can really speak about woman. But she is only a little old woman, who can scarcely pose a problem for a man, being no longer capable of being impregnated nor of being something desirable to men, and she claims a short memory unusual among grandmothers. So he is tempted into making many statements, all of which reduce to the usual ways in which men think of women, as something for them. They are all true, and the old woman lets them be, but the old woman has something to add. If men mean to have woman, if woman is something to be had—and this is not yet impossible—then men had better bring the whip.

> 'And now, as a token of gratitude, accept a little truth. After all, I am old enough for it. Wrap it up and hold your hand over its mouth: else it will cry overloudly, this little truth.'
> "Then I said: 'Woman, give me your little truth.' And thus spoke the little old woman:

"'You are going to women? Do not forget the whip!'"
Thus spoke Zarathustra.[32]

Old women seldom forget, but philosophers have seldom taken their memories or their presence very seriously. She always remembers, unless she has learned to forget with age and prudence. She will die over and over again, sometimes at the hands of Nietzsche's great men. But she always returns. Great men come and go, but there is always an old woman with her broom and her tales. And where she is going, no mortal could tell. The idea of Nietzsche being afraid of an old woman in a nursery rhyme is ridiculous. She is soft and weak and small. Yet she is the corrupting influence, because it is her stories that the young boys hear first. Her stories console them, reconcile them to a world as she finds it. Even her dreams are soft. She lacks rigor. She and the moon together turn men into lunatics, sappy, sentimental, souls. It is she who man must resist to become a man. But there is something unrelenting in her sweeping, some promise that the meek may inherit the earth, no matter how loudly the clarions of war are sounded.

The threat of the old woman with the broom echoes an ancient rumor of another kind of wisdom, of a time when truth was a woman. She was there before the soldiers came. The soldiers erased the old names, the old divinities she served. The Gods of thunder married or raped or disemboweled the old Goddesses, took over their texts, scraped clean the names, and changed the values. All that remains is an old woman who sweeps the cobwebs under the moonlight. This domination marked the first inversion of value, from the old value that honored the creativity that was integrated into the ordinary to a value system that identified creativity with the elite, the men with names. The new robbed the birthright of the old, dominating the weak by force of arms and strength of will. The strong have proclaimed another truth than the old one of the people. Each of the conquerors has a name. They write their names in stone, the graffiti of conquerors who must borrow their scribes from the poets of old times. They have won the battles, transformed the world into the world of men, into their own image. Why then are they so afraid?

But the slaves could not be kept silent, and their morality somehow survived with them, even in captivity. It grew stronger and intensified in its *ressentiment*. This slave morality came to shape from within religion. Weakness and the effeminate returned in the guise of religion. How could the weak and the slave morality have triumphed over so great and powerful an enemy?

Nietzsche proposes an inversion of value, as if the victory must be won again. Perhaps it must be done again. Perhaps they are right to be afraid. Perhaps not all of Nietzsche's despair is a posturing for the benefit of the as yet unborn great men. At the end of every parade, an old woman with a broom follows and sweeps. The nursery rhyme and the fairy tale always turn round again. There is a whisper that the imposition of the values of the great men of Western civilization is crumbling. In the excitement of war, the old woman is overlooked, but that does not mean she has been overcome. The old warrior rests upon the stoop while the old woman sweeps. Or perhaps she rocks by the fire, spinning a tale that is older than war. Grass comes to cover the graves.

There is in Nietzsche no remembrance of the time before history from which these other values emerge. Yet there is a strange romantic nostalgia for that time before time, as if he almost remembers, or is afraid he might remember. Is Nietzsche afraid he might remember? His amnesia covers the origins of the slave's morality that seems to spring from nowhere. The *ressentiment* of the slaves produces a morality so complete and so threatening that it suggests that there is more to know than their simple disconsolation. It is as if they remember that they were once not slaves, and they resent their masters.

> The slave revolt in morality begins when *ressentiment* itself becomes creative and gives birth to values: the *ressentiment* of natures that are denied the true reaction, that of deeds, and compensate themselves with an imaginary revenge. While every noble morality develops from a triumphant affirmation of itself, slave morality from the outset says No to what is "outside," what is "different," what is "not itself"; and this No is its creative deed.[33]

How curious that the will to power, the will to give birth to value, should so continually reassert itself among those whose will is of the lowest sort! Does not this will also demand some examination, some explanation, some origin sufficient to make possible the centuries of resistance to the will to power? Suppose truth is a woman, then perhaps she, and all her kind, have indeed something to hide. Suppose truth was a late name for another woman, a woman named *Sophia*, a woman of wisdom, an old woman who remembers, a witch who remembers.

The oldest memory men have is the memory of forgetting. Always things turn back toward the suppressed memory. There is that in slaves which rebels against mastery, even when they know nothing else. The great build their empires upon the sand of their own forgetting. The building, even Nietzsche's own building, suffers from a great weariness. They build and they build, but they do not understand why it keeps falling apart. They do not remember the old bones buried under the walls. Only the greatest expenditure of energy, bones, and will can serve as a foundation for a building that must always be built anew. And don't forget the whip! The victors do not remember why the building is so tentative. It is necessary for the victors to gather courage and anger, over and over again, to build on foundations that are forever crumbling.

What has been is what will be,
and what has been done is what will be done;
and there is nothing new under the sun.
Is there a thing of which it is said,
"See, this is new"?
It has been already,
in the ages before us.
There is no remembrance of former things,
nor will there be any remembrance
of later things yet to happen
among those who come after.

(Eccles. 1:9–11)

There is a weariness to forgetting. Each accomplishment falls into the hole of its own denial, of a past that has been forgotten. Always the same returns, but what is the same? The great do not return, for their greatness is the result of great effort, of achievement against sameness. What returns is the ordinary and the everyday, with its echoes of a past in which honor was held in common, and the old woman who swept is another name for the goddess. What returns is the same, the continuity of value and meaning in the small things: a sunny day, a green garden, a sleeping kitten. History itself is a rebellion against the ordinary continuity of human existence. The record of wars and the technological evolution of conquest is written over the text of human existence. It is this text beneath men's text that always returns, and it is a weariness to his flesh. History is the determination of old dead white men not to disappear into their own forgetfulness. But there is no remembrance. What they have accomplished has already been done, in the times they have forgotten.

Man forgets as part of the erasure, to ensure a blank slate upon which to write his will. But the effort of forgetting also endangers his own project. There is the danger that his own deeds will also be forgotten. His own act of forgetting reveals that he is dependent upon those who come later, who may also choose to forget him.

I met a traveler from an antique land,
Who said—"Two vast and trunkless legs of stone
Stand in the desert . . . Near them, on the sand,
Half sunk a shattered visage lies, whose frown,
And wrinkled lip, and sneer of cold command,
Tell that its sculptor well those passions read
Which yet survive, stamped on these lifeless things,
The hand that mocked them, and the heart that fed;
And on the pedestal, these words appear:
My name is Ozymandias, King of Kings,
Look on my Works, ye Mighty, and despair!

Nothing beside remains. Round the decay
Of that colossal Wreck, boundless and bare
The lone and level sands stretch far away.[34]

This makes him most vulnerable at the height of his power, when he has achieved that which should assure his immortality. Man has too much power, for the power to forget others is the power also to be forgotten.

The fact that man has the capacity to erase humanity's own origins threatens him, because he recognizes that his own act might also be forgotten. If the origins of human thought can be forgotten, how much more transitory are the momentary victories of a single individual will? There is something that is remembered. Perhaps it is that there was something before. Perhaps it is that there is something one wishes not to remember. Or perhaps it is just a weariness when it comes to remembering. The human project of meaning is rotten to the core with suppressed memory. To this suppression it must always return. And equally, the same returns to man. The value system that Nietzsche must invert will forever return, as long as man is man.

Before there was history, there was that which was forgotten. Before truth there was wisdom. Before the gods there were their mothers. Before man wrote his deeds in stone, there was an old woman sweeping under the moon. We hear an echo, a whisper in the dark. We dream. The whisper is even heard in the corners of Nietzsche—there is something that will return. The time is gone, forgotten. The shape of the forgetting and the shape of the resistance give hints. Man's history is the history of wars and triumphs, of great men and their imposition of sky gods who were warriors like themselves, of the oppression of peoples who came to be their subjects.

Nietzsche is a prophet of those ancient, conquering divinities. Speaking in the age of the death of all those gods, Nietzsche offers a way of understanding that ancient emergence of man's history. By his understanding of man's triumphs, Nietzsche hints at what it triumphs over. The reality of the victory is dependent on the reality of that which was conquered. Nietzsche clarifies the nature of that ancient struggle, that it was essentially a battle of values, of ways of willing, of men who would be great against civilizations that did not value greatness in individuals. The importance of Nietzsche's project is its recognition that the battle did exist, that it was real, and that it has not yet been finished. The loss of memory, which is an attempt to erase the alternative, has not prevented the alternative from continually reemerging. Nietzsche's devaluation of that return testifies to his recognition, and his fear, of its persistence. Instead the loss holds open the possibility of return as long as old women sweep the dust behind the victories. There is a power greater than the will to power, the will to return.

Thus Nietzsche must hope, not merely for the will to power, but for the emergence of a new man. Man is not strong enough to overcome the ordinary.

He is not strong enough to overcome the old woman sweeping the steps. Nietzsche himself recognizes the impossibility of the task of overcoming that which is ordinary in man himself. Man is of the herd and cannot escape his own nature and limitations. More than that, he cannot escape his own history. All forgetting is tentative, as tentative as memory itself. Only when man has been erased will the past be overcome. Only when man has been overcome will there be the possibility of something qualitatively new, something untainted by that ancient shadow.

The despair at the prospect of the return can only be cured by total annihilation of the same. But this is total annihilation of man himself. The integrity of Nietzsche's nihilism leads to his sense of despair at the lack of a possibility of transvaluation and transformation. All men, in their true manliness, will the apocalypse, will the violent end of the world as the revelation and the new beginning. It is the sign of the herd to be content with that which is still possible for human beings. The last man lasts the longest. Zarathustra proclaims: "The earth has become small, and on it hops the last man, who makes everything small. His race is as ineradicable as the flea-beetle; the last man lives longest."[35] Nietzsche's nemesis is the last man. The last man brings despair to Zarathustra because he no longer despises himself.

> Alas, the time is coming when man will no longer give birth to a star. Alas, the time of the most despicable man is coming, he that is no longer able to despise himself. Behold, I show you the *last man*.[36]

The last man is content to be small, content to be simply what he is. He wills no one's annihilation; certainly not his own. Because he does not want to die, nor to kill, he lacks the manly virtues. The last man does not will annihilation and thus cannot will transcendence and the new being.

The great men must always beat the herd to get it to move, and don't forget the whip! Zarathustra the prophet is an example of such a great man. He is the prophet of that which can come next, but he is therefore also the prophet of the annihilation of what is. He stands in a long line of prophets who despise the comfort of those to whom they speak and who offer consolation only when their people are in the midst of destruction. The consolation that they offer is that there is something that will come after. The great men recognize that out of the destruction something new might arise, and for that "something" they are willing to risk everything.

> You higher men, learn this from me: in the market place nobody believes in higher men. And if you want to speak there, very well! But the mob blinks: "We are all equal."
> "You higher men"—thus blinks the mob—"there are no higher men, we are all equal, man is man; before God we are all equal."
> Before God! But now this god has died. And before the mob we do not want to be equal. You higher men, go away from the market place![37]

The higher men must depart from the marketplace, where ordinary men scurry about their business with small words and small smiles, earning their daily bread. The great men, the higher men, are the ones who are committed to hierarchical ranking (because only thus can they be on top). These are the ones who long to climb still higher. But to climb higher, they must destroy.

> With your values and words of good and evil you do violence when you value; and this is your hidden love and the splendor and trembling and overflowing of your soul. But a more violent force and a new overcoming grow out of your values and break egg and eggshell.
>
> And whoever must be a creator in good and evil, verily, he must first be an annihilator and break values. Thus the highest evil belongs to the highest goodness: but this is creative.[38]

The promise that is the lure to the higher men is the promise of yet new heights, the promise that out of the violence comes creation. But the will to do violence, to destroy, is the essential prerequisite, the test of whether one is strong enough to be a higher man. Such a destruction and a will to destroy, even oneself, is possible because of the secret fear of the higher man, that he may in fact still not be high enough. The higher man is a dare, a dare to prove that one is not a small man. To pass this test requires the will to do violence, to destroy the small man, even oneself; to will, at all costs, the one who comes next. The higher man must destroy himself to bring on the new. Out of the nausea at the small, even the smallness of himself, comes the will to go beyond. This nausea is a kind of sinfulness that can only be washed in blood, in the annihilation of all values that do not proclaim that which is over, that which is beyond, that which is higher even than the higher man. The hierarchy promises something more, something that has not yet been thought, something worth risking everything for in order to be a bridge that goes on, beyond God, beyond man.

> Before God! But now this god has died. You higher men, this god was your greatest danger. It is only since he lies in his tomb that you have been resurrected. Only now the great noon comes; only now the higher man becomes—lord.
>
> Have you understood this word, O my brothers? You are startled? Do your hearts become giddy? Does the abyss yawn before you? Does the hellhound howl at you? Well then, you higher men! Only now is the mountain of man's future in labor. God died: now *we* want the overman to live.[39]

Zarathustra suggests three shades of man's being: there is the small man, the higher man, and the *Übermensch*. But the higher man is but a higher form of the small man. The small man is too much like a woman. Man (*mensch*) is a generic that includes male and female in its inclusiveness.

The goal, which is both man and beyond man, is the *Übermensch*, the over-man who has overcome the womanly in man. The *Übermensch* is the one who is beyond the abyss, the gap. He is the one who overcomes the empti-ness that is within man because he is also woman. He is the possibility of man as purified, man as he always meant himself to be insofar as he willed himself to be manly.

This *Übermensch* is a strange half-thought idea, which has been subject to so much confusion, intentional and otherwise. Those who claim Nietzsche for the nazis do so on the basis of an understanding and profound misunder-standing of the *Übermensch*. The nazi claiming of the *Übermensch* for them-selves truncates the dream, limiting the promise to this side of the bridge. It is not the violence of the nazis that separates them from Nietzsche but the smallness of their vision. They did not will to overcome themselves. The violence did not reach deep enough; it was not sufficiently apocalyptic; too much was preserved. One does not need to assume that Nietzsche would mourn the horrible suffering, the intention to commit genocide, to be confi-dent that Nietzsche would reject the nazis. Their vision ultimately commit-ted them to yet another smallness, a triumph of bookkeepers.

Dare one even translate *Übermensch* into English? There are a multitude of images of "supermen" in English; any translation runs into the smallness of the dreams of power that undergird even our fantasies. Superman has been claimed by the comic strips: he wears red tights and flies in defense of truth and justice. Yet there is also something to these images, for there is within man's history the longing for that which is more than man, a longing for the new creation that comes after the apocalypse.

The fascination with the apocalypse haunts the imagery of the *Thus Spoke Zarathustra*. His apocalypse no longer rests upon the promise of God, for even God has become too much of a limitation upon the aspirations of man.

> But let me reveal my heart to you entirely, my friends: *if* there were gods, how could I endure not to be a god! *Hence* there are no gods.[40]

Yet even so, the echoes of revelation and of the violence make clear who is who and what is what. Violence separates the men from the boys. More even than that, violence cleanses the earth, prepares the way to the new beginning, the new creation, the new heaven and the new earth, and the man who has escaped at last from his own uncertainty about who he is to be-come or where he is going. For where he has been, and what he now, is something that cannot be endured. Whatever the cost, man must overcome something in himself that he finds disgusting.

> What is womanish, what derives from the servile, and especially the mob hodgepodge: *that* would now become master of all human destiny. O nausea! Nausea! Nausea! *That* asks and asks and never grows weary: "How

is man to be preserved best, longest, and most agreeably?" With that—
they are the masters of today.

Overcome these masters of today, O my brothers—these small people,
they are the overman's greatest danger.[41]

The nausea is aimed at that in man that still clings to something "womanish," something that therefore cannot lead to the new species, a species of
man without the contamination of woman. Only by woman can the current
species continue, and that is its aim insofar as it is tied to the womanly.
Only by overcoming that of woman in man, a violent cleansing of what
leads to peace and comfort, can the *Übermensch* arrive. Only by overcoming that of woman in the species can man give birth to himself in a new
guise. The confidence that man has in the possibility of death leading to a
new life for man without woman comes to bear in the longing for the end
of time. Then man will go into the throes of birth, though the blood he
sheds will be the woman's, and at last he will beget what the first violence
promised: the son born solely of the father.

> And he who sat upon the throne said, "Behold, I make all things new."
> Also he said, "Write this, for these words are trustworthy and true." And
> he said to me, "It is done! I am the Alpha and the Omega, the beginning
> and the end. To the thirsty I will give water without price from the foun-
> tain of the water of life. He who conquers shall have this heritage, and I
> will be his God and he shall be my son. But as for the cowardly, the
> faithless, the polluted, as for the murderers, fornicators, sorcerers, idola-
> ters, and all liars, their lot shall be in the lake that burns with fire and
> brimstone, which is the second death." (Rev. 21:5–8)

From every war but that one, the earth can recover. All that is most manly,
most terrified by the smallness that overcomes even the greatest, longs for
the clarity of the end. Surely there is that one battle from which nothing can
be saved, in which the victor, because he has destroyed everything, can be
assured of victory. Man in his greatness longs for the holocaust. Only in
that great burning is there any final purity, for that end will burn away even
man. This is why men fight themselves when they plan their wars. Nietzsche,
with his other free spirits, must will nihilism, must will the death of values,
even the value of their own lives. Only when man is strong enough to will
the death of earth itself, of man himself, will the destruction be enough.
This is the final test of courage, of faith in man's ability to give birth by
death. This is the final test of man's god, of whether he is truly stronger
than life and death, whether there truly can be a creation out of nothing.
But this nothing is the nothing that is to be created out of man's will. God,
the great God the Father of all victories, needs man for this purpose, to will
the end of time, the end of man.

All that is manly wills death. All that is manly wills itself toward that which is other than itself. Man is both terrified and yet fascinated by that which is other. This is the only reason the world has survived even this long, because man does not quite will the final destruction. But also, because man does not quite dare, he does not quite dare think through what it is that he wills. *Thus Spoke Zarathustra* is not a simple call to arms, but a project of thought, an attempt to think through what it is toward which man aims. Zarathustra attempts the courage of the emptiness of all the values that he inherits, attempts to think beyond himself. Thus he is the prophet of oblivion, the peculiarly male oblivion that has walked with man since first he rose above woman by means of violence. Zarathustra is the prophet of all that is conceived in violence and that terminates in ultimate destruction.

However, it is not ultimate destruction that frightens Zarathustra, for he above all men is subject to the longing of the man above man/woman and is willing to risk all in the possibility. But in longing for that which is other than man, as that which is other than man and his gods, Zarathustra encounters the possibility that newness turns back into itself. Zarathustra encounters the fear that what comes next is what came first: the eternal recurrence of the same.

> And this slow spider, which crawls in the moonlight, and this moonlight itself, and I and you in the gateway, whispering together, whispering of eternal things—must not all of us have been there before? And return and walk in that other lane, out there, in this long dreadful lane—must we not eternally return?[42]

In the death of *mensch* is the possibility of man. In the death of inclusive humanity is man's hope of overcoming birth and his dependence on the female. But between man and his dream dwells the abyss, which mirrors back to man what he is and bids man to turn and look at where he came from. In his dream a serpent has bitten the man, perhaps the same serpent that spoke in an ancient garden. Man gags on his own sexuality and on knowledge of his sexuality. Only if he will bite off the head of his own being will he overcome himself. This is Zarathustra's greatest hope and greatest fear, that man's own sexuality will turn him back, as the snake of circular time that eats its own tail, from the new beginning.

Zarathustra despairs of the eternal return, longs only to overcome it, to gain the new. Yet his animals are not quite willing to let the eternal return sink into that which is to be passed by. They counsel Zarathustra on the reevaluation even of this. The problem is not the return, but the despair that dares not will even its own turning back, its own going under. Zarathustra must become the prophet of the eternal recurrence of the same. Zarathustra's animals speak:

For behold, Zarathustra, new lyres are needed for your new songs. Sing and overflow, O Zarathustra; cure your soul with new songs that you may bear your great destiny. For your animals know well, O Zarathustra, who you are and must become: behold, *you are the teacher of the eternal recurrence*—that is your destiny![43]

In turning back and proclaiming the return, Zarathustra breaks open the seven seals that have sealed man's way into the future. He finds his own "yes" and "amen," in the rediscovery of eternity, and with this woman Zarathustra can even come to birth. "For I love you, O eternity." At the heart of the return of the same is eternity, and eternity is also a woman. The turning of time over which man has sought to maintain his will brings him back face to face with that which he has willed in willing the other. This other is the face of the feminine, who always already waits beyond the return. This must man fight, but the fight is a lover's quarrel. That which is other than man, which comes before and meets him afterward, is woman.

If ever one breath came to me of the creative breath and of that heavenly need that constrains even accidents to dance star-dances; if I ever laughed the laughter of creative lightning which is followed obediently but grumblingly by the long thunder of the deed; if I ever played dice with gods at the gods' table, the earth, till the earth quaked and burst and snorted up floods of fire—for the earth is a table for gods and trembles with creative new words and gods' throws: Oh, how should I not lust after eternity and after the nuptial ring of rings, the ring of recurrence?

Never yet have I found the woman from whom I wanted children, unless it be this woman whom I love: for I love you, O eternity.

For I love you, O eternity![44]

Zarathustra wills the holocaust, thus he is the prophet of men's doom, of his longing to make himself over, even in death. But he dares to think beyond even that. The apocalypse could be willed because man expected God to step in and make over the world in his own image. Zarathustra wills that which is the end of man, but without God to hide and preserve the male. He, therefore, must face that the new may not be in the image of man's dream, that what may come may be a return, an ancient, ancient return. He thereby renders his promise and his longing ambiguous and open. In his daring, the possibility of opening the way of memory occurs. What is the same that returns? Is it really but a return of Zarathustra, or might the return be itself new?

The will to power is about the will to claim the right to reevaluate even values. It is quite probable that Nietzsche means that power only for men, for his is a vision that reinvokes man's project as against woman, as written over the top of woman. Even when he is not misogynist, or perhaps most when he is not misogynist, Nietzsche is the prophet of man's triumph at all costs. Yet there is, in the clarity of his willingness to face his own vision and see it through, the possibility of reevaluating the project itself. The alternative to Nietzsche and his higher and lower men may yet be the possibility of woman's claim upon the new.

This turning is and is not a turning back. Here the old and the new intersect in the possibility of a return to a time that may never have existed except in women's fairy tales and men's nightmares. The old woman sweeps the cobwebs from the moon. She recalls the alternative to the way things are that exists in the possibility of remembering. She is old, as old as the moon. She cannot be reduced to pregnancy, for her pregnancy is a lunatic pregnancy. She is pregnant with the return, with eternity itself. But now Zarathustra has shown the link between the two, the possibility of return as a preeminent human possibility. The return opens up the future from its closure into men's project. The future opens into the past, opens up the past, makes it possible to rethink that which has been and draw it, or be drawn by it, into a new way of being human. That which is beyond the man will be born in the shadow of men's urge to self-destruction and of women's recovery of her dreams. The song that will be sung will be beyond man, as also songs reach into the beyond, but it will not be the *Übermensch,* the man beyond man/woman, nor will it be a version of a great man. It will not even be a god. Perhaps it will be an old woman sweeping away the cobwebs and remembering.

Suppose truth is a woman. Perhaps then one should be more open to where she came from and where she is going. Suppose truth is a woman. Suppose eternity is a woman. Perhaps then one should ask her name. Perhaps she once knew *Sophia.* Here is an invitation to new stories and new songs that return to the beginning. Perhaps the time has come for a transvaluation of all that men have forced upon the world. Men have forgotten that values belong to singers and to poets, not to warriors. Perhaps it is time for *Sophia* to sing. Perhaps it is time for ordinary men, even for women, to claim the right to create value by their singing. *Sophia's* song never belonged to any man, not even the greatest, but belongs to all who come together in the marketplace and in the kitchen. Nonetheless, the song that will be sung will be beyond man, as all songs reach into the beyond. Like the nursery rhyme, these new lovers of *Sophia* shall throw their song seventeen times higher than the moon. The song will return by and by. This is a song of wisdom that dreams beyond what is to what is possible, a song beyond even the *Übermensch,* who has grown weary of waiting. The song will be of return. But a return to what? Before there were conquerors, there were old women who knew the wisdom of the stars and the moon, and of life and of death. It was those old women who taught the songs, and it was they who will remember, by and by. The song they will sing is a song that will weave the webs that hold together what is with what was with what will be, the fragile weavings of the recurrence of old, old beginnings.

NOTES

1. Friedrich Nietzsche, *Beyond Good and Evil: Prelude to a Philosophy of the Future*, trans. Walter Kaufmann (New York: Vintage Books, 1989), 1.
2. Friedrich Nietzsche, *Thus Spoke Zarathustra: A Book for All and None*, trans. Walter Kaufmann (New York: Penguin Books, 1978), 66.
3. Nietzsche, *Beyond Good and Evil*, 1.
4. Ibid.
5. Ibid., 3.
6. Nietzsche, *Beyond Good and Evil* #1, 9.
7. Ibid.
8. Nietzsche, *Beyond Good and Evil* #2, 10.
9. Nietzsche, *Beyond Good and Evil* #238, 166–67.
10. Peter J. Burgard, *Nietzsche and the Feminine* (Charlottesville: University of Virginia Press, 1994).
11. Peter J. Burgard, "Introduction: Figures of Excess" in *Nietzsche and the Feminine*, 11.
12. Ibid., 14–15.
13. Benjamin Bennett, "Bridge: Against Nothing" in Burgard's *Nietzsche and the Feminine*, 291.
14. Ibid., 289.
15. Ibid., 297.
16. Ibid., 296.
17. Luce Irigaray, *"Ecce Mulier?* Fragments" in Burgard's *Nietzsche and the Feminine*, 325.
18. Luce Irigaray, *Marine Lover of Friedrich Nietzsche*, trans. Gillian Gill (New York: Columbia University Press, 1991), 26.
19. Nietzsche, *Thus Spoke Zarathustra*, 230.
20. Irigaray, *Marine Lover*, 83–84.
21. Nietzsche, *Beyond Good and Evil*, 2.
22. Nietzsche, *Beyond Good and Evil* #19, 25–26.
23. Nietzsche, *Beyond Good and Evil* #44, 54.
24. Friedrich Nietzsche, *On the Genealogy of Morals*, trans. Walter Kaufmann and R. J. Hollingdale (New York: Vintage Books, 1969), 27–28.
25. Ibid., 34.
26. Nietzsche, *Beyond Good and Evil* #52, 65–66.
27. Nietzsche, *Beyond Good and Evil* #42, 52.
28. Nietzsche, *Beyond Good and Evil* #44, 54.
29. Nietzsche, *Beyond Good and Evil* #46, 60.
30. *Mother Goose*, Volland edition.
31. Nietzsche, *Thus Spoke Zarathustra*, 65–66.
32. Ibid., 67.
33. Nietzsche, *On the Genealogy of Morals*, 36.
34. Shelley's *Ozymandias*.
35. Nietzsche, *Thus Spoke Zarathustra*, 17.

36. Ibid.
37. Ibid., 286.
38. Ibid., 116.
39. Ibid., 286–87.
40. Ibid., 86.
41. Ibid., 287.
42. Ibid., 158.
43. Ibid., 220.
44. Ibid., 229.

HEIDEGGER'S POETRY:
BEHIND THE BEGINNING

SOPHIA HAS BEEN THROUGH much. Woman is well established as the second sex, and patriarchy has changed the face of the earth itself. Sexual oppression has been the law of the land for so long that no one is sure any longer whether it is possible to organize a society in any other way. Men no longer have any need to control the women with whom they relate. Social structures are so deeply embedded that women themselves enforce thought control over themselves. Men think; women feel. And only men love her: *philo-Sophia.*

Now women must begin again. But this is worse than reinventing the wheel. For women to think in some way other than a shadow of men's thought, they must redesign thought. But they must do so in the face of a long and well-established standard for what constitutes thought. More difficult than reinventing the wheel is to redesign the wheel in the shape of a spiral. All the weight of successful innovation must be overcome and be overturned. In many ways philosophy is an ideal place to do this, for of all men's rational processes, this endeavor has remained closest to its beginnings. Every philosopher begins by reinventing the wheel. Every philosopher must crawl before he can walk. So, if one would prefer to fly, one must go all the way back to crawling. There is always *Sophia* lurking behind every philosophical enterprise, waiting to help the child learn how to crawl.

All existence, and all of those beings for whom existence is a question (*Dasein*), takes place within a world. Every thought, every question, every statement moves within the context of a world of meaning already constituted. The world, in which we already are, constitutes existence as a meaningful enterprise. The asking of questions, the horizon of possible answers, and the process of wondering itself are already shaped by the world and only afterward by the one in the world.

But if the world can, in a way, be lit up, it must assuredly be disclosed. And it has already been disclosed beforehand whenever what is ready-to-hand within-the-world is accessible for circumspective concern. The world is therefore something 'wherein' Dasein as an entity already *was*, and if any manner it explicitly comes away from anything, it can never do more than come back to the world.[1]

To understand is to come back to the world, a world that preexists the understanding and that gives the terms by which the understanding is an understanding of the world. If the world in which women dwell is a man's world, then the meanings by which she even asks her questions are man's meanings. How then are women to find a way to ask women's questions, in a world in which meanings are the preserve of old dead white men? She must ask her questions from within the context of those already existent meanings, which are those of the old dead white men. Even a breaking of men's traditions must be done in terms that belong to men.

The world encircles and holds women; it establishes her horizons in every direction. It exists as far as she can see. Whatever understanding of herself that she achieves will be achieved within that circle. Though that which is closest to her (the ready-to-hand) has become a problem for her, her questions still take place within the horizon of meanings that encircle her. The world has already given women away to men. She finds herself already defined by her father, her husband, and her sons. The giving of women in marriage only makes explicit the way in which women are already given away to men's definitions of her. Marriage defines women whether she is married or not.

After all her years of marriage to the old dead white men, *Sophia* knows something of the compromises and hidden resources available to her children. And now her daughters have come of age, and the question is whether they will be able to hear her cries from their own marriage beds. Developing a feminist hermeneutics—that is, to take seriously the exclusion of women from the tradition as a point of departure for interpretation—is always done in the context of sleeping with the enemy. The nature of oppression places men and women in opposing camps, while the nature of understanding puts them in the same bed.

Women are not only bound to men in the nature of understanding itself but also by the nature of relationships they find themselves in with men. Women are oppressed by men, but they are also married to them, taught by them, guided by them, parented by them, bound to them by a hundred small commitments. This poses a difficulty. It is hard not to make allowances for those with whom one has the closest relationships. It is hard not to tone down what one might say in deference to a teacher or husband who has always been, after all, supportive. Not surprisingly, much of the most interesting thought originates with spinsters and lesbians, women who have some measure of independence from the nature of relationships with men. Men are frightened by the possibility of women's independence, but women know that even this independence is somewhat illusory as long as the domain of meaning belongs to men. Men lash out at women with jokes, pornographic innuendo, and outright violence to limit the potential for free thought implicit in being "haggard," wild, free, and resistant to courtship.[2]

Women struggle to create spaces, small worlds of meaning within which to begin the process of self-definition, as apart from men as they can. The research they engender weaves powerful new patterns in opposition to patriarchy. Such constructive worlds of meaning provide a context of thought which is truly critical and which can form the foundation for new meaning. Yet even the most secure of women's studies programs exist within the context of larger universities, all of which are dedicated to men's studies.

Such points of beginning are much like a woman keeping her name in marriage, or refusing to be married. The name owned by a spinster is still her father's name; her mother remains nameless. Or, perhaps, she might take her mother's maiden name, and thus invoke her grandfather. To live and think in patriarchy is never quite to escape the inheritance of meaning that belongs to the forefathers. As academics, women work in male-controlled institutions. As thinkers, women speak in patterns of words laid down by the forefathers. At most, women may achieve a generation of woman's thought, but such thought shows training by the generation before them—training in the thought and methodologies of men.

The nature of thought requires relatedness. Women begin with a set of assumptions learned through education, in institutions dedicated to the preservation of old dead white men. Women go on to intensified training designed to give them a framework, a place to begin. This requires immersion in the thought of a man, not so very long dead, perhaps. To this thinker a woman is "married." A woman's thought shares a home with that man. A woman inherits most directly from that man. By virtue of a direct relationship to that man, a woman has the right to participate in current scholarly discussions. She can become a philosopher by virtue of her relationship to one or more old dead white men. Quite probably, by the time she has studied long enough to be credentialed in the area, she will feel that perhaps *her* man was an exception, not quite like the others. Only finally, or for the most rigorous woman perhaps sooner, would a woman have to face up to the fact that sexual oppression exists here, and here, and even here. Aristotle, Heidegger, and even Derrida are produced by and participate in a male-dominated society. She must realize that there is no uncontaminated space to which she may retreat or upon which she may build a separate space. Anyone in the know can detect immediately, by her language and assumptions, the man's world in which she dwells.

It is good to praise the independent thought of spinsters, but it is also necessary to seek a way to change the nature of relationship to the men upon whom women's thought is dependent. Such interpretation requires honesty in admitting that women's thought emerges in relationship, even marriage, to men and their world. The practice of hermeneutics is wedded to men such as Heidegger, Gadamer, Ricoeur, and Habermas. Every time this text mentions hermeneutics, it gets into bed with Heidegger. To say less than this would be to falsify the nature of the relationship that shapes thought. Thought does not emerge in isolation. All new beginnings come from a circular relationship.

> What is decisive is not to get out of the circle but to come into it in the right way. This circle of understanding is not an orbit in which any random kind of knowledge may move; it is the expression of the existential *fore-structure* of Dasein itself. It is not to be reduced to the level of a vicious circle, or even of a circle which is merely tolerated. In the circle is hidden a positive possibility of the most primordial kind of knowing. To be sure, we genuinely take hold of this possibility only when, in our interpretation, we have understood that our first, last, and constant task is never to allow our fore-having, fore-sight, and fore-conception to be presented to us by fancies and popular conceptions, but rather to make the scientific theme secure by working out these fore-structures in terms of the things themselves.[3]

New understandings emerge only by virtue of their ongoing relationship to a concrete, distinct past, a past that is primordial in the sense that it gives us access to the origins of meaning. If women who are thinkers are going to find *Sophia*, it will only be in the context of her marriage to men and to remembering the origins of that marriage. The hermeneutical circle presents itself to women as a vicious circle. The meanings that define philosophy from its very beginning are men's meanings. They are meanings that exclude her participation, denigrate her experience, or deny her very existence as relevant to the philosophical enterprise. The vicious circle can be made, and must be made, productive by refusing to terminate the discussion at the point of man's origins. The circle must spiral inward, finding that which is more primordial, returning again to the historicity of the things themselves. *Sophia* is an old married woman, but she remembers the origins of the relationship constituted by men. We can follow her into the inward opening of the circle which is the spiral.

The task of a feminist hermeneutic is not a denial of relationship but a change in the nature of the relationship to the male-dominated tradition of philosophy. Here, therefore, at the heart of our relationship with current thought and not-so-dead white men, is the point of beginning for a hermeneutic of subversion. Behind and beneath the verses of men's thought, there is an undercurrent of alternative possibilities by whose rejection an overt argument is constructed. The ongoing task of this project is to sing the song in the minor key that shadows every major scale.

Now we can say, we have slept, are sleeping, with the enemy. This is a project of interaction, a family meeting headed by the old dead white men while *Sophia* sits humming in the background while she spins. Within the context of those old dead white men who have most shaped this project, we construct our sub-verses. Now begins a different kind of critical journey. This journey keeps before it an acknowledgment that exclusion of women's reality in-forms this relationship, that even the comfortable assumptions that seem to support the new crop of well-schooled women, also proclaim the ongoing structures of patriarchy. The methodology by which we approach the old dead white men must also work for their sons, for those men who have created the contemporary context. Again, to start with that assumption is not to say that a feminist hermeneutic can be a knee-jerk reaction. Rather we begin with the question raised by the nature of our training in a tradition that has formulated itself in such a way as to exclude women. The question of the meaning of exclusion cannot be answered once and for all. It is a question as concrete as the nature of relationship itself. The process of questioning becomes a hermeneutical process, of interpreting the nature of the relationship in light of its participation in the ongoing project of patriarchy. It is a critical task, an analysis that attempts to get to the root of this particular marriage.

When one explores the ancient texts, one treads upon the graves of one's fathers. Sometimes one can feel them rolling over in their graves, but there is a cheer from the silent, unmarked graves of the women who rest beside them. One persists. When one explores the texts by which one's own scholarship was shaped and matured, the grave is still warm. This is the marriage bed of scholarship. To look at the thinkers who are the immediate context of one's own thought is to try and see oneself thinking in the midst of the process of thought. It is to try to analyze the oppressive nature of marriage in the midst of being married to a man. And one step further, it is an attempt to see through contemporary thought, to the point where it also opens onto an unexpected place of new beginning.

Heidegger's hermeneutical circle constitutes the world as one world, in which everything is homogenized and reduced to the inner coherence of a single common understanding. Only when the later Heidegger confronts the diversity of language and culture, which form the horizon of meaning of all human dwelling, does the hermeneutical circle become explicitly dialogical in nature. In his essay entitled, "A Dialogue on Language: Between a Japanese and an Inquirer," the two speakers explore the way in which the hermeneutical circle can respond to difference.

I[nquirer]: A speaking *from* language could only be a dialogue.

J[apanese]: There is no doubt that we are moving in a dialogue.

I: But is it a dialogue from out of the nature of language?

J: It seems to me that now we are moving in a circle. A dialogue from language must be called for from out of language's reality. How can it do so, without first entering into a hearing that at once reaches that reality?

I: I once called this strange relation the hermeneutic circle.

J: The circle exists everywhere in hermeneutics, that is to say, according to your explanation of today, it exists where the relation of message and message-bearer prevails.

I: The message-bearer must come from the message. But he must also have gone toward it.

J: Did you not say earlier that this circle is inevitable, and that, instead of trying to avoid it as an alleged logical contradiction, we must follow it?

I: Yes. But this necessary acceptance of the hermeneutic circle does not mean that the notion of the accepted circle gives us an originary experience of the hermeneutic relation.[4]

The context of the hermeneutical circle is the living presence of language that undergirds the diversity of men's cultures. Language, with its speaking and above all with its silence, encompasses all the diverse languages that men speak. By highlighting the silence, by letting the spaces of what one cannot say become visible, one enters most fully into the space cleared by language. Diverse languages all share this property of silence in which language shows itself. When there are differences between people, the goal must be to keep one's speaking in relationship to the silence of what is not said. The value Heidegger places on silence opens a way into another kind of silence, the silence of oppression. In the clearing, one may hear voices which have not been allowed to speak but which have long remained in the protection of language. These alternative voices are also available to interpretation if one has the ears to hear.

Heidegger, teacher of our teachers and context of our thought, writes a moment before this one. Heidegger writes in the time of the total victory of patriarchy. In that time, there is much that is not said. Women keep to their home places, unless their men are off killing and being killed in the name of patriarchal justice and fatherlands. There are women who are thinkers, worthy of Heidegger's love and respect.[5] Such women are but a tiny minority, and their thought is carefully formulated in terms defined by men. They think like men, even as good as men, but even so men do not acknowledge them. Suppression of thought in all its many manifestations shapes the societies that rest on the deeper suppression of any truly alternative way to construct society.

Heidegger is a thinker in a culture that has institutionalized violence as a means of silencing memory. This means that we can expect there to be little need for him to write negatively about women, for all that is necessary has already been said. Misogynism is a response to an awareness of threat from women and unnecessary in civilized man at the height of his powers. Even so, and even in Heidegger, there is evidence of a hidden denial built into the structure of his thought. Where is the memory Heidegger has carefully forgotten?

In the context of Heidegger's time, remembrance is dying in gas chambers, where the silence is deafening. The nazis have marched into the foreground of history, which is the background of Heidegger's thought. The silence extends over into Heidegger's writing, which is first of all silent about his relationship to the nazis. There is a deeper silence, however, in the way in which Heidegger seeks the origins of language, as if all of Western culture emerged from Greek thought and language. Heidegger represents the traditions of much of philosophy, for he seeks exclusively his meanings among the Greeks, and this choice itself never becomes available to conscious reflection. The rich meanings that dwell in the Hebrew texts never become a source for his hermeneutics. Insofar as Heidegger seeks what is most original, the choice to exclude the meanings explored at the beginnings of the biblical heritage represents a definite choice, beyond simple dichotomies of philosophy and religion. Given Heidegger's historical context and the genocide of the Jews, this textual choice becomes crucial, even life-threatening. The silencing of victims is the ongoing context from which philosophy emerges, even as the Holocaust serves as the contemporary context from which the later texts of Heidegger emerge. As time passes, it will become more and more difficult to trace the relationship between Heidegger's immortal texts and the sordid reality of Heidegger's collusion with nazism. If Heidegger's personal history is to be made relevant, it must be because the violence is present within the texts themselves. Otherwise, Heidegger's involvement with evil is irrelevant and of interest only to historians.

Heidegger writes in the time of total victory of patriarchy, though strangely enough that total victory still seems to require even more violence. He remains firmly rooted in the assumptions and the commitments of the Western heritage. Heidegger is sometimes seen in the light of breaking away from the traditional way of doing philosophy. Certainly in his later works the way in which he approaches both his own work and the tradition changes fairly dramatically. However, he still carries on the same project, only in a more "originary" way:

> In fact, however, I was concerned neither with a direction in phenomenology nor, indeed, with anything new. Quite the reverse, I was trying to think the nature of phenomenology in a more originary manner, so as

to fit it in this way back into the place that is properly its own within Western philosophy.[6]

Heidegger's project is to trace back the most essential question at the heart of philosophy to its origins.

Heidegger's primary text, *Being and Time*, identifies the central question as the question of the meaning of being. *Being and Time* has the lofty independence of all the great systems. His system is based on the ongoing tradition of thought, yet stands as a point of new beginning even as it goes back to the beginning. Heidegger quotes from Plato at the very beginning of *Being and Time*:

> For manifestly you have long been aware of what you mean when you use the expression "*being*". We, however, who used to think we understood it, have now become perplexed. . . .[7]

Even this question proves to be not basic enough. The real question is, What is the first step? The circular nature of philosophy always asks a question that is more basic than the one with which one begins. *Being and Time* asks and answers but is unable to address, to find the rootedness of asking and answering in the nature of saying itself. Though it asks and answers at the origins of thought in its existential beginnings, the question as question always precedes it. It is not, therefore, at the beginning. The text is always a breath too late in its question, or perhaps too early, because the conditions under which it can be asked are not yet available.

> I only know one thing: because reflection on language, and on Being, has determined my path of thinking from early on, therefore their discussion has stayed as far as possible in the background. The fundamental flaw of the book *Being and Time* is perhaps that I ventured forth too far too early.[8]

In the background of philosophy are the basic questions. The problem is how to address them. Philosophy is always stumbling over its own words, though in another sense it has not even learned how to speak. Somehow there is never an adequate point of beginning, because everything one says takes for granted all the things one has not yet said. The point of beginning must be reexamined in light of the questions raised by the conclusion, by the totality of the project of *Being and Time*. The later Heidegger seeks not so much to talk about Being nor even about language, but to let Saying show itself poetically.

> But if the nearness of poetry and thinking is one of Saying, then our thinking arrives at the assumption that the occurrence of appropriation acts as that Saying in which language grants its essential nature on us. Its vow is not empty. It has in fact already struck its target—whom else but

man? For man is man only because he is granted the promise of language, because he is needful to language, that he may speak it.[9]

There is that which comes to meet man as he speaks. There is a reciprocity in philosophical discourse that hints at something other, by which language grants its essential nature to us. The other is as yet undefined. It is an ontological other, rooted in the very nature of being, of speaking, and of being human. It is a nature and a presence that man has claimed for himself. Heidegger tentatively and with great hesitation, names this other "Saying," that which grants man the promise that he might speak. But there is a subverse hidden in the relationship between man and this precondition of language. The closer man comes to naming this other, the more hesitant he becomes. The relation opens a question as to how man is preceded. Heidegger seeks words that echo with meaning, that open meanings out into the clearing.

> And yet—beyond what is, not away from it but before it, there is still something else that happens. In the midst of beings as a whole an open place occurs. There is a clearing, a lighting. Thought of in reference to what is, to beings, this clearing is in a greater degree than are beings. This open center is therefore not surrounded by what is; rather, the lighting center itself encircles all that is, like the Nothing which we scarcely know.[10]

In this way he seeks to release meaning from the restrictiveness that has been the Western heritage of language. Whereas philosophy has often sought to reduce language to its narrowest meaning, and thus under the control of man, Heidegger seeks to "let language speak." In letting language speak, Heidegger discovers something before man's constructions. The before is an ontological before, not historical. Yet it hints at that which is more primordial than the taken-for-granted world of men.

The assumption that underlies Heidegger's project is the primordial nature of language, language as source of thought rather than language as the product and tool of man. In this case, language that is most true to its nature is also language that speaks most true of whatever is said. This requires following the nature of language in its essential nature as poetry back to the point of origin. The point of origin in language is temporal for Heidegger, because of the nature of *Dasein*, of human existence.

> The existential-ontological constitution of Dasein's totality is grounded in temporality. Hence the ecstatical projection of Being must be made possible by some primordial way in which ecstatical temporality temporalizes. How is this mode of the temporalizing of temporality to be Interpreted? Is there a way which leads from primordial *time* to the meaning of *Being*?[11]

The time implied in temporality is an ontological time, a way of being for *Dasein* rather than a relation between *Dasein* and a particular history. Even so, temporality points to history as the point of origin. History remains present and in a reciprocal relation to that which is now. Past and present move back and forth, and in their movement humans dwell. Language is the repository of this dwelling, the place where the past participates in present human meaning. The past is the ground of the present, and it is available in the words that always retain some relation to their origin. To access the past requires an etymological search in which the multivocity of words is present in its most metaphorical sense as history embodied in poetry.

Heidegger's search for the origins of language draws him to the edge of man's habitation in language. It is at this point that the project hints at an opening for a feminist hermeneutic.[12] The point at which Heidegger's search ends (or begins) is in some sense historical. This historical starting point, the pre-Socratics, is the usual starting point for Western thought. From Heidegger's standpoint, this is far enough back. But it is not the beginning. Instead the Greeks represent the point at which patriarchy began one aspect of its ideological assault upon the peoples that were truly "primordial." The point of philosophy's beginning is the moment of erasure. The totality of the victory had even then begun to exclude the memory of the time before men had triumphed. Heidegger seeks to invoke primordial possibilities for thought, to reach to the origins of meaning as a pathway to meaning as such. His texts, particularly his later works, brush on the edges of the patriarchal worldview in their search for the very source of thought. Yet what he finds is not the beginning but the boundary.

At the boundary the silence speaks very loudly. Our interpretation attempts to identify the way in which that violence is prefigured in the missing presence in Heidegger's thought, especially in his later poetic works and especially at those points in which he touches on the primordial. We seek within the texts for the point at which silence begins, and thereby seek to let the silence speak. Heidegger seeks the primordial possibilities of thought, therefore, we go with him on that search. In *Poetry, Language, Thought*, Heidegger attempts philosophy that is also poetry, and, therefore, poetry that is language speaking in an 'originary' way. The tension between history as the mere inheritance of past facts, and history as the living act of denotative meaning in language, reaches its greatest pitch in the philosophical search for the origin of meaning. At this almost primordial moment the words reverberate with meanings, barely able to stay within the confines Heidegger sets for them.

Poetry, Language, Thought is the text in which Heidegger allows language its greatest play. The text breaks from the systematic analysis of traditional philosophy to let the very sources of meaning disclose themselves. The text is poetry and philosophy and history. Not being bound to conventional understandings of how one does philosophy, the text is freed to follow the word where it will lead. In the essay, "What are Poets For?" the text follows the question to the very edges of the patriarchal worldview in its Greek embodiment. Somehow, this historical point of origin is very close to the present. The essay seeks the past, but it also seeks to understand the present time. The question, taken from Hölderlin's poem, asks after the relationship of poets to this time.

> "... and what are poets for in a destitute time?" asks Hölderlin's elegy "Bread and Wine." We hardly understand the question today. How, then, shall we grasp the answer that Hölderlin gives?[13]

The necessity of asking the question "what are poets for?" reveals the destitution of the modern age. The modern age has lost its relation to language, which leaves it destitute of meaning. Language, in its most essential form as poetry, has become a problem. Therefore, all the enterprises that hinge on language are also problematic. The text leaves the worry of that problem implicit in the destitute time to follow after the question as it is given to a poet.

The poet points to the historical experience that defines this present time. In so doing, the essay draws back to the "end of the day of the gods."

> "... and what are poets for in a destitute time?" The word "time" here means the era to which we ourselves still belong. For Hölderlin's historical experience, the appearance and sacrificial death of Christ mark the beginning of the end of the day of the gods. Night is falling.[14]

Man's ages began to fall into destitution with the advent of Christ. Christ marks the beginning of the end of the gods, and thus of the emptiness of human dwelling. Christ is the zero point, the point that begins to mark the years that have no meaning of their own but that must borrow their meaning from a point in the past that is rapidly disappearing. With every year the point of meaning, by which modern time is referenced, becomes more distant, more difficult to reach.

This moment is also the zero point from which to trace back the origins of the destitution. In this essay, Heidegger begins a familiar journey back to the pre-Socratics. Here, on this familiar territory, which is somehow so close to all philosophical enterprises, but especially to Heidegger, is the point of beginning. Yet this point of origin does not answer questions but raises them. The point of origin is not original enough, but points beyond itself. The text pauses in puzzlement. Heidegger discovers that the destitution of the modern age points back toward an abyss. The nature of being mortal opens a way into the abyss, beyond which it cannot see. The abyss is an event now, that is also in the past. What lies within the abyss?

> Perhaps the world's night is now approaching its midnight. Perhaps the world's time is now becoming the completely destitute time. But also perhaps not, not yet, not even yet, despite the immeasurable need, despite

all suffering, despite nameless sorrow, despite the growing and spreading peacelessness, despite the mounting confusion. Long is the time because even terror, taken by itself as a ground for turning, is powerless as long as there is no turn with mortal men. But there is a turn with mortals when these find the way to their own nature. That nature lies in this, that mortals reach into the abyss sooner than the heavenly powers. Mortals, when we think of their nature, remain closer to that absence because they are touched by presence, the ancient name of Being. But because presence conceals itself at the same time, it is itself already absence. Thus the abyss holds and remarks everything.[15]

The absence is, for Heidegger, a hint of presence, and an ontological promise. Yet the promise cannot be claimed, because both the absence and the presence remain abstract, ahistorical even though they initiate history. The concealment of presence leaves absence at the heart of patriarchy. The absence haunts patriarchy, but patriarchy scarcely notices and considers the absence quite unremarkable. The default of the gods, the abyss, the absence, all circle back upon themselves, with no meaning outside their philosophical formulation.

This character of the discussion of man's midnight, his move into total destitution, marks a point of intersection of this text with a text that is truly 'unremarked.' The historical reality reflected first in the source of meaning at the edge of the abyss and again in the ongoing project of destitution is the reality of an act of conquest. The abyss is no simple lack. It is a concrete removal of that which was the ground of a way of being. The abyss is concrete in its relationship to the history of man's triumph politically and socially, that is also and at the same time the history of thought. The origin of man's thought lies in a series of conquests. Here it all begins. Within the abyss is concealed the blood of the beginning, though one can barely see what is hidden in the dimness of the light at the beginning of man's time. Beyond that we cannot reach, perhaps even poetically, for they have obliterated even the memory of the opponent.

Heidegger can assume that the nature of patriarchy is the nature of thought itself, for the total nature of this heritage represents the total triumph of the patriarchs over all competing representations of the world. To win totally, there must be no way of recalling who it was that lost. What can be recollected is not totally lost. It may begin again, be remembered. Thought also has its genocide. There are consequences, however, to total victory. For the victims, total annihilation. For the victors, a history that stands rootless. In the absence of the history of the battle from which man's history emerges, patriarchy floats, rooted only in its own will to be. The history of patriarchy hangs in such an abyss. The groundlessness of the modern age forms the basis for what Martin Heidegger calls the "destitute time."

> The word for abyss—*Abgrund*—originally means the soil and ground to-ward which, because it is undermost, a thing tends downward. But in what follows we shall think of the *Ab-* as the complete absence of the ground. The ground is the soil in which to strike root and to stand. The age for which the ground fails to come, hangs in the abyss.[16]

Patriarchal history fails to reach the ground. It has cut itself off from its own origins and its memory of the struggle against the primordial ground to deny any other foundation than its own will. Patriarchy exists as a deriva-tive being. Though it can destroy the memory of its ground, its foundations are thereby weakened. Man's history grows out of and remains dependent upon a source that it must destroy. Heidegger is the poet of the complete victory of patriarchy; he sketches the boundaries of the obliteration. He therefore experiences the final failure of patriarchy to find anywhere that it might rest. Heidegger's longing for the ground is genuine even though it finds only the abyss. He cannot see any farther back than the historicity of patri-archy's own self-creation. Where the ground ought to be, there is nothing. Something is missing, and from the standpoint on which Heidegger stands, the missing is what is most needed.

Heidegger follows philosophy in hopes of finding the source of illumina-tion for the world. He finds that philosophy itself points to the priority of language. Language speaks in poetry, in metaphor. It leads the text back to the participation of divinity in the radiance of words. Poetically, Heidegger seeks the gods that gleam at the world's beginning, the poetic sources of a poetic reality. Heidegger points to the methodological priority of poetry as a means of access to the traces of the gods, or origins.

> Poets are the mortals who, singing earnestly of the wine-god, sense the trace of the fugitive gods, stay on the gods' tracks, and so trace for their kindred mortals the way toward the turning.[17]

What gods? The text does not seek just any gods, nor even the god-as-creator that is the traditional subject of philosophical dispute. This great monotheistic conception is a late addition, a product of the narrowing and refinement of the philosophical tradition. Heidegger seeks those gods prom-ised by the nature of poetry, the gods missing in a destitute time in which meaning has narrowed even past the one God. Heidegger's text goes with the singing of the poets to the gods closest to the *Abgrund*.

The default of the gods appears already in the rootlessness of classical thought. Already Socrates is suspicious of the poets and their songs and seeks a god carefully removed from ecstasy and singing. Already Socrates, and his poet, Plato, testify to the destitute time in which all the gods have defaulted. The default of the gods hangs in the abyss, to be found only when philosophy must turn to the poets even to understand itself.

Heidegger's text seeks the origin of thought in the origins of the heritage. It identifies with Hercules, Dionysus, and Christ. It finds the silence before these three. Here it pauses. The gods of which the text sings are a particular group of gods, gods close and involved in the human enterprise of history. Each of these gods is on the boundary of mortal and immortal. Each is in some sense a god and in some sense a participant in human destiny. They trace the boundary between mortal and divine. If anyone can explain the default of the gods, it is these three. The "united three" are in some sense primordial and also capable of touching our time, if only by their default. They mark both the beginning and the end.

> Ever since the "united three"—Herakles, Dionysos, and Christ—have left the world, the evening of the world's age has been declining towards its night. The world's night is spreading its darkness. The era is defined by the god's failure to arrive, by the "default of God."[18]

What Heidegger finds points toward what is missing. The gods are missing. This is the historical context implicit in any original speaking of the "united three," Hercules, Dionysus, and Christ. These three are the heroes of patriarchy's triumph. They are the self-engendered originators of history. Before them is not history, neither remembrance nor philosophy. There is that which is beyond the heroes Heidegger names, but it is unrecorded and unremarked.

The reason for their default, their failure to remain in the world, is implicit in their identity. The "united three" are not an arbitrary collection of gods. They are united in their identity as destroyers of the feminine divine. They have torn themselves out of the ground, sought to terminate all relationship between thought and matter, and left behind them the abyss. Now they, too, disappear into the abyss. They are both the destroyers of the ground, the creators of the abyss, and the seekers of the ground. The longing Heidegger feels is the longing of the gods, to seek that which they also seek to destroy.

Each of the united three stands symbolically tied to myths of the overcoming of the Goddess. Hercules embodies the militaristic victory over the earth. Hercules is the model of the modern hero. His name points back to the woman, the Goddess, Hera, who came before, and after whom he was named. Although Hercules takes his name from a powerful Goddess, Hera, he transforms the meaning of that name to become the hired assassin of the Greek pantheon. In a series of contests arranged by the domesticated Hera, Hercules defeats various representations of female divinity. The most telling is his destruction of Antaeus, the son of Gaia, Mother Earth. Hercules wrestles with Antaeus, who rises again from each fall, renewed by his contact with the earth. Hercules finally chokes Antaeus by holding him away from the renewing power of the Earth.

Hercules, who represents the embodiment of male virtue and strength, gains the victory by his ability to sever the relationship between the Earth and her champions. In his victory the relationship of man to the ground is severed, allowing man to conquer. But this severance also leaves man ground-less. Hercules is the creator of the abyss. It is he who has defeated the earth, and in the defeat, he foreshadows the default of divinity from man's dwelling on the earth.

Hercules symbolizes all those other great victors who create by splitting the heart of the earth. Hercules has many brothers, like Marduk. Like Marduk's triumph over Tiamat, Hercules' fame rests upon brute physical strength and the willingness to use violence against the Goddess.

> Then joined issue Tiamat and Marduk, wisest of gods
> They strove in single combat, locked in battle.
> The lord spread out his net to enfold her,
> The Evil Wind, which followed behind, he let loose in her face.
> When Tiamat opened her mouth to consume him,
> He drove in the Evil Wind that she close not her lips.
> As the fierce winds charged her belly,
> Her body was distended and her mouth was wide open.
> He released the arrow, it tore her belly,
> It cut through her insides, splitting her heart.
> Having thus subdued her, he extinguished her life.
> He cast down her carcass to stand upon it.
> After he had slain Tiamat, the leader,
> Her band was shattered, her troupe broken up . . .
> When he has vanquished and subdued his adversaries,
> Had . . . the vainglorious foe,
> Had wholly established Anshar's triumph over the foe,
> Nudimmud's desire had achieved, valiant Marduk
> Strengthened his hold on the vanquished gods.[19]

Marduk has won, but this is but the beginning of his violence. Even van-quishing the goddess is not enough. Now that she is helpless, she must be torn to pieces. It is her severing that Marduk will call his creation.

> And turned back to Tiamat whom he had bound.
> The lord trod on the legs of Tiamat,
> With his unsparing mace he crushed her skull.
> When the arteries of her blood he had severed,
> The North Wind bore (it) to places undisclosed.
> On seeing this, his fathers were joyful and jubilant,
> They brought gifts of homage, they to him.
> Then the lord paused to view her dead body,
> That he might divide the monster and do artful works.
> He split her like a shellfish into two parts:

> Half of her he set up and ceiled it as sky,
> Pulled down the bar and posted guards.
> He bade them to allow not her waters to escape.[20]

Man's myths tell the story, in many different forms and many different guises, of the creation of the universe of man by the destruction of woman. The destruction is celebrated in song and story of blood spilt and blood not allowed to escape. Sometimes the severing of the Goddess into two halves is hidden in the telling of a spirit that moves across the face of deep waters (Gen. 1:2). Yet there was someone who remembered, someone who knew, for the waters across which God moves is called *tehom*, which recalls the destruction of the ancient Goddess, Tiamat. These waters also were split into two parts to form the firmament above and the firmament below. The destruction of woman is the genesis of man, his creation by the God in whose image he also destroys. The destruction shapes his understanding of himself as the hero of his-story.

Heidegger echoes in his united three an old, old story. But now the mood of the story has changed. The beginning was so long ago, so ancient, that maybe now man has really begun to forget. The forgetting does not leave man easy. Being left alone upon the Earth which no longer responds to his walking, in which neither the snake nor God moves in the garden, man looks at the firmament and sees only the emptiness above and the emptiness below. Man becomes the creator by first becoming the destroyer, only to discover that the two have become one, and the ground has disappeared into the abyss. Perhaps in spite of all that is transcendent about him, he also got his strength from the ground which now has been defeated and disappeared into groundlessness. Hera's hero is defeated by being separated from the ground. Now the victor grows weary in a victory that also separates him from the ground.

The united three unite in their various battles and ways of overcoming the feminine. Dionysus represents an even more total victory over the feminine, in that Dionysus incorporates female divinity into his own maleness, thus annihilating even the claim to her having been. Whereas Hercules is dependent upon his physical ability to destroy the opposition, Dionysus presents a more subtle form of violence. Dionysus overcomes by appropriating the reality and the power of the other into himself. After Dionysus, all that is essentially feminine is subsumed into the male. As Mary Daly warns:

> Moreover, the apparently contradictory aspects of Dionysus—his self-fathering and his femininity—coincide. In the "light" of these elements of the Dionysian myth we can well be suspicious of male fascination with the all too feminine Dionysus, for his mythic presence foreshadows attempts to eliminate women altogether.[21]

Mary Daly's concern is that men wish to take into themselves what they hold to be of value in women. Femaleness then becomes a mere aspect of the totality of the "whole man," the psychological victory in which man triumphs by incorporating the *anima* in the *animus*, and thus becomes whole.

Dionysus's power to alienate and remove female power stems from his own birth. In his birth, man denies the debt he owes to woman for his own being. Dionysus is the son of Zeus and Semele, a mortal woman. But he is not born of Semele, for she is destroyed by Zeus (though of course Zeus's act is blamed on Hera). Zeus saves the fetus, aborted by his own violence, and births it out of himself.

> Had Dionysus been born of Semele, daughter of the Theban Cadmus, he would have been mortal like his mother. Instead, he becomes a god, destroying the barriers dividing mortal from immortal as well as those severing female from male, for the god is sired by a male and delivered from a male.[22]

Woman's integrity is obliterated in this archetypal subordination, a subordination that has annihilated even the possibility of otherness. This subordination and incorporation of the female into the male is repeated and reinforced in the descriptions of Dionysus as being feminine in his beauty and driving women mad with his sensuality. Dionysus is the god who possesses women. The intoxicating rites of Dionysus justify men's fear and disgust at women's unbridled sexuality. Dionysus is like his Hindu compatriots, who swallow the female into themselves, as an "aspect" of their thoroughly male identity. The incorporation hints both that the female has power and transfers that power to male control. In the process, however, the female disappears. The synthesis of male and female is all male.

The final member of the "united three" is Christ. In some ways it is curious that Christ should be included in this triumvirate of Greek gods. By including the Christ, Heidegger points to the Greek origins of Christianity, again rejecting the Jesus who was, after all, a Jew. He also points to a Christ who might offer a metaphor within which "men" might be gathered. The banner of Christ becomes the rallying point for the Lamb's War, for all those who would fight in the name of Christianity against the heathen. This is the Christ who once gathered men into his glorious manhood as Son of the Father-God. The masculinity of the Christ affirms the longing of man for the moment of triumph which is both in the past and not yet accomplished. The Christ is the preexistent Logos, the man who preexisted his mother. This is the man who claims the beginning, the Word made Man, the Word that is the boundary of thought. Heidegger's inclusion of the Christ in the triumvirate with Hercules and Dionysus points to the longing of men to touch immortality and be gathered within it.

Yet the Christ also defaults. Christianity finds no myth that can secure for all men their meaning. Christians constantly seek to come together under the leadership of their male God to do battle with the other. Yet their unity constantly dissolves into squabbles. The Christ defaults. The Christ who would be the uniting of men in their manhood (which is in the image of God) cannot supply the missing opponent. The ancient feminine evil, the source of evil and sin in the world, has already been defeated, over and over again. Her annihilation must be avoided, if the Christians are to continue, but what other victory could ever be complete? Her subordination is always partial and doubtful; the men rest uneasily in the master bedroom. They wait for her rising up. They wait, unable to define even the enemy, for she shares their bed. Only in the witch craze is the enemy clearly defined as woman. But even then, the torture of those millions of women must be erased from memory, and the armies of Christ are unemployed again.

The Christians wait and wait for the final battle, the battle of Armageddon, but it never quite arrives. In the meantime, history is empty of divinity; the gods have fled and destitution is upon us. The default of the Christ leaves this time destitute. The Christ is the one for whom men wait, anxiously, hoping to be gathered into parousia but, therefore, the more aware of the emptiness of the destitute time. Where is the whore of Babylon when one needs her? Where is "Babylon the great, mother of harlots and of the earth's abominations" (Rev. 17:5) who will call the Christ into his final triumphant return? In that battle for a new earth at last the ambiguity, the absence of the clarity of battle, will be overcome. But she does not arrive, and the time is destitute so that men must fight each other instead of her, in Christ's name.

Mary Daly, like Martin Heidegger, sees an underlying commonality between Christ and Dionysus, though the value they attach to this commonality is different. Daly looks behind and beneath Christ to the remnants of the Mother of God, who is overcome and tamed by her reduction to a mere vessel for the God's incarnation. In Christ, the Goddess has taken up her own annihilation. Eve, Mother of Life, becomes Mary, mother of God, but the nature and meaning of motherhood has been so reduced that this represents Mary's complete lack of divinity. So totally has the Mother's memory of herself been erased that she is grateful to be allowed to touch the divinity of man.

Having eliminated Mary, the ghost of the Goddess, it sets up a unisex model, whose sex is male. Jesus, androcracy's Absolute Androgyne, is male femininity incarnate. Unlike Dionysus, whom he spiritually incorporates, he is not a member of a pantheon of female and male peers. He is the Supreme Swinging Single, forever freed from challenge by Forceful Furious Females.[23]

Mary, the mother of Jesus, represents woman reduced to her patriarchal function as vessel for the male seed. Jesus takes from her his humanity, excluding his mother from his divinity even while incorporating into himself all aspects of her humanity, so that ultimately all that she is becomes his.

Heidegger has traced the default of the gods without realizing what their default reveals. He stands at the beginning and finds no source, only the default even of the path. The path disappears into the abyss, and, therefore, the future becomes destitute. The modern age, the other end of the path, is a time without divinity. The male gods prove barren. They leave us with their own hollow victory. They leave us destitute of all divinity. The "united three" have disappeared, because they have fulfilled their sole function in assuring the victory of patriarchy. The ground has been defeated. The earth is severed from its origin. Now there is no longer any ground. The battle is won. There is no longer any battle. In this victory even the battle itself is erased. Therefore, there is nothing—only the emptiness that once was called the ground but now can be called nothing but the *Abgrund*, the ground that is no longer.

Once the Goddess is conquered, the gods are no longer needed, and, therefore, they disappear. The longing that Heidegger feels is misplaced. He longs for a return of the gods, for their engaging once more with the world. But the gods have no need to return, for their victory is already complete. Man has triumphed and the gods have gone off into the abyss, leaving him the emptiness of his victory. With Hercules, Dionysus, and Christ, the symbolic triumph over the divinity of the world is mythically complete. They have nothing more to do with the world. The world is dead, and because it is dead, men can build their skyscrapers and drop their bombs on each other. Yet underneath it all is an emptiness.

> The default of God means that no god any longer gathers men and things unto himself, visibly and unequivocally, and by such gathering disposes the world's history and man's sojourn in it. The default of God forebodes something even grimmer, however. Not only have the gods and the god fled, but the divine radiance has become extinguished in the world's history.[24]

The gods have fled because they have succeeded in overcoming the divine radiance they gathered from the ground. The feminine divine has passed, and even the gods who conquered her mourn. Heidegger's longing does not reach deeply enough into the abyss. He follows the traces of the gods without noticing the bloody footprints beneath. All Heidegger notices is that he missed the battle and his gods have gone. Like all poets, he strives to remember, but this is one memory that withdraws even from the poets.

The gods have fled as fugitives from the violence still spreading from their destruction of the Goddess. The innocence with which they battled the dragon had consequences far beyond their own expectations. Not even the gods can stop the violence they have initiated. Therefore, they flee. What is left is the darkness and godlessness of the destitute time. They leave behind their poets who can sing of no glorious victory but only of the empty triumph of Auschwitz. The line begun with the united three ends in the destitution of gas chambers. Here even the poets lose their voice. Auschwitz is the triumph of meaningless death, of victories counted up by accountants, of the dead reduced to numbers. All the songs have been sold and language itself is reduced to acronyms, the meaning of which no one tries to remember.

In the absence of the gods, myth-making becomes a lost art. Heidegger turns to the poets for their intuitive sense that something is missing and that the traces can be followed. Poets do trace the abyss, the absence of the gods, which might otherwise go unnoticed. Yet the tradition of poetry to which Heidegger is committed is necessarily bound to male voices. Such poetry is bound by the abyss of the negation of the Goddess. Poetry also becomes mere collections of words. Poetry discovers no divinity. In the absence of divinity, it feeds upon itself. It creates no myths but multiplies and feeds on its own emptiness. Even so, poetry, by naming the *Abgrund,* testifies that the ground is missing and thereby makes possible thinking about the ground. Thus do poets reach first into the abyss. However, poetry as originary of new meanings, as the source of myth and that which allows for the shining forth of the divine radiance, is not yet possible. Only that poetry that roots itself in prehistorical memory and the primordial possibility can reach the ground.

Heidegger has begun to answer the question "What are poets for?" The poets of patriarchy reach into the abyss and no further, for these poets follow after the gods and worship at the traces of violence that are their heritage. They long for the ground only to witness again the victory of their gods. Therefore, they find only emptiness, for the gods themselves are groundless and without matter. Heidegger is never quite able to bridge poetry and thought, for these two are separated by what they dare not acknowledge even with a thought. Only those who listen for the song and hear what is missing in the poetry can begin to participate in the underground tradition. Yet those poets who listen in patriarchy still refuse to ask, "What is woman for?" Or rather they have already answered in such a way as to close themselves off from the only ones who can answer such a call. The subverses, which must be excavated from the apparent triumph of patriarchy, can be seen and heard from any point within the dominant culture for anyone willing to hear between the lines. The abyss, in which women dwell and which dwells within woman, speaks for herself.

To hear between the lines is to engage in a hermeneutics of subverses. Such a hermeneutics listens for the holes and contradictions in the beauty of patriarchal longing. A hermeneutic of subversion, to be successful, requires an archaeology of ideas. Until we know more of the mysteries that Dionysus appropriated, we have not the historical resources to uncover the Dionysian incorporation of feminine divinity. The stories of women running wild hint at the refusal of women to be domesticated within the strictures of the Greek pantheon. She resists and her resistance is recorded with a shudder of horror in Euripides' *Bacchae*.

> Now, at the foot of Cithaeron,
> the two hamlets, Hysiae
> and Eurythrae, are invaded,
> the women are attacking,
> plundering. They tear children
> from their houses, and whatever they put
> on their backs stays there,
> without straps, even bronze and iron.
> They carry fire on their hair
> and weren't scorched. Now the men
> had had enough: in rage, they rose,
> took up their weapons. What we see
> next is dreadful, lord.
> The men throw their spears, and draw
> no blood; the women, though, let loose
> their *wands*, and *wound* the men and
> the men run! . . . Women defeating men!
> Certainly a god was in it.
> The women went back then
> to the springs the god had gushed
> out of the earth, and washed away
> the blood, the snakes licked the drops
> from their cheeks.[25]

Dionysus is a new god. Yet his newness covers a much more ancient memory of women's power, now recalled only in the threat of women running loose. What remains for us is even less. Heidegger is pulled toward the past, which does not go far enough back.

The underground tradition discloses itself only in relationship to the meanings of prehistory in which history is grounded. Every poetic sighing hints and points to a historical actuality, and beneath that historical actuality is the evidence of woman-centered traditions that were destroyed. The tombs of history must be turned over to disclose the older dead. The dust must be shaken from the mourning clothes that have wrapped the corpses for aeons. The corpses rise; they walk freshly into the new morning; their song is the song that women have been whispering through all the time between. It is the poets who mourn those who are dead, and it will be the poets who will herald their new birth. When the poets make myths that do not belong to them, but to the divinities they announce, the ancient undead goddesses, we will all learn to sing.

It is possible to recognize the Goddess even in a patriarchal age. It requires a search for the subverses, an uncovering of the poetry that is buried in the text. Subversion is bound to the text. One does not and cannot make up new meaning. New meanings grant to the fathers the victory; they participate in the groundlessness of the fathers. We are the children of the fathers who fought and won against the ground, and our poets are trapped in the void that results. We must dream new dreams, but we cannot make it all up. As philosophers we return to the origins of the meanings that no longer satisfy us. The women will lead us, and the people on the margins of the conquerors' victories will show us the way, as they reach into the old with their new dreams. For this purpose all kinds of archaeological and etymological uncoverings must take place, those which dig in the ground, those who seek to preserve the memories of the first peoples, and those which dig into men's texts. Making up new meanings without an ear for subversion assumes that there are no other stories than those of the fathers, that we are the first to realize that it is possible to be free of the father's yoke. Yet between us and the ancient unremembered past there have been a host of many who have tried to recall, and in their recalling shared the fate of their mother's people. There was never a time when women did not dream and when men did not have to resist dreaming. There was never a time when the past was over and done with, when suppression was no longer necessary. Even now, even in the destitute time, there are poets. Even now the genocide of peoples with ties to alternatives, who still live with an ear to the ground, continues. The purpose of a subversive hermeneutic is to hear the ground beneath the *Abgrund*, to hear the echoes of the silenced women in the voices of those who silenced them. The purpose of a subversive hermeneutic is to give the children of the fathers who destroyed a way through the father, through the destruction, to the Mother.

In this project Heidegger participates, though his participation is shaped by his own need to keep silent about the ongoing erasure of the voices of those dying again. He is not the poet for whom we wait, but among those poets through whom we must pass for the singers of old songs to be born. He points at the abyss as the starting point of thought and frees thought from its subjugation to the technical rationality of the ideological fact. He pursues the nature of thinking and speaking, making a space for language to speak for itself. In that opening there is a space for the ground, though he attempts to maintain the "united three" and their guard. They will fail him by virtue of the longing that is still also a longing for new blood. His ambivalence, the longing implicit to the enterprise of thought itself, betrays him.

The methodology of subversion follows Heidegger's lead to the point at which history, the history of thought, begins. Here is the boundary of history and prehistory. Those spinsters and researchers who have dared to look into the history which history attempted (and continues to attempt) to deny and to destroy, these, our sisters, precede us. Heidegger leads us to that point where the inevitability of history opens into the abyss, our Mother. This is the pathway that leads trustingly into the void of men's meanings, in confidence there is still more of the story waiting to be told.

The key to subversion is the removal of the inevitability that represents the father's control of the doing of history. What was, remains possible. The past is our reservoir of meanings that can open up the future. The opening up of the historical corpus to the enlivening insights of prehistory provides new points of access into original meanings. The history of man is a history of closing down access, of claiming that the past is over and done with, and that the future belongs to the strong. Subversion treats the past as a collection of odd bits held in the hand of an interpreter like a kaleidoscope. Turn the kaleidoscope and the picture changes. In the process the pieces of the past remain intact, yet emerge in new patterns. With a twist of the hand, a startling new image emerges. A feminist hermeneutic of subversion is that twist of the hand, in which an as yet undetected world of meaning comes alive. The past is the origin of meanings, and it can be retold, even now, even yet.

The new kaleidoscopic patterns speak of ancient, primordial meanings as dwelling among us. Against Heidegger's despairing conviction that the gods have fled, yet also in light of what his text reveals about the emptiness left by their departure, the ground is re-membered. The ground is the most ancient of old deities, the dis-membering of her body is the story told in history. This story is a story of men's severing of matter and *Mater*. It is a story that testifies to the metaphorical destruction of the ancient feminine. It is also the story of the actual, physical destruction of peoples and of cultures, of the repetition of genocide. It is yet again a story of the destruction of the world of living and nonliving reality in her dismemberment and annihilation. Subversion is the story of the resilience and resistance of all those that patriarchy sought to destroy. And thus his story can be her story as well. The past testifies to the unremitting emergence of women's memories of power and, therefore, the need for their continual subordination. Women can remember; women can sew their members back together and spin a new future.

It might seem confusing that in patriarchy "the true sin is forgetting" this deed, since its ideologies deny that there ever was, is, or can be female divinity, whose existence would be a prerequisite condition for her murder. However, since the fathers' ritual is the realm of reversals, such confusion should be expected. The purpose of such contrived confusion is to prevent us from committing the "true sin" against patriarchal rule/ritual, that is, remembering that as long as we are alive the Goddess still lives. The radical "sin" is re-membering the Goddess in the full sense, that is, recognizing that the attempt to murder her—mythically and existentially— is radically wrong, and demonstrating through our own be-ing that this deed is not final/irrevocable.[26]

Now is the time for the poets to seek words that are hidden with her repression. The silence always sings, even after the gas chambers, if the meaning of their deadly fumes can be reopened.

The sexual subordination of women provides patriarchy with an easily identifiable enemy. This primordial rape serves as the prototype for the subsequent pattern of violent suppression. The united three point to the meanings of women's subordination. Women take the blows aimed at the threat of the reemergence of matristic cultures and the Goddess. Matristic cultures are identified by the status they grant women. Therefore, women become the obvious target. However, the wrath of patriarchal culture against matristic societies is not just aimed at women. Any people that becomes identified in any way with the gynocentric heritage becomes the target of patriarchal society's vengeance.

The apparently irrational oppression of women, Jews, people of color, primitive societies, and sexual "deviants" discloses the special access that these peoples have to the excluded history. These excluded peoples retain connections with the ground via stories, myths, songs, and rituals, by their very being. Here lies the root of the hermeneutical privilege of the oppressed. The fathers know who carries the promise, and why they are dangerous. The resilience and survival of oppressed peoples is a testimony to the limits of the fathers' power. Their continual return is a constant source of irritation to the fathers, for it testifies that patriarchal closure on meaning is never complete. The path to the future can be traced by means of the knowledge of who the fathers would destroy. The nazis have revealed to us that even the biblical narratives, and the traditions of the Jews, hold memories intolerable to an oppressor. Our task is never to forget, but even more, our task is to remember that which the gas chambers were intended to erase.

The history of oppression is both a smoke screen and also a hint. It discloses what the fathers continue to find dangerous. However, there is little hope as long as the oppressed themselves focus on the fact of their oppression, unable to remember the special relationship to matristic cultures that make them powerful—and dangerous. Liberation lies in remembering. Freedom cannot be achieved on the father's terms. Rather, one must draw on those sources of power that reach back and back and back, even beyond the groundlessness of the fathers. Freedom can only be found in the recovery of what is missing, in the discovering of that which makes the fathers groundless. And then we must sing!

Even at the heart of the triumph of patriarchy there is a route into an alternative text. The methodology of subversion can be identified by its willingness to play with those elements of the text that reach before and beyond. In Heidegger, the elements that point into the background are identified by the longing. What the longing longs for cannot be named within the noise and violence of patriarchy. The closest Heidegger's patriarchal text can overtly come is to the boundary: the longing for the point of intersection. Hercules, Dionysus, and Christ intersect with the memory of the Goddess only as her destroyers. They represent the last point of the Goddess, the first point of patriarchy. Heidegger's longing is not for the Goddess, except dialectically. He longs to participate in that destruction, to follow in the footsteps of the matricides. His longing is filled with bewilderment at the disappearance of the victor, the one who defaults in the absence of a victim. The inability of patriarchal heroes to exist independently shows in their fading footsteps. They fall into the abyss left by her absence.

Such a reading of his text necessarily goes beyond Heidegger's apparent intentions. Yet it is not foreign to his project. Heidegger opens history. He is aware of the multivocity of the metaphors he invokes. Within that openness of meaning other meanings, even meanings that stand in conflict with accepted meanings and ordinary assumptions, have a place. The nature of Heidegger's project is a dialogue: with language, with the past, with the future.

> Each man is in each instance in dialogue with his forebear[er]s, and perhaps even more and in a more hidden manner with those who will come after him.[27]

Perhaps this is not quite the future Heidegger had in mind, yet it is nonetheless the future that draws on Heidegger and therefore draws what he has to say into the future, in dialogue.

The hidden dialogue speaks after the openness implicit in texts and beyond the intentions of the author. The nature of this particular dialogue is problematic precisely because the history of philosophy is an attempt to prevent women from intervening in the progress of patriarchal philosophy. To subvert the meaning is to take it away from the old dead white men, and make it say something else entirely—not entirely unrelated, but entirely resisted. A hermeneutic of subversion makes visible the hole, the abyss, of the longing as an event of significance within the text. It also changes the meaning of the abyss. The continuing presence of the abyss as conceived by Heidegger dialectically points at what is missing. Just as the lack of a biblical term for female divinity proves highly significant in interpreting the relation of the ancient Hebrews to their matristic neighbors, Heidegger's poetry provides an access to that which cannot be said by the romantic old men of our civilization.

Perhaps any patriarchal text has the capacity of opening into otherness, though the proof of this can be found only in the doing. The methodology offers a way. A feminist hermeneutic is a revolutionary, subversive act that establishes a dialogue between the overt text and another negated text. The longing in Heidegger's text hints at a more primordial possibility. There are other hints which lead us back. What we seek are those points in a text which disclose negation. Wherever there is something to be negated, there is something to be feared and something to be hated. In a patriarchal text, that which is feared or hated might point to a minority voice that has been suppressed.

A longing that cannot be satisfied by the terms of the system within which it arises points beyond the text. Heidegger's text, for example, poses a mystery which the text cannot answer. The longing points a way, but the way disappears from view. The task of a subversive feminist hermeneutic is to examine the symbols that embody the longing. The symbols cast their own shadows, quite apart even from Heidegger's own intentions. Here may be found hints of women's past buried amidst the shadows, waiting to be excavated. When brought to light, the direction of the travel is reversed. No longer does one go outward after a distant grail; rather, the travel spirals inward into the forbidden.

What is forbidden is the fruit given to Eve. Patriarchy fears the fruit and therefore names it evil. Even the God fears its allure, and therefore forbids it absolutely. To eat of the fruit is to defy the patriarchal God. Invariably, conceptions of archetypal evil hint at the original object of rejection, which is the Goddess. The fruit of the tree of knowledge of good and evil is the fruit of the Goddess. She is named "evil incarnate" even though she is absent from the text. She is present in the text only in the person of her serpent. Even to name her would be to grant her too much power. Later, when the serpent becomes associated with Satan and the Devil, the original identification with the Goddess is lost. The Devil is too powerful a title to be granted a woman, for then it would have to be acknowledged that a feminine divinity threatens God himself. Nonetheless, the Devil's ontological Otherness points at the textual exclusion of the Goddess.

Archetypal evil is the hated and despised enemy that is suspected to be lurking everywhere. The association with the Goddess is now thoroughly suppressed. Against such an enemy, any violence, any immorality, can be justified. Every aspect of life and death is condemned for its association with her. Every enemy takes on something of her substance. Herein lies the source of man's viciousness in warfare, for every enemy begins to look like the Devil, and the Devil is always associated with her. Regardless of the goals of the rhetoric, every war repeats Hercules' feat and becomes a war on women and children. The process of negation is never complete: evil must be destroyed over and over. The fear and hatred of ontological evil is an irrational, ghastly residue of vigilance, constantly seeking to erase shadows of her form.

In the end, the only tool that can successfully assuage the fears of the fathers is genocide, the destruction of some group of people seen to embody some element of her being. Because evil is perceived in ontological terms, any actions taken in the name of the good is justifiable by reference to the despicable potential of the bad. Any act can be justified by the need to eliminate the existence of evil, and every such immoral act reenacts the first genocide by which patriarchy emerged.

Texts carry the symbols by which the hated otherness can be identified with the ancient enemy of man. For feminist re-searchers, these clues become the means of access to the almost forgotten shadows which lurk in patriarchal texts, which hint at subversive possibilities. The "trick" is to learn to recognize the signals of suppressed dialogue in its dialectical longing which is both a longing for the *mater*, the ground—and a longing for her blood.

The longing within Heidegger's text is dialectically allied with the forces of hate and genocide. Historically, his association with the Third Reich follows from the romanticism of his nostalgia for the primordial past from which Western culture originated. Heidegger does not worship violence, but the symbol of the united three points to the genocidal roots of the West to which his longing draws him. All who turn to the sources of Western culture are infected with the masked symbols of its violence. Heidegger's texts long for, yet do not follow, the footsteps of the gods to their ground. The missing gods themselves stand in the way. Heidegger reaches into the abyss after the ground and mourns that he is too late. The structure implicit in the textual symbols reveals that his mourning is ambivalent. The footsteps he wishes to follow are united in the destruction of the ground, in obliterating her existence. Genocide is the subverted text of his poetry.

A hermeneutic of subversion gains its power from knowledge of the process of negation by which the Goddess is excluded from consciousness. We can deepen that consciousness, by making clear the awareness of the Goddess implicit in that which is not said. The result is controversy, not conclusions. This is not a conspiracy theory that has the whole of Western thought sitting in conscious exclusion of the Goddess. Heidegger does not reject the ground in active collusion with the nazis, nor is he necessarily a woman-hater in his personal or public life. Rather his thought, by participation in patriarchy, is unable to see its own shadow. His metaphors, his search into language, are all shaped by the patriarchal project of exclusion. Interpretation opens up dimensions beyond the obvious. Feminist hermeneutics exhibits the power that was always implicit in interpretation. Behind the texts of men's authority, hidden in the multiple meaning of the symbols they employ, there are shadows. We do not deny the interpretations which properly belong to the surface of the text. Rather we shine the intense light of our anger upon the surface of the text, so that the shadows are as evident as the intentionality of the words.

Is it legitimate to use texts to say what they do not intend? Clearly such interpretations are illegitimate. They are born out of wedlock, and, therefore, they are free of the locks of the fathers. Subversion represents an uprising of bastards, of the disinherited. Women's texts are missing: They have been stolen, denied, destroyed. Patriarchal texts have been given us instead. Therefore, we will reconstruct from their shadows a bastard inheritance.

The interpretations are not therefore arbitrary. They speak to the very depths of the text, are buried in the nature of these distinct symbols. The nature of subversive thinking is that it highlights the alternatives. Both the surface and the background speak in high relief by virtue of the contrast. Unlike the fathers, we do not pirate nor destroy the texts that deny women's legitimacy. Rather the subversion remains always in conversation with the original. It serves to preserve even Heidegger, as he stands, as providing a context for exploring the background. We move into and beneath the *Abgrund*, following that which will forever draw the gods in after itself. The text remains as a signpost on the *Abgrund* as Heidegger left it.

Every patriarchal text, by the nature of its sexism, by the necessity of its support for the monologue, stands in dialectical relationship to the denial. The reversal of the texts is a necessary precondition of the re-searching of the foundations of the current power structures. The methodology of subversion continues to reclaim our memory from the very heart of patriarchal texts and thought. Recognizing the power inherent in the reversal frees us to respond to our own training and collusion with current institutions without betrayal of the promise of a new point of departure. We cannot yet abandon the texts of patriarchy's ascendancy. Indeed we must be among those who refuse to forget women's exclusion, for the patterns and symbols of denial are our access to the destruction of our mothers. And the gods testify by their fear and hatred and longing that destruction is not even now quite complete. What was done may yet be undone. This is the fugitive hope we follow beyond the default of the gods.

NOTES

1. Martin Heidegger, *Being and Time*, trans. John Macquarrie and Edward Robinson (New York: Harper and Row, 1962), 106–7.
2. Mary Daly, in *Gyn/Ecology: The Metaethics of Radical Feminism* (Boston: Beacon Press, 1990), develops the etymology of this word in a way that liberates

the word from its use to insult and control women. See pages 14–17.

3. Heidegger, *Being and Time*, 195.
4. Martin Heidegger, "A Dialogue on Language between a Japanese and an Inquirer," in *On the Way to Language*, trans. Peter Hertz (New York: Harper and Row, 1971), 51.
5. See, for example, the discussion of the relationship between Hannah Arendt and Martin Heidegger in Elzbieta Ettinger, *Hannah Arendt Martin Heidegger* (New Haven: Yale University Press, 1995).
6. Heidegger, "A Dialogue on Language," *On the Way to Language*, 9.
7. Heidegger, *Being and Time*, 19.
8. Heidegger, "A Dialogue on Language," *On the Way to Language*, 7.
9. Martin Heidegger, "The Nature of Language," *On the Way to Language*, 90.
10. See Heidegger's "The Origin of the Work of Art," in *Poetry, Language, Thought*, trans. Albert Hofstadter (New York: Harper and Row, 1971), 53.
11. Heidegger, *Being and Time*, 488.
12. This hint has not been totally ignored. See Luce Irigaray, *L'Oubli de l'air chez Martin Heidegger* (Paris: Minuit, 1983).
13. Heidegger, "What Are Poets For?" *Poetry, Language, Thought*, 91.
14. Ibid.
15. Ibid., 93.
16. Ibid., 92.
17. Ibid., 94.
18. Ibid., 91.
19. The *Creation Epic* of the Akkadians, tablet IV, 93–127, trans. E. A. Speiser, in James B. Pritchard, ed., *The Ancient Near East: An Anthology of Texts and Pictures* (Princeton, N.J.: Princeton University Press, 1956), 34–35.
20. The *Creation Epic* of the Akkadians, tablet IV, 128–40, *The Ancient Near East*, 35.
21. Daly, *Gyn/Ecology*, 66.
22. William Blake Tyrrell, and Frieda S. Brown, *Athenian Myths and Institutions: Words in Action* (New York: Oxford University Press, 1991), 61.
23. Daly, *Gyn/Ecology*, 88.
24. Heidegger, "What Are Poets For?" *Poetry, Language, Thought*, 91.
25. Euripides, *Bacchae* 752–67.
26. Daly, *Gyn/Ecology*, 111.
27. Heidegger, "A Dialogue on Language," *On the Way to Language*, 31.

CONCLUSION:
SPINNING THE CANON

THIS IS THE END. But wouldn't it be curious if it should turn out to be a beginning?

Imagine that human civilization were to take a turn toward a new value system, perhaps a value system based on women's truth, not men's. What a curious, presumptuous claim! Let us choose some text that centers itself in women's thought, and that includes some discussion, with quotations, of the texts of the Western (male) philosophical heritage. Imagine that women's texts have replaced men's texts, and then that the men's texts are lost. Imagine even that the reversal results in the erasure of what came before. Perhaps then all these male thinkers and writers are known only through the fragmentary remains of what women have to say about them. What a curious view of these works by Plato, Anselm, and so forth, such a society would inherit! Written works are subject to the preservers, those who come after, who edit and revise, suppress and preserve what comes before. If nothing were preserved directly of men's works, our view of their ideas would be very different, very strange indeed. Our reconstruction of their works would necessarily be tentative, but it could be done. This is the premise upon which this work is based. The possibility of erasure applies to all texts and all cultures.

The transmutation of time and social structures gives us a responsibility to the texts that we inherit. Just as there is the possibility of a revisionist history, one that seeks to re-create all history in its own image, so also there might be revisionist interpretation. Revisionist interpretation would take texts and erase the alternatives. Revisionist interpretation is possible, because all texts are always subject to interpretation, to revision, to ideological appropriation. The very writing of a text is a process of revision, interpretation, and ideology. The public appearance of a text signifies only a pause in the writing of the text; it is not the conclusion. Interpretation is a part of the process of the text in its essential nature. When a text is closed down rather than being opened up by an interpretation, the text becomes a monument to an ideology.

Revisionist history erases and closes down alternative meanings and voices. Its intention is to deny access to a people, a way of life, an alternative too threatening to be included in the dialogue. The alternative history that we offer as the basis for this project is the product of a new vision of what came before, of the alternatives that honored women and included them in power. This alternative has been, and may still be, too threatening to be open to consideration. Our Western philosophical texts are revisionist texts. They were written, or perhaps preserved, because they served the fathers' purposes in the erasure of alternatives. Yet the record of the alternative is present as a subvoice of the text. It is to this subvoice, this subverse, that we have dedicated our work.

In the very idea of a subverse, there is an acknowledgment of an overt voice in the text. Texts speak with many voices. This is the presupposition that underlies the possibility of interpretation. The day is long gone when one can speak of an authoritative, indubitable "true" text. The text-in-itself has gone the way of the thing-in-itself. It may be necessary to posit such a thing, but we have no access to it. Likewise, the notion of judging interpretations in light of the intentions of the author has become problematic, given that the author's intentions are only available as text or as interpretations. Even so, though one may debate the meaning of the text, that debate has not the right to erase the voice of the text from the conversation. There is an irrevocable givenness and objectivity of a text that ought not be erased or denied. What gives the text its own integrity is its nature as event and as "objection" over-against interpretation.

Living white men are, of course, most concerned that their texts may be violated by an opening of interpretation to everyone and everything. If texts are opened to all interpretations, then soon the texts may become indistinguishable from something they were never meant to mean. Even as, grudgingly and with tremendous resentment on the part of the academic establishment, literary criticism has opened the nature of interpretation to the dangers of deconstruction and cultural critique, the question of limiting the extent of interpretation arises. At what point does a textual interpretation become inappropriate?

It is difficult for those whose texts have disappeared under the weight of the old dead white men's ruminations to be very sympathetic with this concern. The erasure and misappropriation of texts has been the standard response of the tradition to any alternative ways of thinking or reflecting. Finally, only the standard texts of the old dead white men and their authorized interpreters qualify. The very process of interpretation has locked out alternatives and ensured that only the interpretations that continue and support patriarchal presumptions are "legitimate" uses of the texts. The concern about misappropriation is equally a fear of loss of control. The fear of the bastardizing of texts is a guilty projection of those who know what it might mean for the sins of the fathers to return upon the heads of their sons.

This project is a hopeful response to the concern about the possible loss of the classical heritage in the modern age. A heritage cannot be permanently lost. The ideas that the fathers thought they had thoroughly erased turn out to maintain their integrity even in the face of centuries of denial of their reality. Texts, ideas, ways of thinking have the capacity, always and forever, to return to haunt those who have erased them. The nature of interpretation is to stay in conversation with that which it opposes. Interpretation emerges out of the nature of the text, of every text, as conversation. Insofar as interpretation silences that with which it speaks, it violates the nature of the text. This is precisely what the texts of Western philosophy have done. The old texts, the missing texts, speak beneath and behind the silencing. Every time someone attempts to call back the dead, to trace their murder within the texts, there will be someone who will claim that this violates the texts, that it makes them say something other than what was intended. The fathers would like to make old murders sacred, immune to prosecution. The attempt to create appropriate "criteria" for the interpretation of texts is no final protection for the preservation of the heritage. Texts that erase contain within themselves the footprints of that which they have erased. The dead, no matter how misappropriated, come back to haunt the living.

The fathers need not worry. Our interpretations of the texts both assume and revoke the overt directionality of the texts. Our only access to the other layers of meaning is through the surface meaning with which they stand in opposition. The power of the reversal is directly proportional to the awareness the reader has that the text has been reversed. For this reason we tend to speak as if there were a clear intentionality in the text, an intentionality that may belong more to the tradition than to the text. Then we place that directionality in conversation with a radical alternative, which is nonetheless also within the text. The text becomes problematic, but it does not disappear. The text becomes not the object but a partner in the conversation. It lives in its opposition to our positioning. It is active in its problematic responsiveness. The reader turns to the text and the text turns to the reader, for both are participants in the conversation.

Is our interpretation of the texts "right"? It is not in agreement with the overt meaning of the texts. Rather it is a conversation between possibilities of meaning suggested by the text. The text becomes *con-text*. Within that context is an opening into meaning. Texts are multivocal. They contain within themselves a multiplicity of meanings. Does this mean that all interpretations are equal? The question is a peculiar one, for it assumes the text is an object to which things are done, namely interpretations. A text is a conversation. Some conversations are more like monologues, some are full of malapropisms, some are like the conversations between strangers, but every conversation reveals something about the nature of the speaking. The better the conversation, the more alive the participants in that conversation, full of nuance and difference, irreducible to any single meaning. Our conversation with the texts of the old dead white men is a loving conversation, meant to make them roll over in their graves, that is, to come alive again in conversation with those of us who are not happy with how they left our world.

It is clear that we regard the texts that we inherit as already interpreted, even in the selectivity of their preservation. These are the texts of the old dead white men, both in the sense that they were written by old dead white men and that they are preserved by the fathers as a means of maintaining a certain kind of world. To place the texts in relation to women is already a violation of the texts, which had (and continue) to regard women as a subset of wider, more "philosophical" issues. Our claim is that the absence of women from among the authors, and the way in which the texts do or do not treat women, is pivotal to the understanding of the text and to the world texts create. Here is where we begin our conversation, with a silence and denial that we think can lead into an alternative world of meaning. The conversation understands that the very fact of the conversation moves us both away from what the text "wants" to mean and into the text in a new way. The conversation is implied in the text, but only as a dysfunctional family will avoid the subject that is most central to its problem. This is an argument with the texts and with most of the tradition that has regarded the absence of women as accidental to the texts. Even now it is hard for anyone to place the absence of women, or the negative appropriations of women, as important in a philosophical or hermeneutical sense. To do so is already to violate the texts in their implicit claim to the unimportance of the issue.

In some sense our interpretation is subject to the criticism that we have imposed upon the texts a twentieth-century concern with the rights and views of women. This is a true criticism, in that the texts of these times did not concern themselves with the issue of women's rights, as understood in this time and in this place. Yet the criticism is also reflective of the ideological bias of the twentieth century, that regards all previous times as limited in the nature of their truth by virtue of being the product of a historical time and thus reducible to their historical context. Past texts did not see themselves as reflecting merely a time but as addressing the timeless and universal claims of philosophy. To impose pon them a claim that they are only responsible for issues of a single time is to render them something other than philosophical texts, to reduce their truth claims to the status of merely historical interest.

The objection to raising the question of women's claim on philosophy to historical texts is, even as a historical claim, a curious claim, for it assumes that women were not around or of importance "back then." This claim assumes that women only became of importance in the modern age when men decided they were worthy of consideration. There is a chauvinism implicit in the assumption that our own time *does* regard women of importance and the assumption that women of past times did not object to their secondary status. Both of these claims have problems even as historical claims. Such claims about the superior status of women in the twentieth century do not reflect the greater flexibility, say, of God language in Anselm's texts as opposed to modern, exclusively patriarchal, language about God.

More important than the shortsightedness of the rejection of women's struggles for acknowledgment prior to our own time, there is a hermeneutical issue at stake. Our interpretation is committed to texts as living texts, even those texts written by old dead white men. The texts are not reducible to historical contexts. They make claims against us. We are they. They continue to shape our reality, and we address them because by doing so we have access to our contemporary world. We are what we are because they speak, now. These are the substance of our understanding of ourselves. What we offer to the next generation will be shaped by how we understand who they are and what they say. Like Plato's philosopher kings, we might wish to erase the past and begin anew, but as soon as we even say that we hear the contradiction. It is we who would do the erasing, and thus our erasing will reflect that which we would remove.

We must teach our students, and these are still the best truths we have. The texts live by their capacity to continue to address and be addressed by their audiences. Even to abandon them would simply be to adopt paler shadows of their meanings. History is the story of the present, told in the form that brings it to consciousness. The past lives can speak in its texts, and in speaking to it we come to understand ourselves.

This is not a determinism, as if our present is simply caused by the past. Rather we exist in the conversation between meanings, which we access by those old conversational partners, the philosophers. The fact that our texts are the way they are sets the terms of the conversation, even when we wish it did not. So it becomes of crucial importance, if we would open our future, that we open our past. We must speak with the past, but we must do so in new ways. To do this we must reopen the multiplicity of voices that have been forced underground by the ideological commitments of the present preservers. It was to their benefit to claim that the texts "mean" a certain thing, for they therefore could close off the way into alternative futures that is always implicit in texts. The concern with the misappropriation of the classics is itself ideological. Yet to say this, as if the naming of its ideological bias negated its right to claim truth, misses the point. The identification of bias should suggest that there are other ways. It should not be an excuse to turn off this biased way also. Every ideology stands in relation to what it denies as well as to that which it affirms. Turn the ideology over, and one finds a door, a way into the alternative.

Our conversation tries to keep in view the ideological bias that is in closest conversation with that which is our own ideological bias. We begin with a bias toward the possibility of an alternative way of constructing human society, which is somehow connected with a focus upon women's reality. Or rather, we begin with a rejection of that possibility which we discover within the ideological bias of the classical texts. The interest of patriarchy in suppressing women suggests that women are dangerous or that thinking about women's situation can lead to a possibility that threatens patriarchy. That possibility we claim. But our claiming of the alternative always stands in relation to the rejection by the texts as claimed by a patriarchal tradition. Ours is a conversation with another who would not hear us but whose texts introduce us to ourselves even so, even if they would not do so willingly.

These texts exclude the voice of women. Was this the motivation that led to the texts? Perhaps so or perhaps not. Perhaps only the exclusion of women's voice motivated their preservation. Perhaps even they wrote in the hope of preserving, secretly, that which we now discover. It does not matter, nor could we ever be sure which was true. All the possible intentions are hidden in the ongoing role these texts play in our culture. Whatever these texts meant in the past, they speak now because they serve as a basis for a society that is committed to a patriarchal project. The exclusion of women from these texts continues to speak for and to men, because they legitimate women's exclusion from the determination of meaning in the present, and above all in the future. Thus the texts are, essentially and concretely, the texts of old dead white men, by old dead white men, to preserve the claims to superiority of living white men.

By naming the ideological bias we attempt to reopen a conversation that underlies the bias. A bias is a claim on truth, a claim in a conversation, which can open as well as close off meaning. The structure of the text as a claim on truth stands over and against the interpreter, and especially over and against such interpreters as we. Because we are not in agreement with the overt claim, the structure of the interpretation as a conversation can be consciously before us. Into this conversation the reader is invited. The reader is invited into the process of interpreting the text, and, because what we offer is not the authoritative version of the text, the reader may well disagree and stand by the text in its over-and-against character. Yet because what we offer, over and against the text, is also a truth claim, the reader is also invited into the text as a dialogue.

The old dead white men have moldered too long in their graves, while still holding on to their texts. Now the texts will be set free, to seek new partners in dialogue. The tendency of texts to become old and heavy is not implicit in the nature of texts, but in the property rights exerted over them by the authority of authorship. Suppose that these texts belonged to us all. Suppose that we stood in a tradition that held to the openness of texts. Wouldn't we then dare to dream that *über* the *Mensch* was a pathway to the little old woman who sweeps under the moon? Wouldn't we wander back with Socrates into the cave, leaving the sun behind? Wouldn't our students construct their own dialogues, in which Kierkegaard the magician pulls out one more trick and turns God into a woman? Then our sacred canon of philosophy would, like the sacred biblical canon, grow by accretions of new meanings. In the possibility of adding meaning to texts, there is great danger but also great possibility. We call on those who would be a part of the building of texts to come and to participate in the conversation that is our heritage. Then it will be no wonder that the men in charge will be worried!

Women are storytellers at heart. Women have gone through a long drought in which their stories have been taken over by texts. Even the fairy tales have been taken from the grandmothers and collected, collated, and pinned to the names of the men who then own them. It will be hard to become accustomed again to the telling of stories. When the old dead white men give over the keys to their castles, the dragons return. Can truth survive the opening into story? Can a text dance? Can *Sophia* sing? And if she does begin to sing, who will write the verses?

Truth calls to the story, though in a different way than the truth of correspondence. Truth as a story is an opening into world. When one hears truth, one recognizes it, but this is not the recollection of a preexistent truth that Socrates offers us. Rather one recognizes it as one might walk into beauty. Truth is a slow building of wonder at the intricate interwoven nature of wholeness. Truth happens when one is surprised, when one is transformed, when one comes home. One recognizes the pond around the bend. We come home to truth, pouring over the little details that make us aware of our belonging, just so, just here.

We are most at home when we are surprised by truth. Indeed truth is stranger than fiction, and perhaps this is the major difference. We come home and nothing is the same. This we ask of our stories: surprise us with truth we both recognize and resist. That which reduces to what we expect lacks the over-and-against character of truth's singing. Men too long have listened to each other's voices. Their discourse drowns in the reworking of what they already all agree upon. Their differences are in danger of becoming trivial. What they need is to speak with truth, and for that they need to go back to the beginning. Woman is man's opportunity to start philosophy all over.

But who is this "woman"? "Woman" is not to be taken as an ontological entity. Nor is "woman" an abstract idea.

If she confines herself to asking the question of woman (what is woman?), she might merely be attempting to provide an answer to the honorable male question: what does woman want? She herself still remains the *object* of the question.[1]

The formal construction of woman, as having a womb, as sometimes being mothers, as men's sexual partners and objects, as the virgin and the whore and the lesbian, can be traced through many of the philosophical images of the old and new philosophers. Yet these images of woman do not touch the concreteness of women in their lived historical experience. Nor do these images make a way for women to reclaim any part of the heritage of thought and discourse that belongs to philosophy. Instead, finding definitions of woman in male thought is like overhearing a conversation in a locker room. The idea of Woman, the very being of woman, is distant from women. It belongs to men, who find women less troublesome in their universal form. The whole idea of ideas and particulars belongs to men and to men's thought. Men own the ideas and women wear them awkwardly.

What we seek is an epic poem within the interaction of idea and particular, of men's denial of women's reality and men's claiming of women's physiological structure qua "woman." In an epic poem the levels of interaction make of the idea a possibility for action. Woman, then, is not something that one *is*, it is something in which one participates and is transformed by the participation. That a woman bleeds is a fact, a concrete, a particular. That a woman is as one who is contaminated by blood is a traditional ontological understanding of woman. If, by bleeding, one participates in the divine feminine, as the blood that infuses the universe with life, the fact of bleeding is returned to the one who does, in fact, bleed, as a possibility for meaning. The individual woman is not Woman, but discovers Woman as a possibility before her, a reaching into the fact, and into the symbol, and into the history of the symbol, to create a poem which can be lived. Such a poem is poetry-as-praxis. Such a poem is a myth. Having said this frees women to drop their blood, so to speak, in public. Such a saying is to reclaim, by concrete social change, the possibility of doing what they are as a revolutionary act of affirmation. By such poetry, by myth, the world is transformed.

The loss of the play of words that belongs to the human species occurred in conjunction with the loss of women's symbolic power in the world. The ontological meaning of the Woman was, and is, a historical enterprise, even as it is a symbolic enterprise, for history is the symbolic enterprise par excellence. The concrete, physical suppression of women is a consequence and response to the need to overcome her power as symbol and as maker of symbols. Thus the hidden, and not so hidden, use of Woman as symbol in the philosophical texts is not irrelevant. Feminists have finally begun to catalog the vast collection of misogynist sayings and statements made by the respectable forefathers of our systems of thought and being. More recently, feminists, such as Mary Daly and Luce Irigaray, have begun to uncover the ways in which woman has been dismembered, and her parts transformed into caves and oceans. What they show us is shocking, and the shock of rereading profound and seminal works of men in terms of their fascination and disparagement of the female body has the power to wake us from our reified admiration of their spiritual accomplishments. Such readings bring the great men down to the level of the kind of misogyny women understand and have learned to deal with, and this is a major accomplishment. What is needed, what is still needed, is some way of going on from there to the construction of new meanings. Otherwise, again, women are stuck with the horror of being the object of men's dismemberment. Women's image of themselves remains a catalog of men's abuse.

As Daly points out, however, the very word "dismemberment" hints at the possibility that can liberate women in the midst of their existence in the living texts of men's construction. What can be *dis*-membered, can be *re-membered*. Texts are historical, not as the mere past, the over-and-done-with, but as the active interaction of symbol and practice in the human construction of the world. And, what is constructed can be re-constructed. History is humanity's greatest poem: the attempt to understand ourselves as action and as meaning. The ideas and systems of the old dead white men walk among us, acting with us, making us what we are, opening or closing us to what we might be. "Woman" is the symbol, not of some reification of the female as body, but of the essential drama we are still in the process of telling. "Woman" is what history is about, the "Woman" that was dismembered, and the "Woman" we are about to remember.

What a grandiose claim to be made about one's humble cleaning lady, the old woman and her broom! Woman *is* not something. We don't know what the idea means, or who the woman is, as a content or metaphysical entity, or even as an ontology of female existence. What we claim her as is the locus of the intense collusion of meanings, which has generated in the past and continues to generate in the present, the male construction of meaning, as one of hierarchy, competition, power, and violence. "Woman" is the symbol of men's construction of meaning as a coherent, world-defining event, as his-story, and as history. The necessity of constructing the world in terms of self and other, of man and woman, of conqueror and conquered, comes to symbolic meaning in the suppression and distortion and dissembling about the word "Woman." Therefore, the placing of the philosophical texts of that world constructing act we call history in relation to "Woman," first as idea and then as concrete woman, liberates women into their own possibility of acting as world historical agents. What is at stake is the possibility of rebuilding the world from the ground up. What is at stake is the evolution of man into something else, something as yet unimagined by men. Even more, what is at stake is the revolution of woman into world singer.

Prehistory is an idea that occurs within the context of the ongoing, historical acts of resistance by women to men's domination. Men's control is largely a matter of control of memory. Every generation of women is taught to forget that their mothers were not happy, were not satisfied, and that they resisted. Every generation of women begin again, thinking that theirs is the first generation to attempt liberation. Every generation finds its mothers a drag on its own ambition. Every generation "has it better" than the generations before them. This is the concrete structure of forgetting, which is always specific and which serves ideology as much, if not more, than remembering. Men's history is above all a selection process, a Dr. Mengele standing at the head of the line and separating those ideas which will "work" from those ideas which are best forgotten. By forgetting, concrete present men "for-get," they get beforehand the meanings they want and need to control the future. Forgetting prehistory forgets not something in the distant past before history, but forgets the meanings that are "pre" and apart from whatever is to be preserved by the fathers. The prohibitionists and the witches, the gnostics and the maneads, are all prehistory, meaning that they come before the forgetting, and stand apart from the story that belongs to men's story.

Beneath and behind and around that story which belongs to the fathers is the larger shadow of prehistory. This is the claim that before all the civilizations we call the "beginning" of civilization, there existed other societies: powerful, creative, "advanced" societies that honored women as divinity and empowered women as leaders and self-defining participants in their own sexuality of reproduction. The facticity of prehistory is probably the biggest battle of meaning to be fought in our memory. In archaeology, in anthropology, in mythology, in religion, the struggle to claim a coherent, intelligible, factual example of a fundamental alternative to patriarchy is being waged. The most powerful weapon men have is still the power to erase this memory, even as it is being formed, and to make a mockery of those researchers who present the possibility. In the ruins there are hints, and in the ridicule there is confirmation that it may have been possible, it may still be possible, to live in a society in which advances in all forms of social existence are consistent with the rejection of male domination. The very act of positing such a reality, no matter how dim and distant that reality is, constitutes a revolutionary act.

Our own project rests on a commitment to that exploration of ancient texts and shadowed cities. Our project poses the claimed reality of prehistory as the grounds for mythmaking. Prehistory is a kind of history, thus it exists as symbol and as "fact." It exists as symbol, as a metaphor for that otherness, that alternative within the text. The texts we explore carry possibilities for interpretation, reversal, sub-versal. Our interpretations follow the "spirit" of the text, as a multivocal texture of initiation and response, of discourse both acknowledged and denied. Within that spirit we discover other spirits. The texts create history as meaning and become our door into alternative meaning, also as history. This other history is prehistory, as the history that is not, not anymore or at least not here and not now. Prehistory is, in a certain sense, ahistorical. The "pre" in prehistory is originating and primordial. Its priority exists alongside and over and against history. Prehistory as it exists in relation to the texts of philosophy does not need a knowledge of archaeological digs but of the lure and resistance to the other possibility of human existing, the possibility represented by woman.

It is prehistory, the myth of the concurrent alternative pathway through history, that is our way of reclaiming the texts of the old dead white men. If these texts can be rewritten from within, without in turn violating their otherness to the project, then women can make them their own. It is as though one were to discover by happenstance that once there was a magical grandmother, one whose very existence promised a model for living a life. One might ask one's grandfather, and ask and ask and ask. All that the grandfather would say might be negative and demeaning, but one might hear in those comments also the power of what went before. One would become very sneaky, asking about things that appeared unrelated but that would allow one to garner details about what the grandfather would not say. And in the still darkness of the attic full of things that might have been hers, and that might be things of power which were intended for the granddaughter, one might put together a possible other, the grandmother, who might also be one's mother, or one's sister, or even one's self. Soon in everything that was said, one would begin to hear echoes of that lost possibility, and then one would add to it one's own dreams. The grandmother is too tenuous to be merely real and thus too tenuous to be really dead. One sees her now, sweeping the cobwebs from the stars.

How is fantasy to be distinguished from reality in such a case? Reality has long ago been claimed by those who grant to women no independent existence. A woman's fantasies are more necessary than bread in barren times. But she must test herself, and will test herself, against the hardness of the men's denial of her reality and her fantasy. Even so, the right to engage in illicit conversations with the old philosophers requires the willingness not to pretend that we think these subverses are what the text "really says." The dialectical nature of the enterprise we have just finished is essential. The subverses are just that, are subversive, and they test their reality, not by agreement but by the truest kind of disagreement. The reader must choose, and the authors of this piece must keep the choice present, so that what comes of the interpretation is left open. This is what Socrates did *not* say, not just any not saying, but the not saying that is very close, even in reversal. Here is the delicacy in the secret fantasy of woman, to spin tales while respecting that men are unwilling participants.

We would hope that, if this works, others might dare to try spinning tales around the old dead white men's texts. Texts have gone through a long period of rigidity, of separation from their sources in dialogue and conversation. But perhaps not all that rigidity was inherent in the nature of text as in the nature of the technology and social agreement that shaped and preserved and maintained the texts. The ideology that made reproduction the matter of producing exact copies, instead of corrupt copies, produced the printing press that guaranteed the author's control over his offspring. The structures of economics that were grounded in the private ownership of everything, women, children, ideas, and texts, created its own subsidiary concerns for accurate transmission and attempts to guarantee the author's prior right to interpretation.

There will be new technological and social experiments, as yet unknown. Perhaps in the future there will be new kinds of preservation, preservation of texts in something other than rigid, immutable formulations which rest forever in museum collections of the relics of old dead white men. Perhaps in the future, as in the past, authors' names will indicate schools of thought, or initiating voices in conversations. Perhaps in the future, an author like Heidegger will be more like Moses, in which collections of voices are woven and rewoven. Perhaps someday the voice of divinity will be recognized in multiple voices, some perhaps even contradictory, rather than in homogenized renderings that purport to proclaim a single authoritative truth.

There are those who already object to the watering down of the corpus of classical texts that shape the Western heritage. For them, the very existence and inclusion of alternative, minority voices in the curriculum of civilization is an affront. Our enterprise in some sense stands with them, with those who return in love and commitment to the voices that have stood the test of time. We return to the classics, with an insistence that history lives, either consciously or unconsciously, and that by studying the classics we come to self-consciousness of our past and our present and our future. In another sense, however, our defense of the classics will but move the battle closer to home. The classics we discuss are laid open for the emergence of just that multiculturalism which is most dangerous because it is closest to the heart. If we can learn to interpret the old dead white men in such a way as to open them into the revolutionary discussions being introduced by women and by people of color and by first peoples, we may make the old dead white men too dangerous to be discussed. This enterprise is thus an open invitation to all those who have some reason to be suspicious of the ideologies of the powers that be, to encourage our fellow thinkers to turn again to the texts that underlie and inform those ideologies. What has been closed can yet be opened.

So how does one do such a thing as we have done? Every strong value invites reversal. The values that underlie the formal systems of truth can be used as new points of departure. The stronger the position created, the more it poses itself in relation to its dialectical other. But why have we assumed that a position has only one other alternative? Texts are multivocal, with all kinds of hidden possibilities. To access those possibilities, look for the language that proclaims the worth of the truth being proclaimed. Watch not only for those values which the author claims as of worth but also for those truths of negative value which are rejected. What an author proclaims as evil or valueless is a clue, especially for women.

Arguments rest on metaphors, both implicit and stated. Metaphors call for poetic response and appropriation. The world calls to humans to sing it songs. Singers and mythmakers and storytellers have long known that each good telling invites another. We have long settled for exclusive truth. Let us have many beginnings! Sometimes one needs a beginning ex nihilo to reach into the silence of the nothingness which even now re-creates itself. Sometimes one needs a turtle upon which to stack the universes. Sometimes one needs an evolution out of apes to remind us of our debt to and interconnection with other animals. Sometimes one needs a story that the fossils were put there by an enterprising deity with a peculiar sense of humor. Sometimes one needs the world to exist in a womb of a Mother. Sometimes even one needs that woman be born out of man—but only on second Sundays when there is a prolonged eclipse of the moon. We have come out of the cave into the blinding brightness of the Sun too long. The task of the new interpreters will be to dare to take us back into the darkness.

This book, in other words, does not claim to have given the right or correct meaning of these texts, but the wrong interpretation consistently carried through. From there we can regain our sense of humor about deconstruction and textual authority and old dead white men. From there we can regain our sense of seriousness about creating symbols that dance with the earth and move us to new songs and new dances and new ways of designing our urban dwellings. We invite other wrong interpretations, as long as they sing, and love what they oppose.

All that we have written is dedicated first and foremost to *Sophia*, the goddess whose name is a subverse in the long love affair men have had with *philo-Sophia*. It is she who has taught us to listen to words that are spoken and words that are not spoken. She points the way for the return of the philosophical witches, those ancient wise women who have cackled their way through the alternative history, which is prior and independent of men's truth. When women become again philosophers they also will learn to cackle

at the presumptions of the old dead white men. They will be spinsters, spinning webs of meaning, attaching their webs to the old tomes and old tombs,
but also catching a truth or two if it should wander too close. They will be
the new thinkers, these dreamers and spinsters, these lovers of *Sophia*. It is
for them that this book is written. May they, and She, find the power to
laugh between the lines, to go back to loving old dead white men, and to
rewrite the future in Her name.

NOTE

1. Gayatri C. Spivak, "Displacement and the Discourse of Woman," in *Displacement: Derrida and After*, ed. Mark Krupnick (Bloomington: Indiana University
Press, 1983), 185–86.

BIBLIOGRAPHY

PLATO BIBLIOGRAPHY

Arendt, Hannah. *The Human Condition*. Chicago: University of Chicago Press, 1958.

Berger, Pamela. *The Goddess Obscured: Transformation of the Grain Protectress from Goddess to Saint*. Boston: Beacon Press, 1985.

Caragounis, Chrys C. *The Ephesian* Mysterion: *Meaning and Content*. Uppsala, Sweden: GWK Gleerup, 1977.

Craig, Leon H. *The War Lover: A Study of Plato's* Republic. Toronto: University of Toronto Press, 1994.

Derrida, Jacques. *The Post Card: From Socrates to Freud and Beyond*. Translated by Alan Bass. Chicago: University of Chicago Press, 1987.

Dow, Sterling, and Robert F. Healey. *A Sacred Calendar of Eleusis*. Cambridge: Harvard University Press, 1965.

Engelsman, Joan C. *The Feminine Dimension of the Divine*. Philadelphia: Westminster Press, 1979.

Foley, Helene P., ed. and trans. *The Homeric Hymn to Demeter*. Princeton, N.J.: Princeton University Press, 1994.

Garland, Robert. *Introducing New Gods: The Politics of Athenian Religion*. Ithaca: Cornell University Press, 1992.

Gimbutas, Marija. *The Goddesses and Gods of Old Europe: Myths and Cult Images*. Berkeley: University of California Press, 1982.

Graves, Robert, ed. *New* Larousse *Encyclopedia of Mythology*. London: Prometheus Press, 1968.

Harrison, Jane. *Prolegomena to the Study of Greek Religion*. New York: Meridian Books, 1955.

Irigaray, Luce. *Speculum of the Other Woman*. Translated by Gillian C. Gill. Ithaca: Cornell University Press, 1985.

Kraemer, Ross S. *Her Share of the Blessings: Women's Religions among Pagans, Jews, and Christians in the Greco-Roman World*. New York: Oxford University Press, 1992.

Lefkowitz, Mary R. *Women in Greek Myth*. Baltimore: John Hopkins University Press, 1986.

Lincoln, Bruce. *Emerging from the Chrysalis: Studies in Rituals of Women's Initiation*. Cambridge: Harvard University Press, 1981.

Mylonas, George. *Eleusis and the Eleusinian Mysteries*. Princeton, N.J.: Princeton University Press, 1961.

Nichols, Mary P. *Socrates and the Political Community: An Ancient Debate*. Albany: State University of New York Press, 1987.

Ophir, Adi. *Plato's Invisible Cities: Discourse and Power in the* Republic. Savage, Md.: Barnes and Noble, 1991.

211

Parke, H. W. *Festivals of the Athenians*. Ithaca: Cornell University Press, 1977.

Plato. *Plato's Republic*. Translated by G. M. A. Grube. Indianapolis: Hackett Publishing, 1974.

———. *The* Republic *of Plato*. Translated by Allan Bloom. New York: Basic Books, 1991.

———. *The* Republic *of Plato*. Translated by Francis M. Cornford. London: Oxford University Press, 1945.

———. *Symposium*. Translated by Alexander Nehamas and Paul Woodruff. Indianapolis: Hackett Publishing, 1989.

Rice, David G., and John E. Stambaugh. *Sources for the Study of Greek Religion*. Atlanta: Scholars Press, 1979.

Sayre, Kenneth M. *Plato's Literary Garden: How to Read a Platonic Dialogue*. Notre Dame: University of Notre Dame Press, 1995.

Spretnak, Charlene. *Lost Goddesses of Early Greece: A Collection of Pre-Hellenic Myths*. Boston, Beacon Press, 1992.

Strauss, Leo. *The City and Man*. Chicago: University of Chicago Press, 1964.

Tyrrell, William B., and Frieda S. Brown. *Athenian Myths and Institutions*. New York: Oxford University Press, 1991.

Vernant, Jean-Pierre. *Mortals and Immortals: Collected Essays*. Edited by Froma Zeitlin. Princeton, N.J.: Princeton University Press, 1991.

Ward, Benedicta. *Anselm Of Canterbury: A Monastic Scholar*. Oxford: SLG Press, 1973.

Wasson, R. Gordon, Albert Hofmann, and Carl A. P. Ruck. *The Road to Eleusis: Unveiling the Secret of the Mysteries*. New York: Harcourt, Brace, Jovanovich, 1978.

Wheelwright, Philip, ed. *The Presocratics*. New York: Odyssey Press, 1966.

White, Nicolas P. *A Companion to Plato's* Republic. Indianapolis: Hackett Publishing, 1979.

Zaidman, Louise B., and Pauline S. Pantel. *Religion in the Ancient Greek City*. Translated by Paul Cartledge. Cambridge: Cambridge University Press, 1992.

ANSELM BIBLIOGRAPHY

Allen, Prudence. *The Concept of Woman: The Aristotelian Revolution 750 BC–AD 1250*. Montreal: Eden Press, 1985.

Anselm, Saint. *Basic Writings: Proslogium, Monologium, Cur Deus Homo, Guanilo's* In Behalf of the Fool. Translated by S. N. Deane. La Salle, IL: Open Court Publishing, 1962.

———. *The Letters of Saint Anselm of Canterbury*. 3 vols. Translated by Walter Fröhlich. Kalamazoo, Mich.: Cistercian Publications, 1990–94.

———. *The Prayers and Meditations of Saint Anselm*. Translated by Benedicta Ward. New York: Penguin, 1973.

Baumstein, Paschal. "Revisiting Anselm: Current Historical Studies and Controversies." *Cistercian Studies Quarterly* 28, nos. 3–4 (1993): 207–29.

Blamires, Alcuin, ed. *Woman Defamed and Woman Defended: An Anthology of Medieval Texts*. Oxford: Clarendon Press, 1992.

Bridenthal, Renate, and Claudia Koonz, eds. *Becoming Visible: Women in European History*. Boston: Houghton Mifflin, 1977.

Claster, Jill. *The Medieval Experience: 300–1400*. New York: New York University Press, 1982.

Eadmer. *The Life of St. Anselm: Archbishop of Canterbury.* Edited and translated by R. W. Southern. Oxford: Clarendon Press, 1962.

Evans, Joan. *Life in Medieval France.* Oxford: Oxford University Press, 1925.

Gross, Susan H., and Marjorie W. Bingham. *Women in Medieval/Renaissance Europe.* St. Louis: Glenhurst Publications, 1983.

Hartshorne, Charles. *Anselm's Discovery: A Re-Examination of the Ontological Proof for God's Existence.* La Salle, Ill.: Open Court, 1965.

————. *The Divine Relativity: A Social Conception of God.* New Haven: Yale University Press, 1948.

Hick, John, and Arthur C. McGill, eds. *The Many-Faced Argument: Recent Studies on the Ontological Argument for the Existence of God.* New York: Macmillan, 1967.

Hollister, C. Warren. *Medieval Europe: A Short History.* 6th ed. New York: McGraw-Hill Publishing, 1990.

Kamuf, Peggy. *Fictions of Feminine Desire: Disclosures of Heloise.* Lincoln: University of Nebraska Press, 1982.

Labarge, Margaret W. *A Small Sound of the Trumpet: Women in Medieval Life.* Boston: Beacon Press, 1986.

McNamer, Elizabeth M. *The Education of Heloise: Methods, Content, and Purpose of Learning in the Twelfth-Century.* Lewiston, Me.: Edwin Mellen Press, 1991.

Morris, Thomas V. *Anselmian Explorations: Essays in Philosophical Theology.* Notre Dame: University of Notre Dame Press, 1987.

Rowling, Marjorie. *Everyday Life in Medieval Times.* New York: G. P. Putnam's Sons, 1968.

Southern, R. W. *Saint Anselm: A Portrait in a Landscape.* Cambridge: Cambridge University Press, 1990.

————. *Saint Anselm and His Biographer: A Study of Monastic Life and Thought.* Cambridge: Cambridge University Press, 1963.

Vaughn, Sally N. *The Abbey of Bec and the Anglo-Norman State 1034–1136.* Suffolk: Boydell Press, 1981.

————. *Anselm of Bec and Robert of Meulan: The Innocence of the Dove and the Wisdom of the Serpent.* Berkeley: University of California Press, 1987.

————. "Anselm: Saint and Statesman." *Albion* 20, no. 2 (Summer 1988): 205–20.

Warner, Marina. *Alone in All Her Sex: The Myth and the Cult of the Virgin Mary.* New York: Vintage, 1983.

KIERKEGAARD BIBLIOGRAPHY

Crites, Stephen. *In The Twilight of Christendom: Hegel vs. Kierkegaard on Faith and History.* Chambersburg, Penn.: American Academy of Religion, 1972.

Kant, Immanuel. *Critique of Pure Reason.* Translated by Norman Kemp Smith. New York: St. Martin's Press, 1965.

Kierkegaard, Søren. *Concluding Unscientific Postscript.* Translated by David Swenson. Princeton, N.J.: Princeton University Press, 1968.

————. *Fear and Trembling* [with *Repetition*]. Edited and translated by Howard V. Hong and Edna H. Hong. Princeton, N.J.: Princeton University Press, 1983.

————. *On Authority and Revelation: The Book on Adler, or a Cycle of Ethico-Religious Essays.* Translated by Walter Lowrie. New York: Harper and Row, 1966.

————. *Philosophical Fragments.* Edited and translated by Howard V. Hong and Edna H. Hong. Princeton, N.J.: Princeton University Press, 1985.

————. *The Point of View for My Work as an Author: A Report to History.* Translated by Walter Lowrie. New York: Harper and Row, 1962.

————. *Repetition* [with *Fear and Trembling*]. Edited and translated by Howard V. Hong and Edna H. Hong. Princeton, N.J.: Princeton University Press, 1983.

Makarushka, Irena. "Reflections on the 'Other' in Dinesen, Kierkegaard and Nietzsche." In *Kierkegaard on Art and Communication*, edited by George Pattison, 150–59. New York: St. Martin's Press, 1992.

Ricoeur, Paul. *Interpretation Theory: Discourse and the Surplus of Meaning.* Fort Worth: Texas Christian University, 1976.

Starhawk. *The Spiral Dance: A Rebirth of the Ancient Religion of the Great Goddess.* Rev. ed. San Francisco: Harper and Row, 1989.

Taylor, Mark Lloyd. "Ordeal and Repetition in Kierkegaard's Treatment of Abraham and Job." In *Foundations of Kierkegaard's Vision of Community: Religion, Ethics, and Politics in Kierkegaard*, edited by George Connell and C. Stephen Evans, 33–53. Atlantic Highlands, N.J.: Humanities Press, 1992.

Nietzsche Bibliography

Ackermann, Robert J. *Nietzsche: A Frenzied Look.* Amherst: University of Massachusetts Press, 1990.

Bennett, Benjamin. "Bridge: Against Nothing." In *Nietzsche and the Feminine*, edited by Peter J. Burgard, 289–315. Charlottesville: University Press of Virginia, 1994.

Burgard, Peter J. "Introduction: Figures of Excess." In *Nietzsche and the Feminine*, edited by Peter J. Burgard, 1–32. Charlottesville: University Press of Virginia, 1994.

Derrida, Jacques. *Spurs Nietzsche's Styles.* Translated by Barbara Harlow. Chicago: University of Chicago Press, 1979.

Gillespie, Michael A., and Tracy B. Strong, eds. *Nietzsche's New Seas: Explorations in Philosophy, Aesthetics, and Politics.* Chicago: University of Chicago Press, 1988.

Graybeal, Jean. *Language and "the Feminine" in Nietzsche and Heidegger.* Bloomington: Indiana University Press, 1990.

Irigaray, Luce. *"Ecce Mulier?* Fragments." In *Nietzsche and the Feminine*, edited by Peter J. Burgard, 316–31. Charlottesville: University Press of Virginia, 1994.

————. *Marine Lover of Friedrich Nietzsche.* Translated by Gillian Gill. New York: Columbia University Press, 1991.

Kofman, Sarah. "Baubô: Theological Perversion and Fetishism." Translated by Tracy B. Strong. In *Nietzsche's New Seas: Explorations in Philosophy, Aesthetics, and Politics*, edited by Michael A. Gillespie and Tracy B. Strong, 175–202. Chicago: University of Chicago Press, 1988.

Krell, David F. *Postponements: Women, Sensuality, and Death in Nietzsche.* Bloomington: Indiana University Press, 1986.

Nietzsche, Friedrich. *Also Sprach Zarathustra: Ein Buch für Alle und Keinen.* Stuttgart: Alfred Kröner Verlag, 1964.

————. *Beyond Good and Evil: Prelude to a Philosophy of the Future.* Translated by Walter Kaufmann. New York: Vintage Books, 1989.

————. *The Birth of Tragedy and The Case of Wagner.* Translated by Walter Kaufmann. New York: Vintage Books, 1967.

————. *The Gay Science*. Translated by Walter Kaufmann. New York: Vintage Books, 1974.

————. *On the Genealogy of Morals and Ecce Homo*. Translated by Walter Kaufmann and R. J. Hollingdale. New York: Vintage Books, 1969.

————. *Thus Spoke Zarathustra: A Book for All and None*. Translated by Walter Kaufmann. New York: Penguin Books, 1978.

————. *The Will to Power*. Translated by Walter Kaufmann and R. J. Hollingdale. New York: Vintage Books, 1968.

Oliver, Kelly. *Womanizing Nietzsche: Philosophy's Relation to the "Feminine."* New York: Routledge, 1995.

Shapiro, Gary. *Alcyone: Nietzsche on Gifts, Noise, and Women*. Albany: State University of New York Press, 1991.

Spivak, Gayatri C. "Displacement and the Discourse of Woman." In *Displacement: Derrida and After*, edited by Mark Krupnick, 169–95. Bloomington: Indiana University Press, 1983.

HEIDEGGER BIBLIOGRAPHY

Daly, Mary. *Gyn/Ecology: The Metaethics of Radical Feminism*. Boston: Beacon Press, 1990.

Ettinger, Elzbieta. *Hannah Arendt Martin Heidegger*. New Haven: Yale University Press, 1995.

Graybeal, Jean. *Language and "the Feminine" in Nietzsche and Heidegger*. Bloomington: Indiana University Press, 1990.

Heidegger, Martin. *Being and Time*. Translated by John Macquarrie and Edward Robinson. New York: Harper and Row, 1962.

Heidegger, Martin. *On the Way to Language*. Translated by Peter D. Hertz. New York: Harper and Row, 1971.

————. *Poetry, Language, Thought*. Translated by Albert Hofstadter. New York: Harper and Row, 1971.

Irigaray, Luce. *L'oubli de l'air chez Martin Heidegger*. Paris: Les Editions de Minuit, 1983.

INDEX